長谷川豪作品集

Go Hasegawa Works

TOTO出版

Go Hasegawa Works

First published in Japan on February 24, 2012
Third published in Japan on December 10, 2016

TOTO Publishing (TOTO LTD.)
TOTO Nogizaka Bldg., 2F,
1-24-3 Minami-Aoyama, Minato-ku,
Tokyo 107-0062, Japan
[Sales] Telephone: +81-3-3402-7138
Facsimile: +81-3-3402-7187
[Editorial] Telephone: +81-3-3497-1010
URL: http://www.toto.co.jp/publishing/

Author: Go Hasegawa
Publisher: Toru Kato
Book Designer: Yoshiaki Irobe
Printer: Sannichi Printing Co., Ltd.

Except as permitted under copyright law, this book may not be reproduced, in whole or in part, in any form or by any means, including photocopying, scanning, digitizing, or otherwise, without prior permission. Scanning or digitizing this book through a third party, even for personal or home use, is also strictly prohibited. The list price is indicated on the cover.

ISBN978-4-88706-323-5

A House

The vertical pillar extends to the far heavens.
The horizontal beam extends to somewhere unknown.
People dwell where the vertical and the horizontal intersect,
awed by trees, fearing beasts and groping for their coordinates.

At night, when the wind steals into the room,
the child, sleeping, wakes up to love.
In the morning, when the sun jumps into the room,
the child folds up its dream many times over.

The tail of the past is in the fog.
The antenna of the future is in the clouds.
And yet the cosmos is always here
with no need to depend on rockets.

Descending the stairs we feel the land warm.
The land continues to the sea and the sea to the lands of other countries.
Ascending the stairs we find the sky spreading wide.
The sky continues to the stars. The stars wink in silence.

The house is quietly pregnant with its family
and repeatedly breathes deeply.

Shuntaro Tanikawa

家

タテの柱は遥かな天へと伸びてゆく
ヨコの梁は知らないどこかへ伸びてゆく
垂直と水平の交わるところに人は棲む
木を畏れ獣を恐れ自分の座標を探りながら

夜　風が部屋に忍びこむと
子どもは眠りながら愛に目覚める
朝　太陽が部屋に飛びこんでくると
子どもは夢を幾重にも折りたたむ

過去の尻尾は霧のなか
未来の触角は雲のなか
でもロケットに頼らなくても
宇宙はいつも今　ここにある

階段を下りると地面が暖かい
地面は海へ　海は他国の地面に続く
階段を上がると空が広い
空は星へ　星は黙って目配せする

家はひっそりと家族を孕んで
深い呼吸を繰り返している

　　　　　　　　　　　谷川俊太郎

House in a Forest	10
House in Sakuradai	26
House in Gotanda	42
House in Komae	58
Apartment in Nerima	74
Pilotis in a Forest	90
Townhouse in Asakusa	106
House in Komazawa	122
House in Kyodo	138
Nippon Design Center	154
Belfry in Ishinomaki	162
A House————Shuntaro Tanikawa	4
Credits	171

森のなかの住宅	10
桜台の住宅	26
五反田の住宅	42
狛江の住宅	58
練馬のアパートメント	74
森のピロティ	90
浅草の町家	106
駒沢の住宅	122
経堂の住宅	138
日本デザインセンター	154
石巻の鐘楼	162
家―――谷川俊太郎	4
クレジット	171

Go Hasegawa Works　|　長谷川豪作品集

House in a Forest ｜ 森のなかの住宅

This weekend house was built in a forest in Karuizawa. Standing between a promenade on the north side and a brook on the south side, the house allows the residents to enjoy the rich natural environment. Using a simple gabled-roof volume, I designed all of the various sizes of rooms, including the living room and the kitchen, with a gabled ceiling. Between the gabled roof and ceiling, there was an open or attic-like space. By inserting a skylight in the top of the roof, the attic provided the rooms below with a soft quality of sunlight and produced a greenhouse-like atmosphere in the shade of the trees. There is also a staircase leading to a lookout deck on top of the roof, and from one room, you can look up at a scene of the sky on the opposite side through a window with a depth of a few meters. The light and landscape that are visible from every room through the ceiling change moment by moment according to the movement of the sun, and each unique experience makes it seem as if the rooms are independent and scattered throughout the forest. Due to the attic space, your attention is drawn upward at a slant when standing in the kitchen. Embedded in the form of this familiar house shape is a diagonally expanding awareness.

軽井沢の森のなかに建つ週末住宅。北側を遊歩道に、南側を小川に挟まれた敷地のなかで、自然豊かな森の環境を楽しめる住宅が求められた。単純な切妻屋根のヴォリュームを建て、そのなかに並べる居間、台所といった大小さまざまな部屋もすべて切妻形の天井とした。切妻屋根と切妻天井の間には隙間＝小屋裏がある。屋根頂部に天窓を設けているため、この小屋裏は、その下の部屋に柔らかい光や木陰を落とす温室のようになったり、屋根の上の物見台に上がるための階段室になったり、あるいは一方の部屋から反対側上空の景色を見上げることができる奥行き数mの深い窓になったりしている。各部屋の天井に差し込む光や風景は太陽の動きに合わせて刻一刻と変化し、それぞれの経験はまるで森のなかにバラバラに置かれた部屋のように独立したものになっている。またキッチンに立つと、小屋裏を介しスーッと斜め上に意識が広がっていく。家型という馴染みのある形のなかに、斜めへの意識の広がりが埋め込まれている。

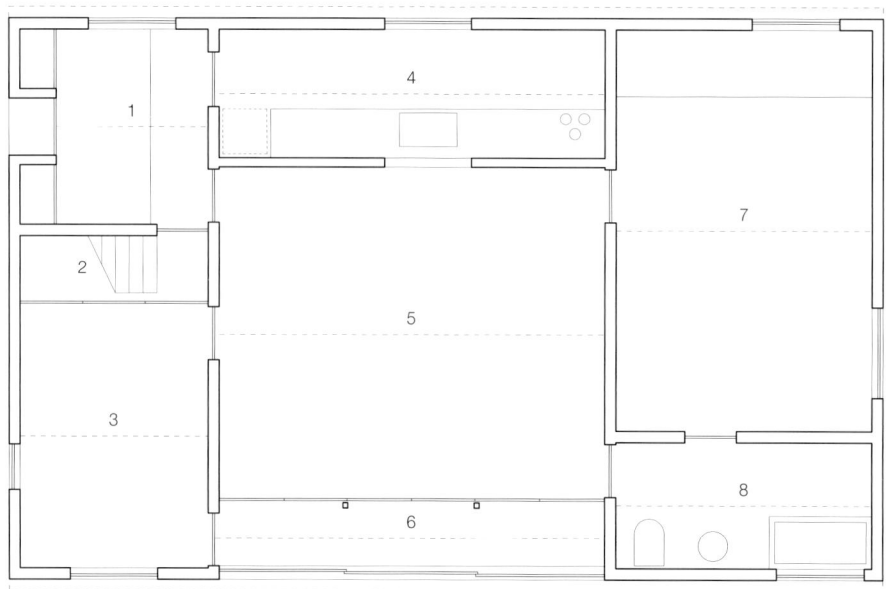

Plan 1:100   1: entrance 2: storage 3: guest room 4: kitchen 5: living room 6: deck 7: bedroom 8: bathroom 9: staircase 10: roof deck

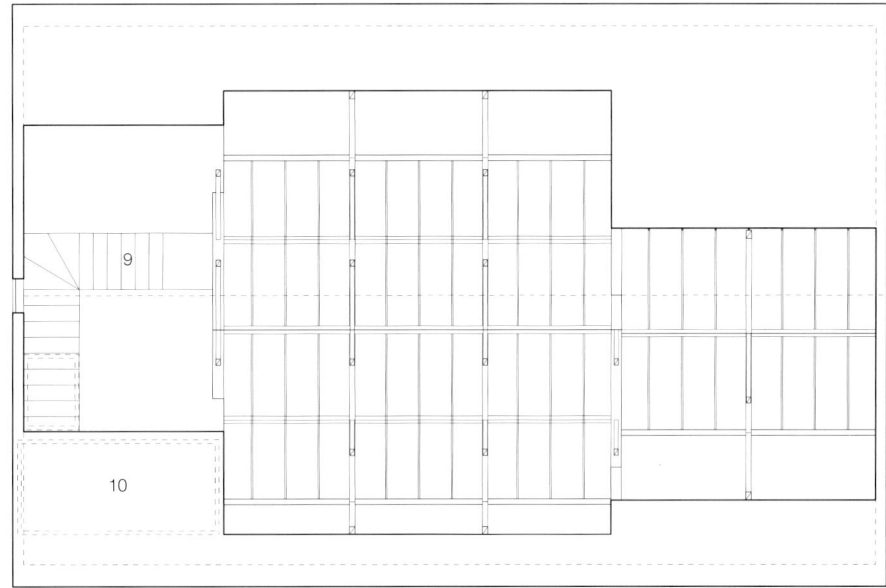

attic

平面図 1:100　　1:玄関　2:収納　3:客室　4:キッチン　5:リビング　6:縁側　7:寝室　8:浴室　9:階段室　10:物見台

Section 1:100   1: entrance 2: staircase 3: guest room 4: roof deck 5: bedroom 6: bathroom

断面図 1:100　　1:玄関　2:階段室　3:客室　4:物見台　5:寝室　6:浴室

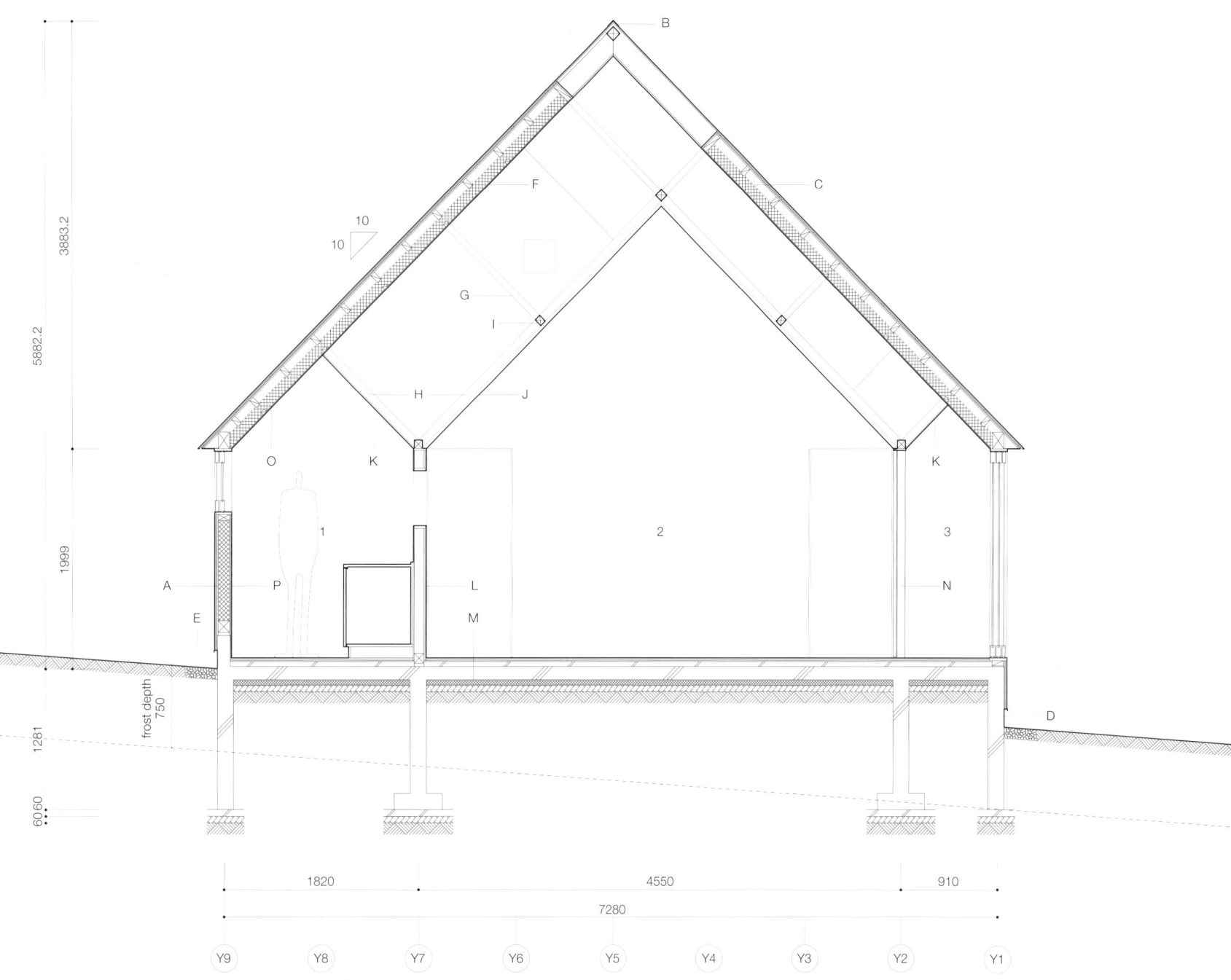

A—External walls: Corrugated galvanized steel sheeting t=0.4mm | Furring strips: 10×30mm @455mm | Asphalt roofing 22kg/m² | Structural plywood t=12mm | Column: 105×105mm | Insulation: Glasswool t=100mm (24kg/m³) B—Skylight: Double corrugated polycarbonate t=0.7mm | Coping: Bent galvanized steel sheeting t=0.4mm C—Roof: Corrugated galvanized steel sheeting t=0.4mm | Furring strips: 10×30mm @455mm | Asphalt sheeting 22kg/m² | Underlayment: Structural plywood t=12mm | Purlins: 45×90mm | Rafters: 90×180mm @1820mm | Insulation: Glasswool t=100mm (24kg/m³) D—Foundation: Exposed concrete E—Gravel paving: Crushed stone w=300mm t=100mm F—Ceiling: Plasterboard t=9mm, polyurethane paint G—Strut: 60×60mm @1820mm, polyurethane paint H—Angle braces (also ceiling furring): 75×75mm @1820mm, polyurethane paint I—Deflection stoppers: 60×75mm, polyurethane paint J—Ceiling: Acrylic boards t=3mm laminated with veneered maple slices K—Glass ceiling: Clear laminated glass t=6mm (3+3mm) L—Walls: Structural plywood t=12mm+lauan plywood t=9mm with veneered maple slices t=0.2mm M—Floor: Maple flooring t=12mm | Underlayment: Structural plywood t=12mm | Floor joists: 45×45mm @303mm (mortar in between joists t=30mm+buried polyethylene pipe) | Concrete trowel finish t=120mm | Insulation: Styrofoam t=50mm | Double polyethylene film sheeting t=0.2mm | Crushed stone t=60mm N—Columns: 75×75mm, oil stain clear lacquer finish O—Ceiling: Lauan plywood t=9mm, oil stain clear lacquer finish P—Wall: Structural plywood t=12mm, lauan plywood t=9mm, oil stain clear lacquer finish

A—外壁：ガルバリウム鋼板 t=0.4mm小波葺き｜横胴縁：10×30mm @455mm｜アスファルトルーフィング 22kg/m²｜構造用合板 t=12mm｜柱：105×105mm｜断熱材：グラスウール t=100mm(24kg/m³)　B—天窓：ポリカーボネート小波 t=0.7mm 2重貼り｜笠木部分おさえ：ガルバリウム鋼板 t=0.4mm マゲ　C—屋根：ガルバリウム鋼板 t=0.4mm小波葺き｜横胴縁：10×30mm @455mm｜アスファルトルーフィング 22kg/m²｜野地板：構造用合板 t=12mm｜母屋：45×90mm｜登り梁：90×180mm @1820mm｜断熱材：グラスウール t=100mm(24kg/m³)　D—基礎：コンクリート打放し　E—犬走り：砂利敷き w=300mm t=100mm UP　F—小屋裏天井：プラスターボード t=9mm UP　G—束材：60×60mm @1820mm UP　H—方杖(兼天井下地材)：75×75mm @1820mm UP　I—方杖たわみ止め：60×75mm UP　J—天井：アクリル t=3mm メープル突板貼り加工品　K—ガラス天井：透明合わせガラス t=6mm(3+3mm)　L—壁：構造用合板 t=12mm＋ラワン合板 t=9mmの上メープル突板 t=0.2mm貼り　M—床：メープルフローリング t=12mm｜構造用合板 t=12mm｜根太：45×45mm @303mm(根太間にモルタル t=30mm＋架橋ポリエチレン管埋設)｜コンクリート直押え t=120mm｜断熱材：スタイロフォーム t=50mm｜ポリエチレンフィルム t=0.2mm 2重敷き｜砕石 t=60mm　N—柱：75×75mm OSCL　O—天井：ラワン合板 t=9mm OSCL　P—壁：構造用合板 t=12mmの上ラワン合板 t=9mm OSCL

Section 1:50　1: kitchen 2: living room 3: deck　矩計図 1:50　1：キッチン　2：リビング　3：縁側

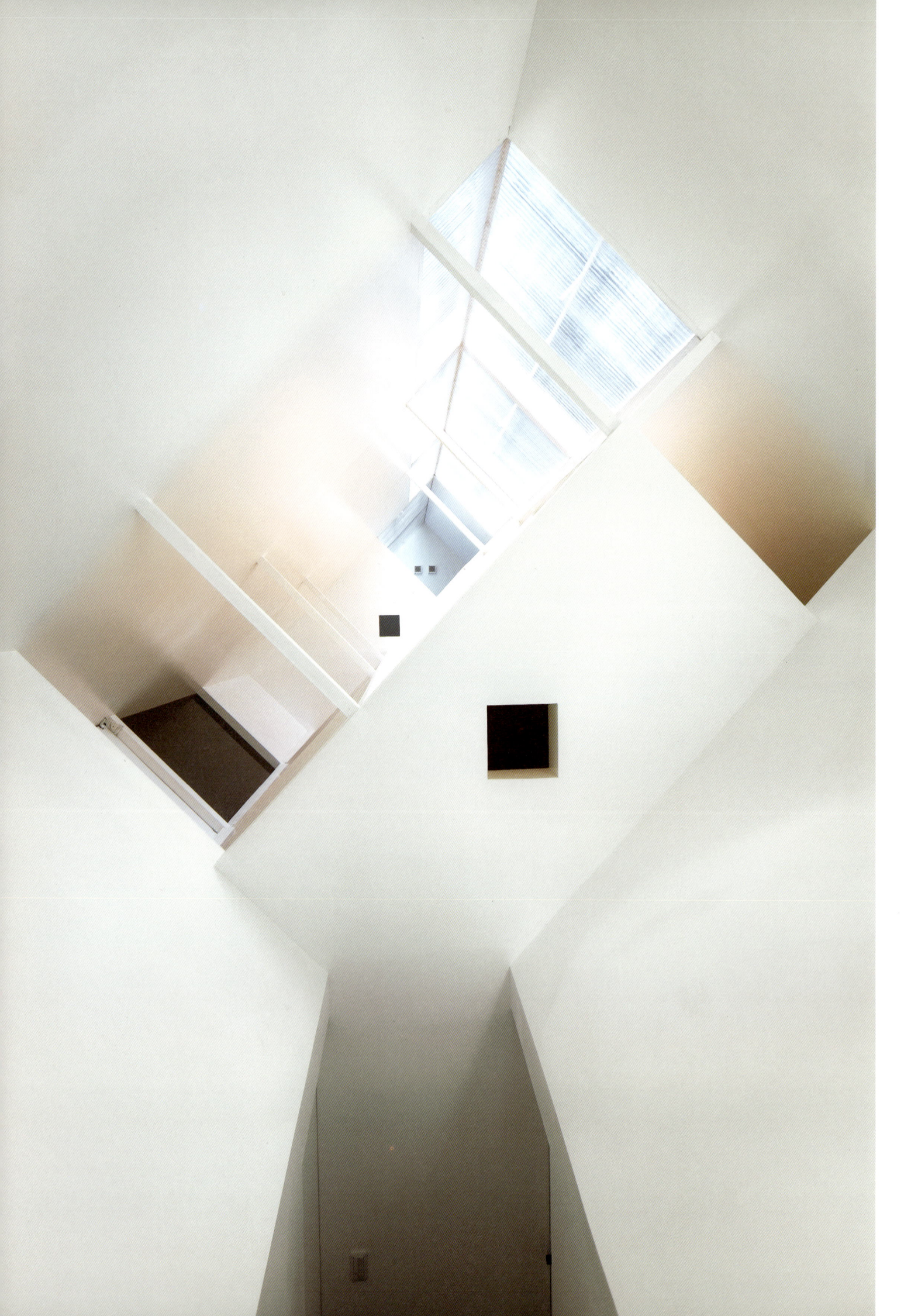

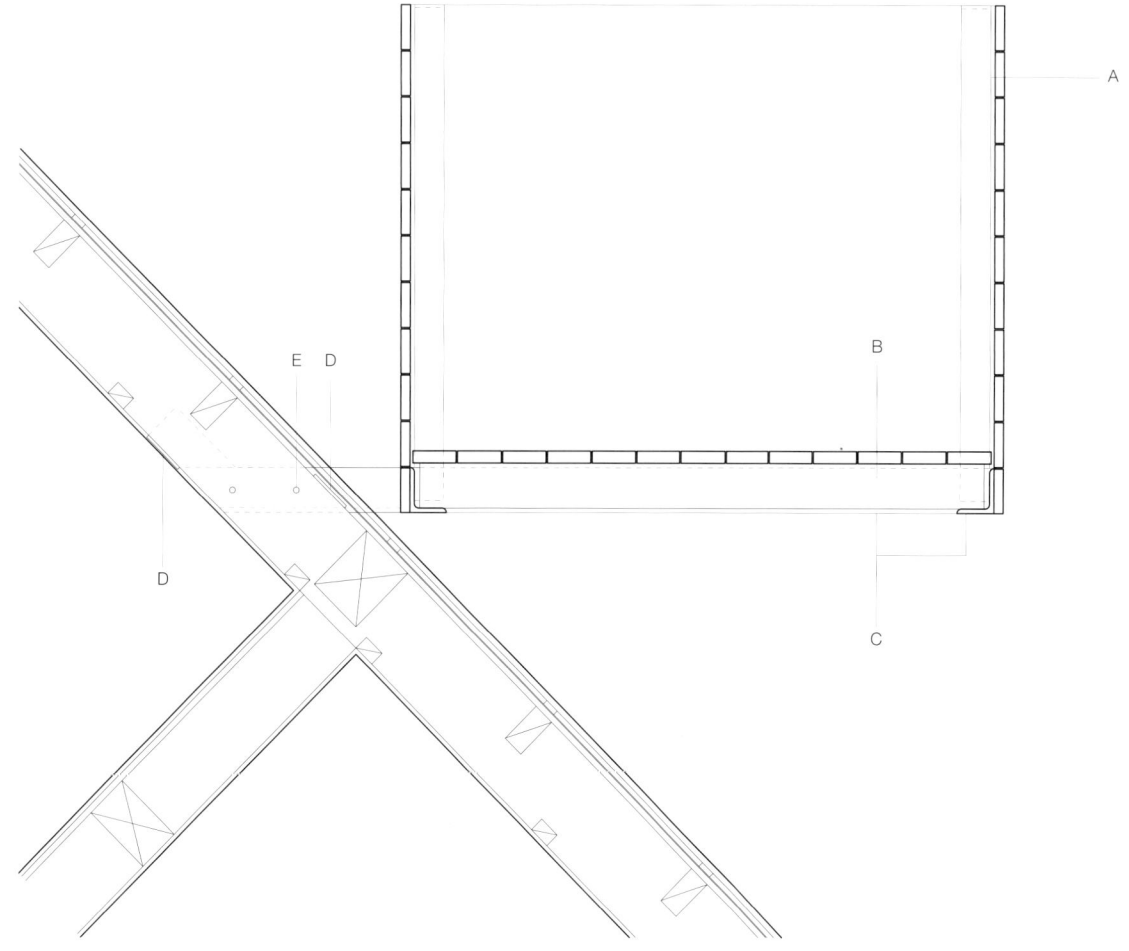

A—Balustrade: Ipe 89 × 19t, oil stain clear lacquer finish | Balustrade post: Steel □60 × 30 × 3.2t @910mm, edge closer, hot dip zinc, oil paint   B—Floor: Ipe 89 × 19t, oil stain clear lacquer finish | Floor joist: Ipe 90 × 45mm @455mm, oil stain clear lacquer finish   C—Base: Steel L-90 × 75 × 9t, hot dip zinc, oil paint   D—Cleat: Steel plates 90 × 90 × 6t, hot dip zinc   E—Hexagon head bolt 2-M12

A—手摺：イペ 89×19t OSCL｜手摺子：St □-60×30×3.2t @910mm 小口フサギ 亜鉛ドブヅケ OP　B—床：イペ 89×19t OSCL｜根太：イペ 90×45mm @455mm OSCL　C—土台：St L-90×75×9t 亜鉛ドブヅケ OP　D—転び止め：St PL-90×90×6t 亜鉛ドブヅケ　E—六角ボルト 2-M12

Detail of roof deck 1:15　物見台詳細図　1:15

Site plan 1:1000　配置図 1:1000

House in a Forest

Location: Karuizawa, Kitasaku-gun, Nagano
Principal use: Residential
Site area: 1,049.99m^2
Building area: 85.59m^2
Total floor area: 89.75m^2
Number of stories: 1
Structure: Timber frame

森のなかの住宅

所在地：長野県北佐久郡軽井沢町
主要用途：専用住宅
敷地面積：1,049.99m^2
建築面積：85.59m^2
延床面積：89.75m^2
規模：地上1階
構造：木造

House in Sakuradai ｜ 桜台の住宅

Built in a relaxed residential district of a regional area, this house was designed for a couple and their two children. Both the husband and wife are elementary school teachers, and they wanted a house equipped with a spacious workshop where they could prepare educational materials and one in which they would always have a vague sense of the family's movements. I created a garden around the square, two-story building, which is located in roughly the center of the lot. Placing the individual rooms and wet area on the first floor, and the living and dining area on the second, I also created an atrium completely covered by a skylight in the middle of the house, and installed a large table there that occupied almost the entire space. The bright first-floor table area, which seems to be outside, functions as a second living room, and as it is surrounded by the other rooms, forms a loose connection between the private rooms, and the first and second floor. You can sit in a chair at the corner of the table, and with your lower body in the small private room, and your upper body in the large, bright table space, you can experience two different spatial scales at the same time. Due to these two distinct areas, each member of the family can spend their time exactly as they see fit and still feel a sense of unity in regard to the house.

地方のゆったりとした住宅地に建つ、夫婦と子供2人のための住宅。施主夫妻は小学校の教師をしており、要望としては教材の準備などができる広いワークスペースが欲しいということと、いつもなんとなく家族の気配が感じられる住宅にしたいということだった。敷地のほぼ中央に2階建ての四角い建物を配置して、建物の外周に庭をつくった。また1階を個室と水廻り、2階をリビングダイニングにして、さらに建物の真ん中に全面トップライトをもつ吹抜けの部屋をつくり、その部屋いっぱいに大きなテーブルを設けた。外のように明るい1階のテーブルの空間は個室に囲まれたもうひとつのリビングになり、個室同士、さらには1階と2階を柔らかく関係づけている。テーブルの隅の椅子に座る。下半身は小さな個室に、上半身は明るい大きなテーブルの空間に属し、2種類の空間のスケールがひとつの身体に重なる。そうした2種類の空間をもつことで、家族それぞれが思い思いに過ごしながら、この住宅全体を一体的に感じることもできる。

Site plan 1:1000　配置図 1:1000

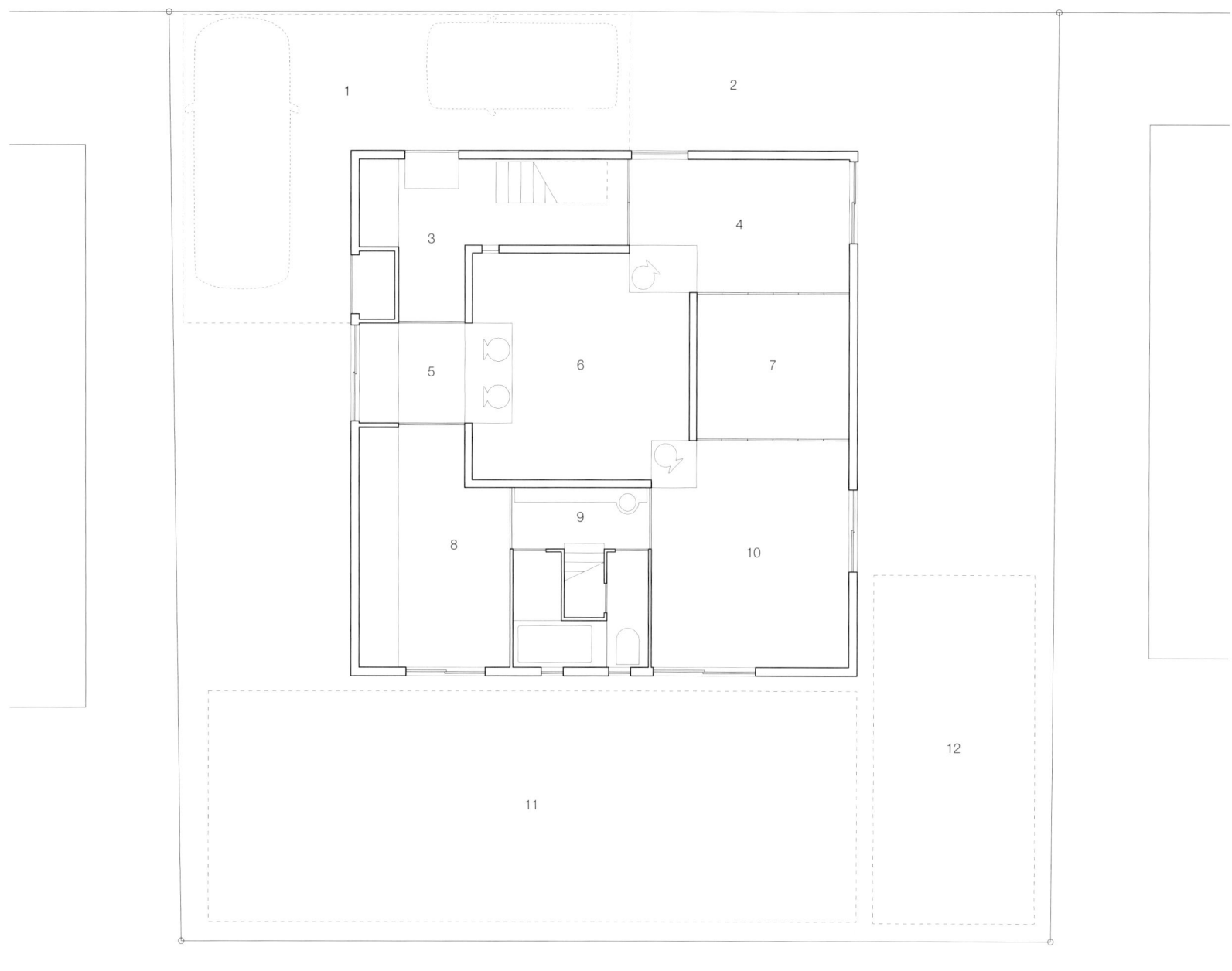

1st floor

1: parking 2: approach 3: entrance 4: children's room 1 5: study room 6: table 7: closet 8: bedroom
9: washroom 10: children's room 2 11: garden 12: farm 13: guest room 14: hall 15: void 16: dining kitchen 17: living room

Plan 1:100

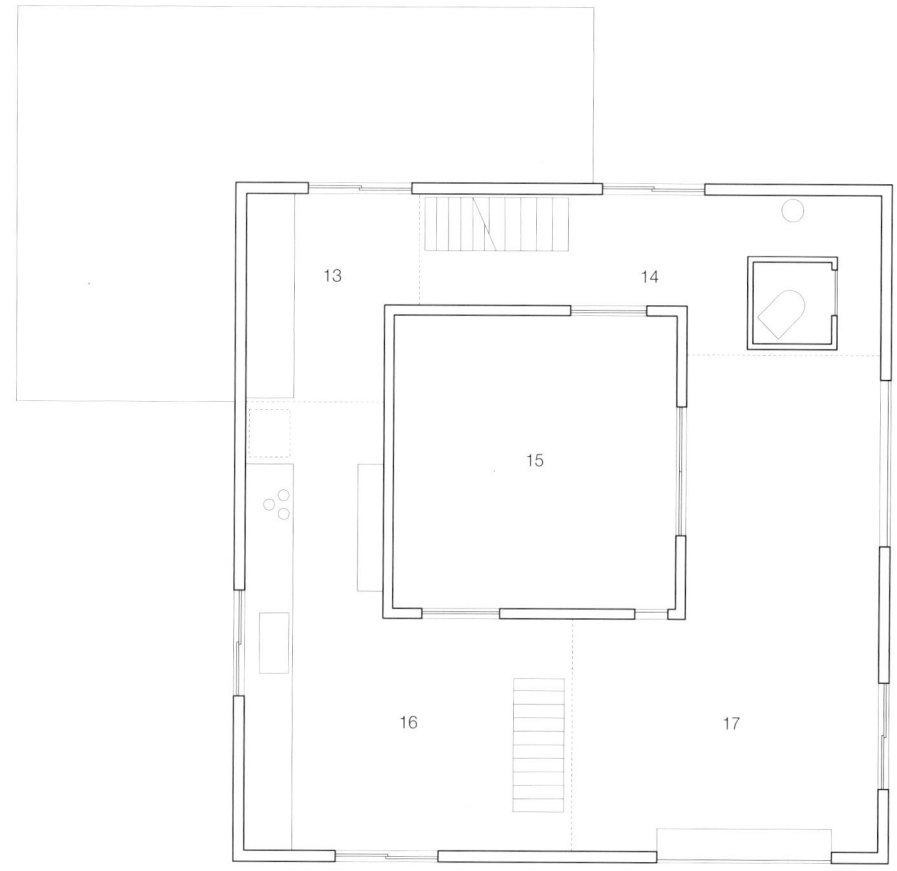

2nd floor

1:駐車場　2:アプローチ　3:玄関　4:子供室1　5:書斎　6:テーブル　7:クロゼット　8:寝室
平面図　1:100　　9:洗面室　10:子供室2　11:芝　12:畑　13:客室　14:ホール　15:吹抜け　16:ダイニングキッチン　17:リビング

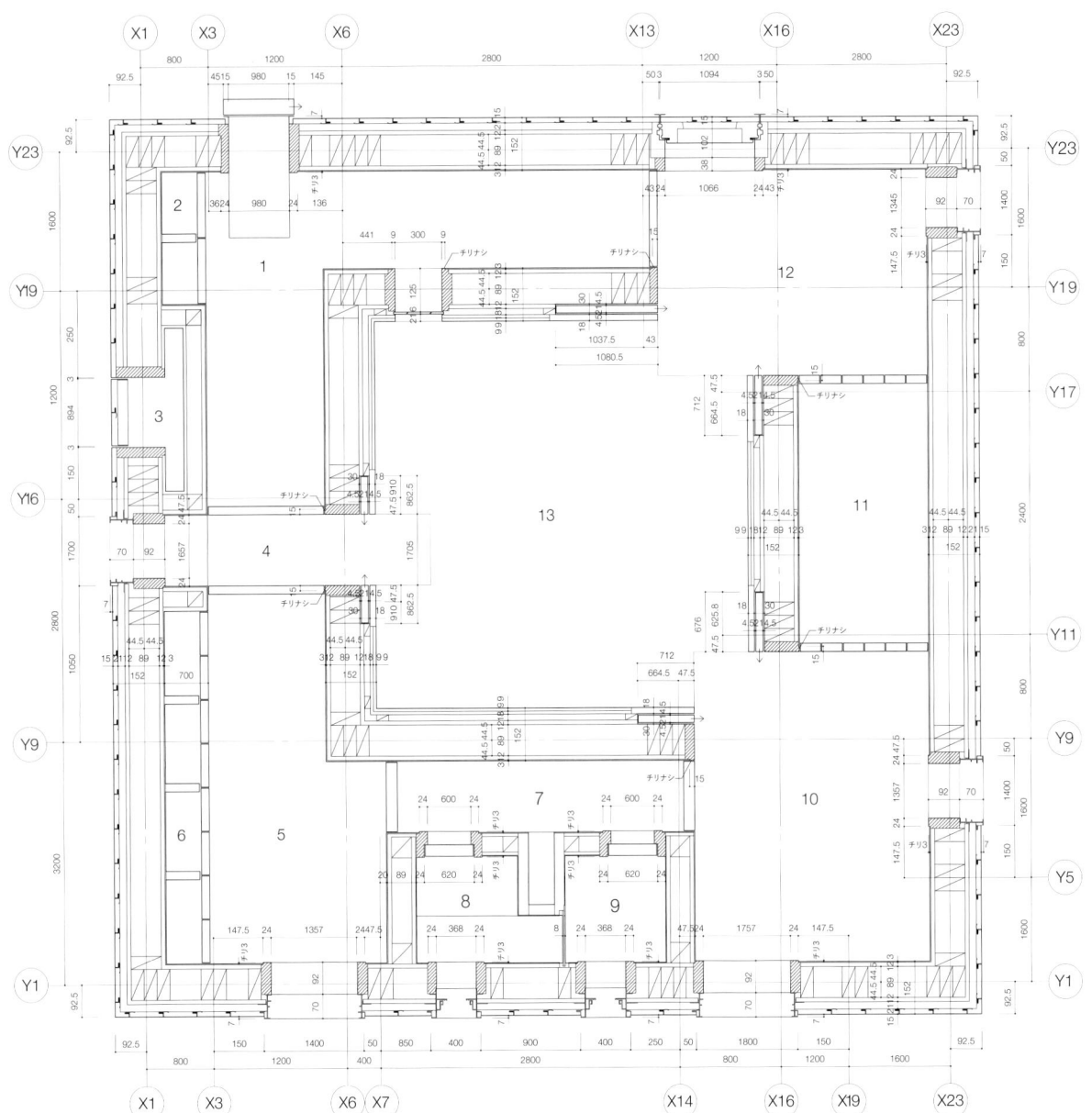

1st floor

1: entrance 2: shoe storage 3: store room 4: study room 5: bedroom 6: storage 7: washroom 8: bathroom 9: toilet
10: children's room 2 11: closet 12: children's room 1 13: table 14: hall 15: guest room 16: dining kitchen 17: living room 18: void

Horizontal detail 1:20

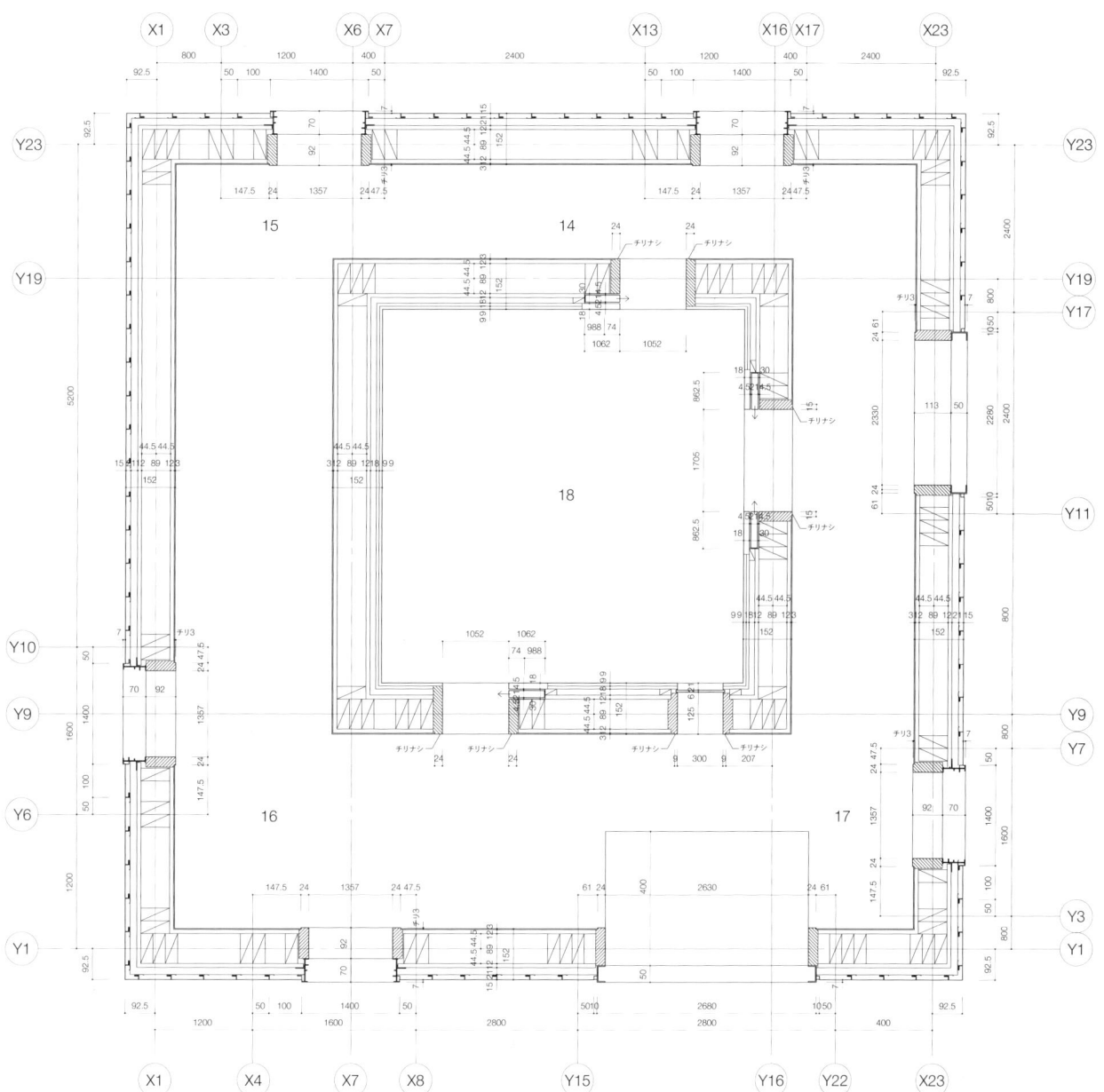

枠廻詳細図 1:20

1:玄関 2:靴箱 3:倉庫 4:書斎 5:寝室 6:収納 7:洗面室 8:風呂 9:トイレ 10:子供室2
11:クロゼット 12:子供室1 13:テーブル 14:ホール 15:客室 16:ダイニングキッチン 17:リビング 18:吹抜け

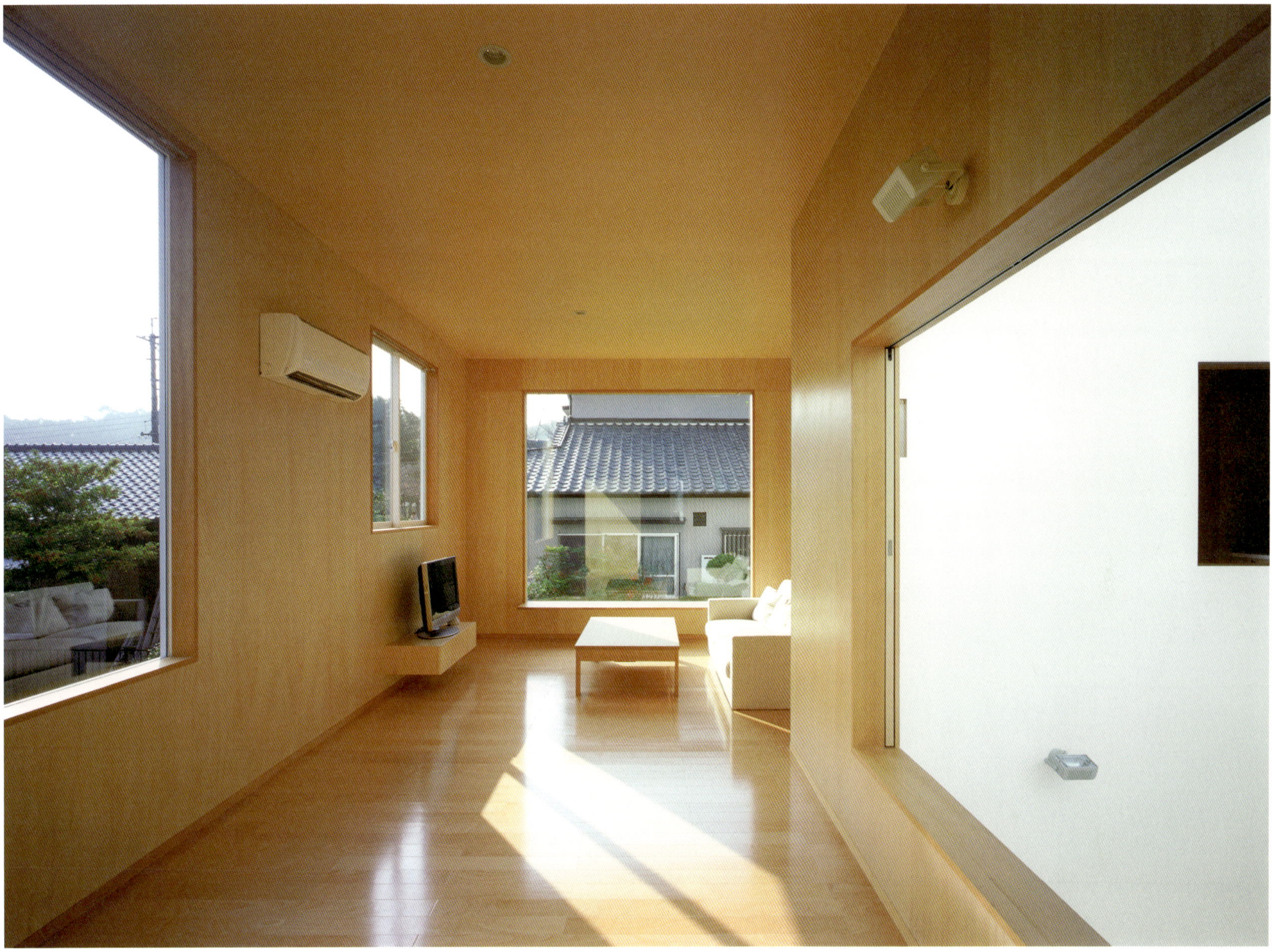

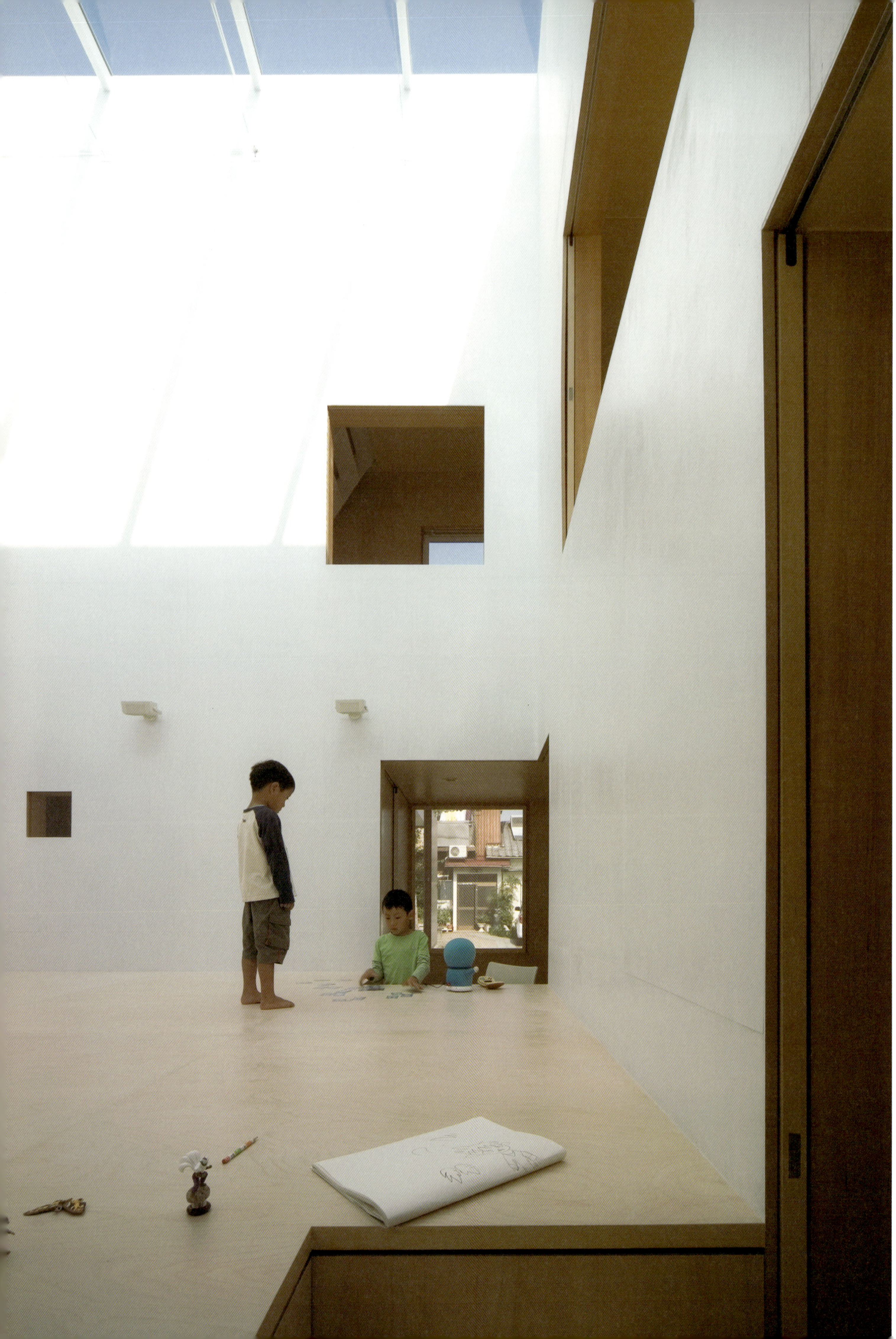

37

A—External walls: Colored galvanized steel sheeting spandrel t=13mm (vertical, jointless) | Furring strips: 40×10mm @400mm | Moisture permeable waterproof sheeting | Structural plywood t=12mm | Jamb: 2"×4" (38×89mm) @400mm | Glasswool t=90mm (16kg/m^3) B—Coping: Bent colored galvanized steel t=0.5mm C—Skylight flashing: Bent colored galvanized steel t=0.5mm | Skylight peripheral framing: Steel 100×100mm t=2.3mm D—Top light: Double float glazing t=16mm (8+8mm), solar protective film | Skylight support: Steel 100×50mm t=4.5mm @1000mm, polyurethane paint E—Parapet: Fiber reinforced plastic waterproofing t=2mm, topcoat finish F—Rooftop floor: Fiber reinforced plastic waterproofing t=2mm, topcoat finish | Double waterproof plywood t=12mm | Joists: 2"×4" (38×89mm) @400mm | Structural plywood t=12mm | Joists 2"×8" (38×186mm) @400mm | Insulation: Glasswool t=140mm (16kg/m^3) G—Standardized aluminum sliding window sash H—Flashing: Bent colored galvanized steel t=0.5mm I—Floor: Concrete trowel finish t=100–150mm J—Sunshading tent K—Ceiling: Plasterboard t=9mm, acrylic emulsion paint | Ceiling joists: 10×40mm @400mm L—Wall: Structural plywood t=12mm, basswood plywood top t=3mm, polyurethane paint M—Floor: Cherrywood flooring t=12mm (painted) | Electrical floor heating panel t=12mm (glasswool on underside of heating panels) | Structural plywood t=12mm | Binding beam: 2"×8" (38×186mm) @400mm N—Wall: Lauan plywood t=9mm, oil paint O—Table board: Lauan plywood t=21mm, birch top t=9mm, polyurethane paint | Joists: 60×60mm @800mm P—Floor: Cork tile t=4mm (painted) | Underlaying plywood t=5mm | Structural plywood t=12mm | Floor joists: 30×40mm @400mm | Girders 30×40mm @400mm | Insulation: Glasswool t=50mm (24kg/m^3) | Concrete slab t=150mm | Polyethylene film t=0.2mm | Crushed stone t=60mm Q—Floor: Lauan plywood t=9mm

Section 1:50   1: rooftop terrace 2: dining kitchen 3: hall 4: bedroom 5: entrance 6: table

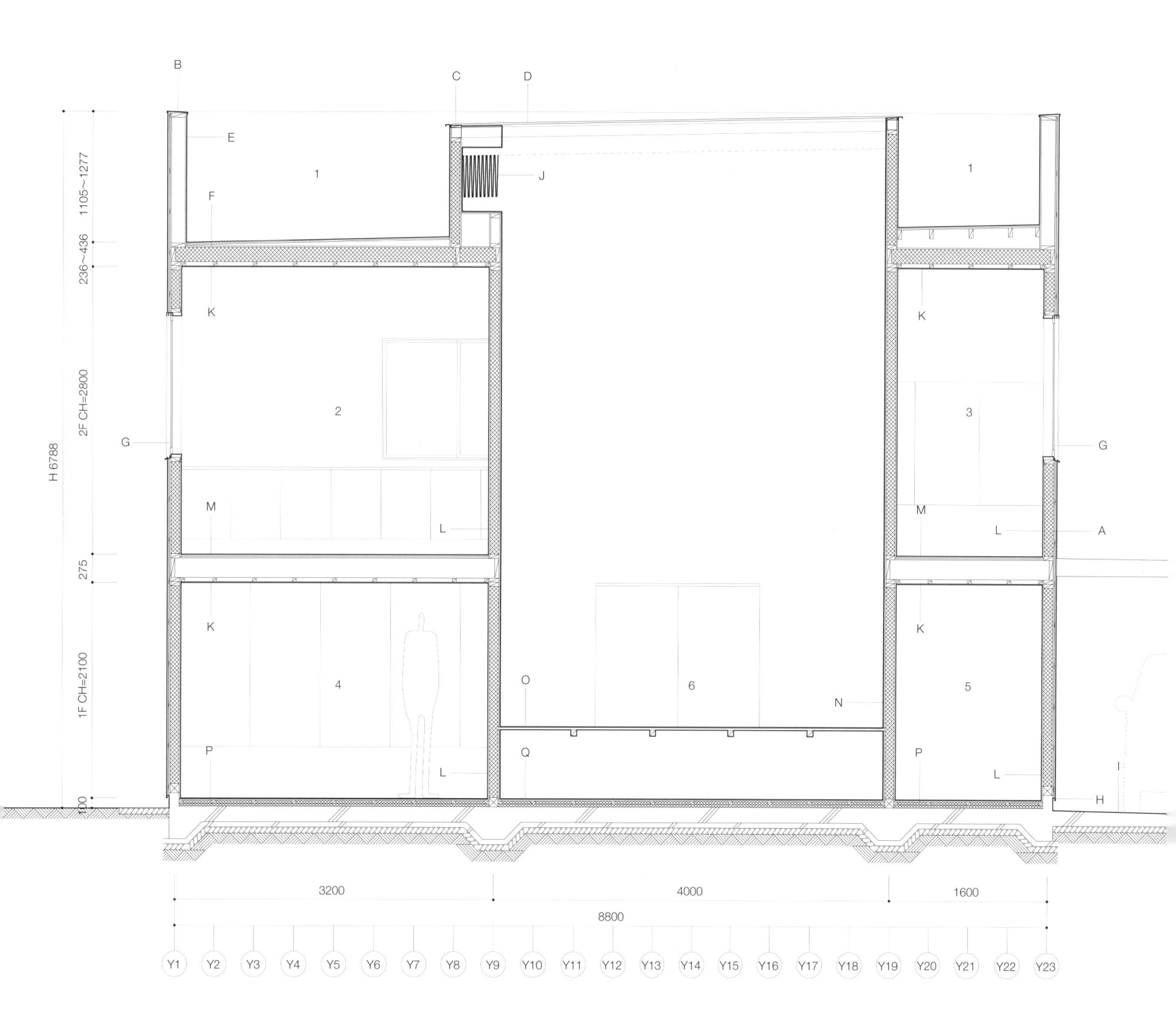

A—外壁：カラーガルバリウム鋼板スパンドレル t=13mm（縦貼、目地ナシ）｜胴縁：40×10mm @400mm｜透湿防水シート｜構造用合板 t=12mm｜縦枠：2"×4"(38×89mm) @400mm｜断熱材：グラスウール t=90mm（16kg/m³）　B—笠木：カラーガルバリウム鋼板 t=0.5mm マゲ　C—トップライト水切り：カラーガルバリウム鋼板 t=0.5mm マゲ｜トップライト四周枠：St-□100×100×2.3t　D—トップライト：合わせガラス t=16mm(8+8mm) 熱線反射フィルム貼り｜トップライト受け材：St-□100×50×4.5t @1000mm UP　E—パラペット立ち上がり：FRP防水 t=2mm トップコート仕上げ　F—屋上床：FRP防水 t=2mm トップコート仕上げ｜耐水合板 t=12mm 2枚貼り｜根太：2"×4"(38×89mm) @400mm｜構造用合板 t=12mm｜小梁：2"×8"(38×186mm) @400mm｜断熱材：グラスウール t=140mm（16kg/m³）　G—引き違い窓：アルミサッシ既製品　H—水切り：カラーガルバリウム鋼板 t=0.5mm マゲ　I—床：土間コンクリート金ゴテ仕上げ t=100-150mm　J—日除けテント　K—天井：プラスターボード t=9mm AEP｜野縁：10×40mm @400mm　L—壁：構造用合板 t=12mmの上シナ合板 t=3mm UP　M—床：サクラフローリング t=12mm(塗装品)｜電気床暖房パネル t=12mm(床暖房パネルの下部のみグラスウール敷き込み)｜構造用合板 t=12mm｜小梁：2"×8"(38×186mm) @400mm　N—壁：ラワン合板 t=9mm OP 拭き取り　O—テーブル板：ラワン合板 t=21mmの上バーチ合板 t=9mm OP 拭き取り｜根太：60×60mm @800mm　P—床：コルクタイル t=4mm(塗装品)｜捨て貼り合板 t=5mm｜構造用合板 t=12mm｜根太：30×40mm @400mm｜根太下地材：30×40mm @400mm｜断熱材：グラスウール t=50mm(24kg/m³)｜コンクリートスラブ t=150mm｜ポリエチレンフィルム t=0.2mm｜砕石 t=60mm　Q—床：ラワン合板 t=9mm

矩計図　1:50　　1：屋上テラス　2：ダイニングキッチン　3：ホール　4：寝室　5：玄関　6：テーブル

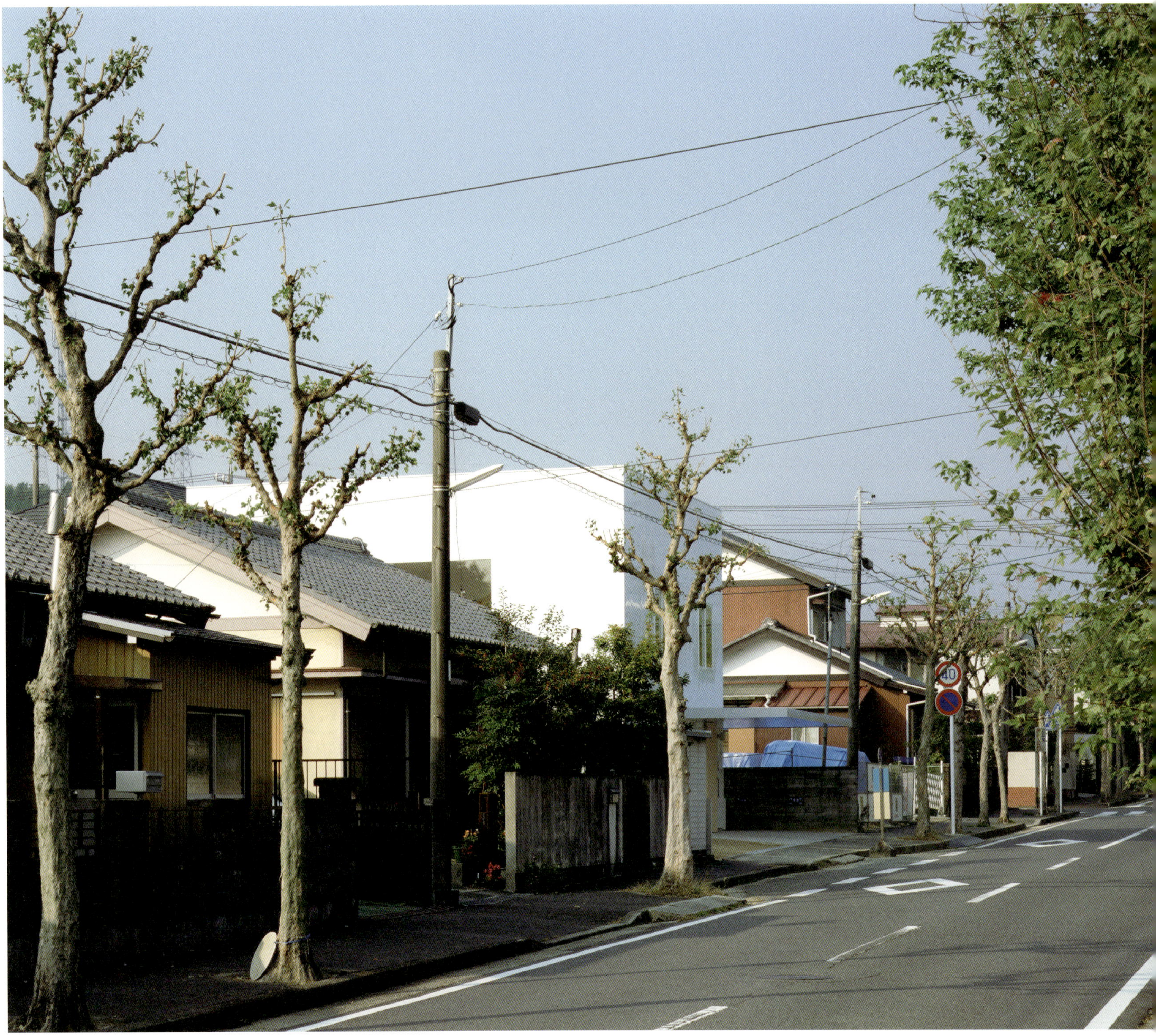

House in Sakuradai

Location: Mie
Principal use: Residential
Site area: 246.42m²
Building area: 89.13m²
Total floor area: 138.88m²
Number of stories: 2
Structure: Timber frame

桜台の住宅

所在地：三重県
主要用途：専用住宅
敷地面積：246.42m²
建築面積：89.13m²
延床面積：138.88m²
規模：地上2階
構造：木造

House in Gotanda | 五反田の住宅

This house, built for a young couple, stands on a small lot in the center of Tokyo. The corner lot, with an area of 48 square meters, is in a densely populated neighborhood with a mixture of buildings of various sizes and types, including factories, office buildings, and detached houses. I started by dividing the house into two wings – a south wing with three stories and a floor space of 16.83 square meters, and a north wing with four floors and a floor space of 9.18 square meters. Between the wings I created an alley-like space with a width of about 1.2 meters which I covered with a glass roof, and designed a hall that houses the front entrance and a staircase. On the roadside surface of the hall, I installed a large front door with a height of approximately ten meters. When the door is open on a nice day, sunlight and wind flow through the hall. And while on the spiral staircase, you have the sense that your body occupies a space between your own house and the adjacent house, and as you ascend or descend the steps, you can experience both the inside and the outside as you move from a room in the south wing to the gap between the house and the neighboring house, a room in the north wing, and the hall. Without realizing it, you transcend the boundary line of the lot, and the contours of the building, and rather than being aware of the structure itself, you have the sense that you are living in the landscape of the town.

東京都心の小さな敷地に建つ若い夫婦のための住宅。敷地面積48m²の角地で、工場や事務所ビル、戸建て住宅など種類も大きさもバラバラな建物が混在して建つ過密な地域にある。まず建物を2棟に分け、南棟を11畳の3階建て、北棟を6畳の4階建てとした。2棟の間には幅1.2mほどの路地のような空間があり、そこにガラスの屋根をかけ、玄関と階段室を兼ねたホールとしている。ホールの道路側の面には建物と同じ高さ約10mの大きな玄関扉を設置しており、天気の良い日にはこの大きな扉を開放してホールを光と風が流れる空間にする。また螺旋階段は途中で身体が自分の家と隣家との隙間に出るようにしているため、階段をくるくる上り下りすると、南棟の部屋から、隣家との隙間、北棟の部屋、ホール……といったように、インテリアと街を交互に体験することになる。無意識のうちに敷地境界や建物の輪郭を超えて、建物のなかというよりは、街の風景のなかで暮らしているように感じられる。

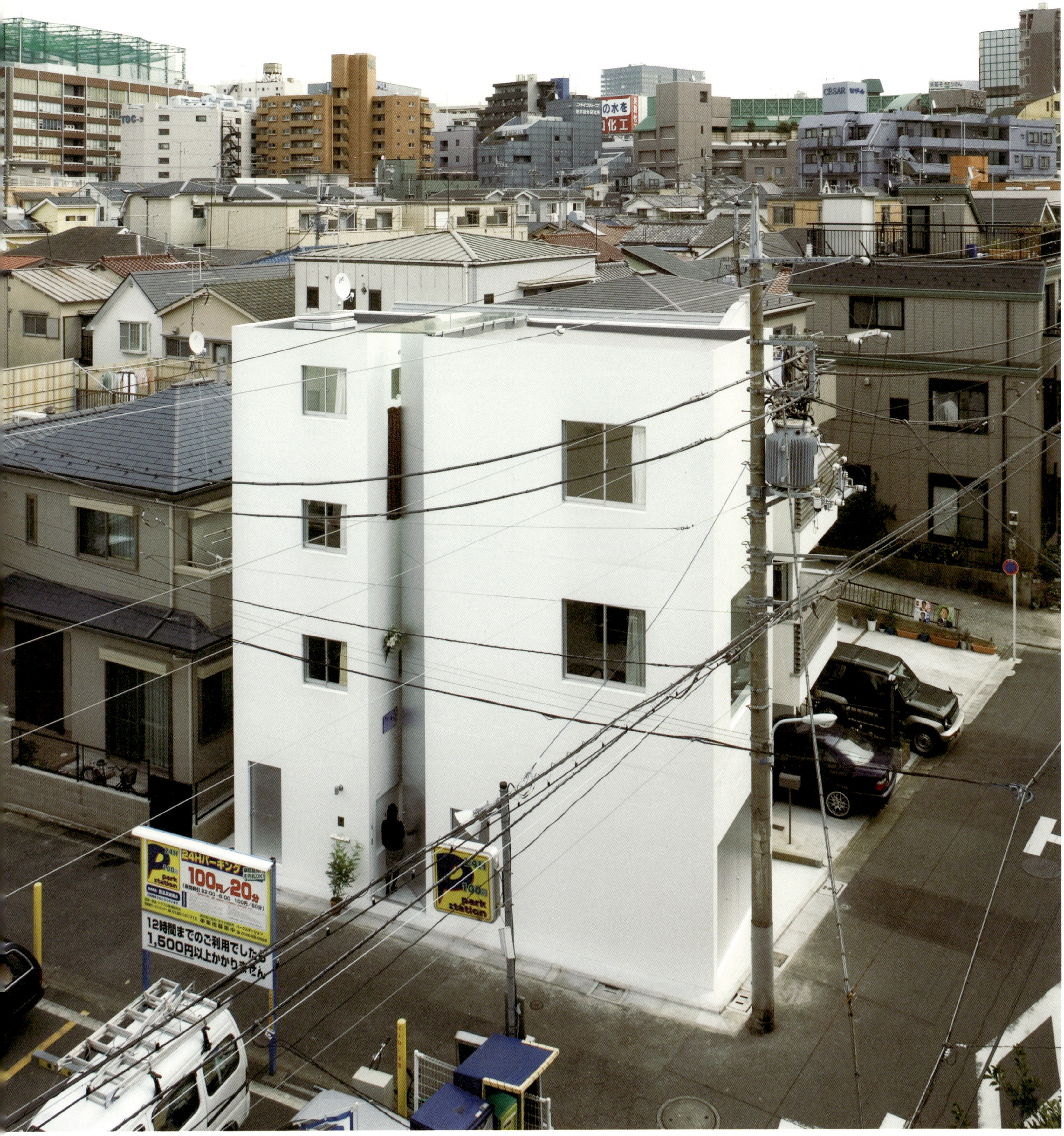

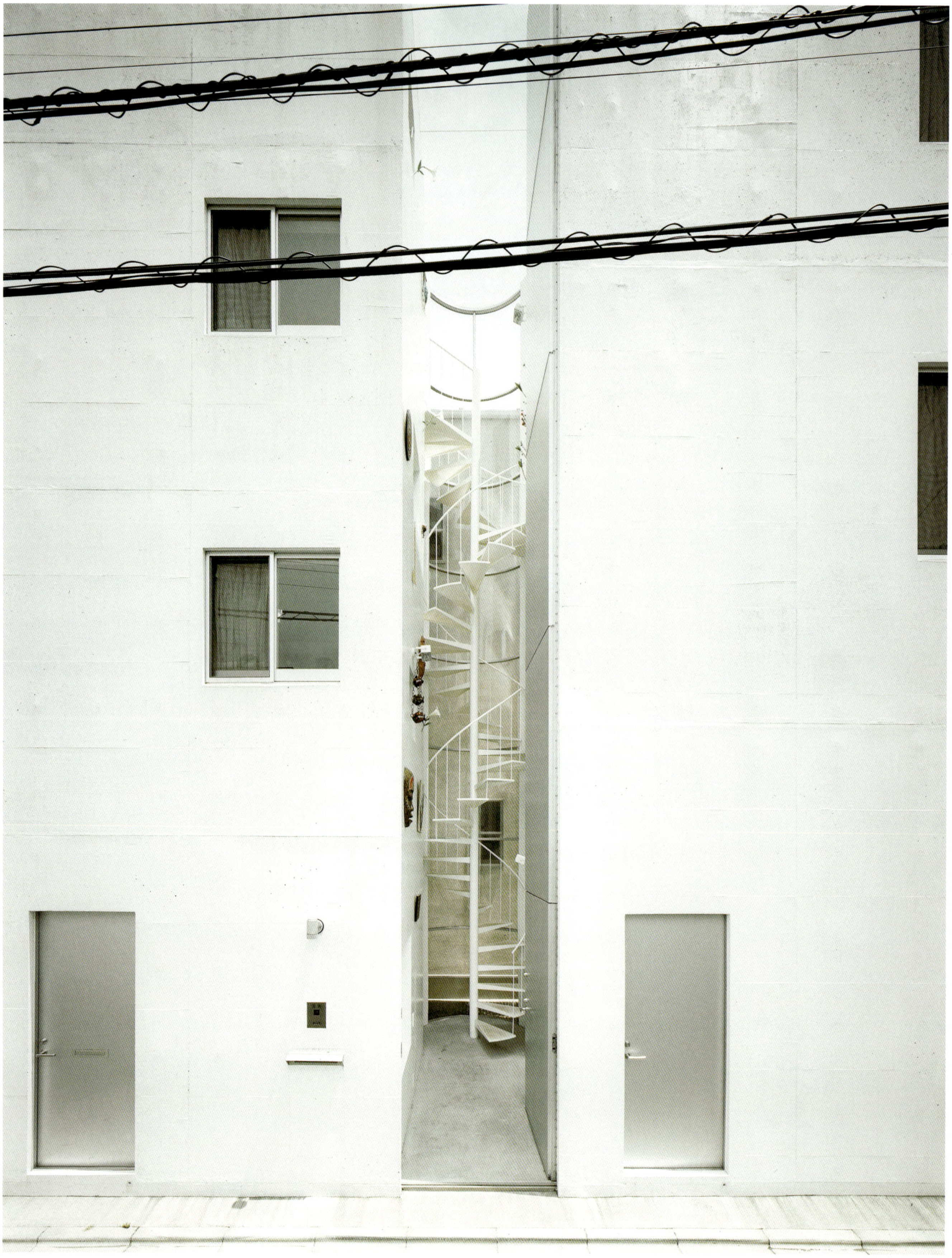

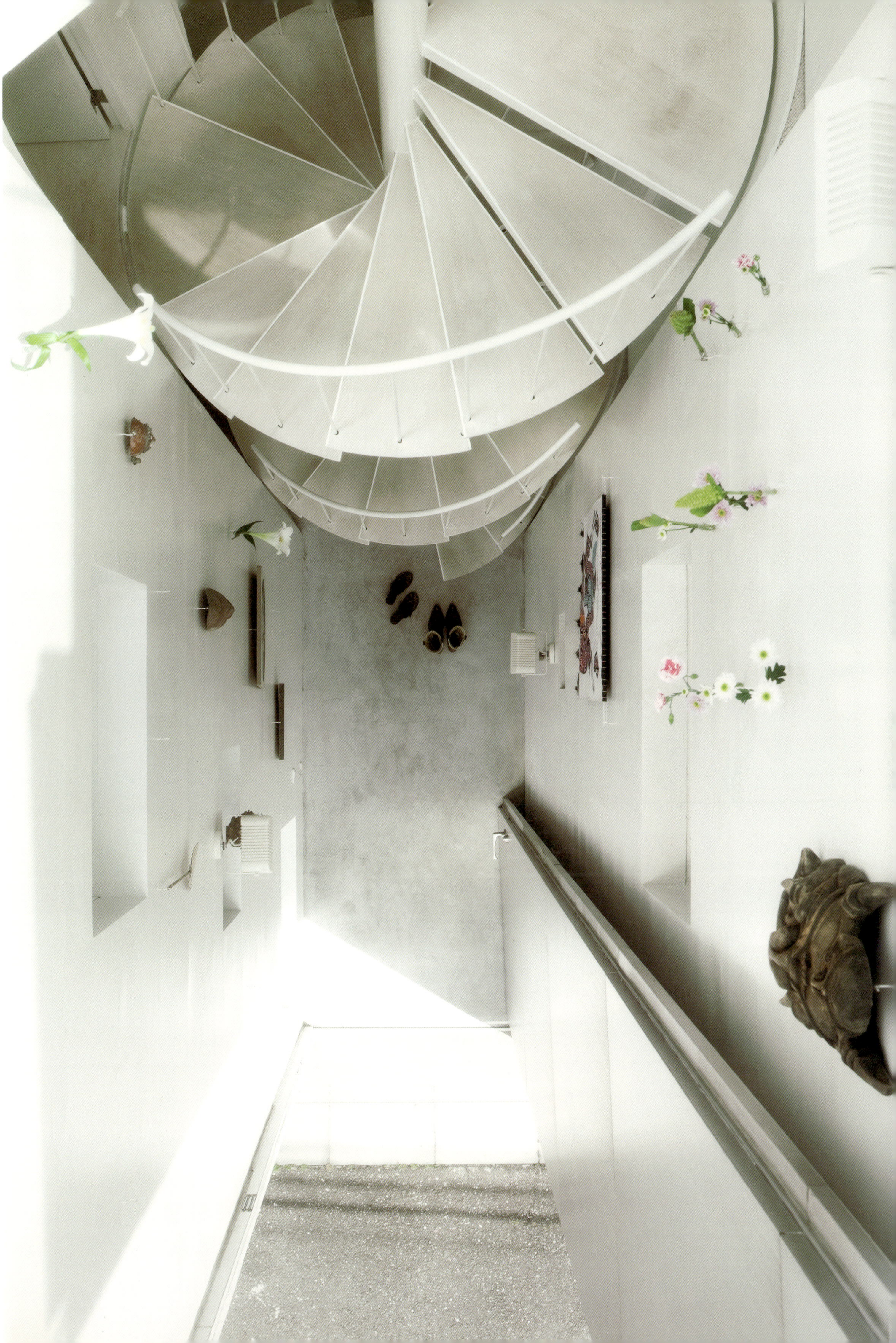

A—External walls: Exposed concrete (standard formwork), polyurethane paint B—Skylight: Double reinforced glass t=20mm (10+10mm) C—Rooftop waterproofing: Waterproof membrane t=2mm | Extra layer of concrete t=0–120mm | Concrete slab t=150mm D—Fixed window: Transparent glass t=10mm E—Bifold door: Douglas fir t=42mm, polyurethane paint F—Standard aluminum sliding window sash G—Ceiling: Waterproof plywood t=12mm, fiber reinforced plastic waterproofing t=2mm, topcoat finish H—Walls/bathtub: Waterproof plywood t=12mm, fiber reinforced plastic waterproofing t=2mm, topcoat finish I—Ceiling: Plasterboard t=9mm, acrylic emulsion paint J—Walls: Plasterboard t=12.5mm, acrylic emulsion paint K—Floor: Carpet t=8mm L—Ceiling: Exposed concrete putty mended, acrylic emulsion paint M—Floor: Birch plywood t=9mm, oil stain, wax N—Floor: Tile t=9mm O—Floor: Cypress flooring t=19mm, oil stain, wax P—Ceiling: Exposed concrete Q—Wall: Exposed concrete R—Floor: Concrete trowel finish, wax S—Wall: Exposed concrete (ribbed formwork), putty mended, polyurethane paint T—Floor: Concrete trowel, water-repellant finish U—Floor: Concrete trowel finish (water gradient t=0–50mm)

A—外壁：コンクリート打放し（普通型枠）UP B—トップライト：強化合わせガラス t=20mm（10＋10mm） C—屋上防水：シート防水絶縁工法 t=2mm | コンクリート増打ち t=0–120mm | コンクリートスラブ t=150mm D—はめ殺し窓：透明ガラス t=10mm E—折戸：ベイマツフラッシュ t=42mm UP F—引き違い窓：アルミサッシ既製品 G—天井：耐水合板 t=12mm の上FRP防水 t=2mmトップコート仕上げ H—壁・浴槽：耐水合板 t=12mm の上FRP防水 t=2mmトップコート仕上げ I—天井：プラスターボード t=9mm AEP J—壁：プラスターボード t=12.5mm AEP K—床：カーペット t=8mm L—天井：コンクリート打放し パテ補修の上AEP M—床：バーチ合板 t=9mm OS WAX N—床：タイル t=9mm O—床：ヒノキフローリング t=19mm OS WAX P—天井：コンクリート打放し Q—壁：コンクリート打放し R—床：コンクリート金ゴテ仕上げ WAX S—壁：コンクリート打放し（化粧型枠）全面パテ補修の上UP T—床：コンクリート金ゴテ仕上げ撥水材塗布 U—床：コンクリート金ゴテ仕上げ（水勾配t=0–50mm）

Section 1:50   1: bathroom 2: bedroom 3: dining kitchen 4: living room 5: study room 6: garage 7: office 8: hall

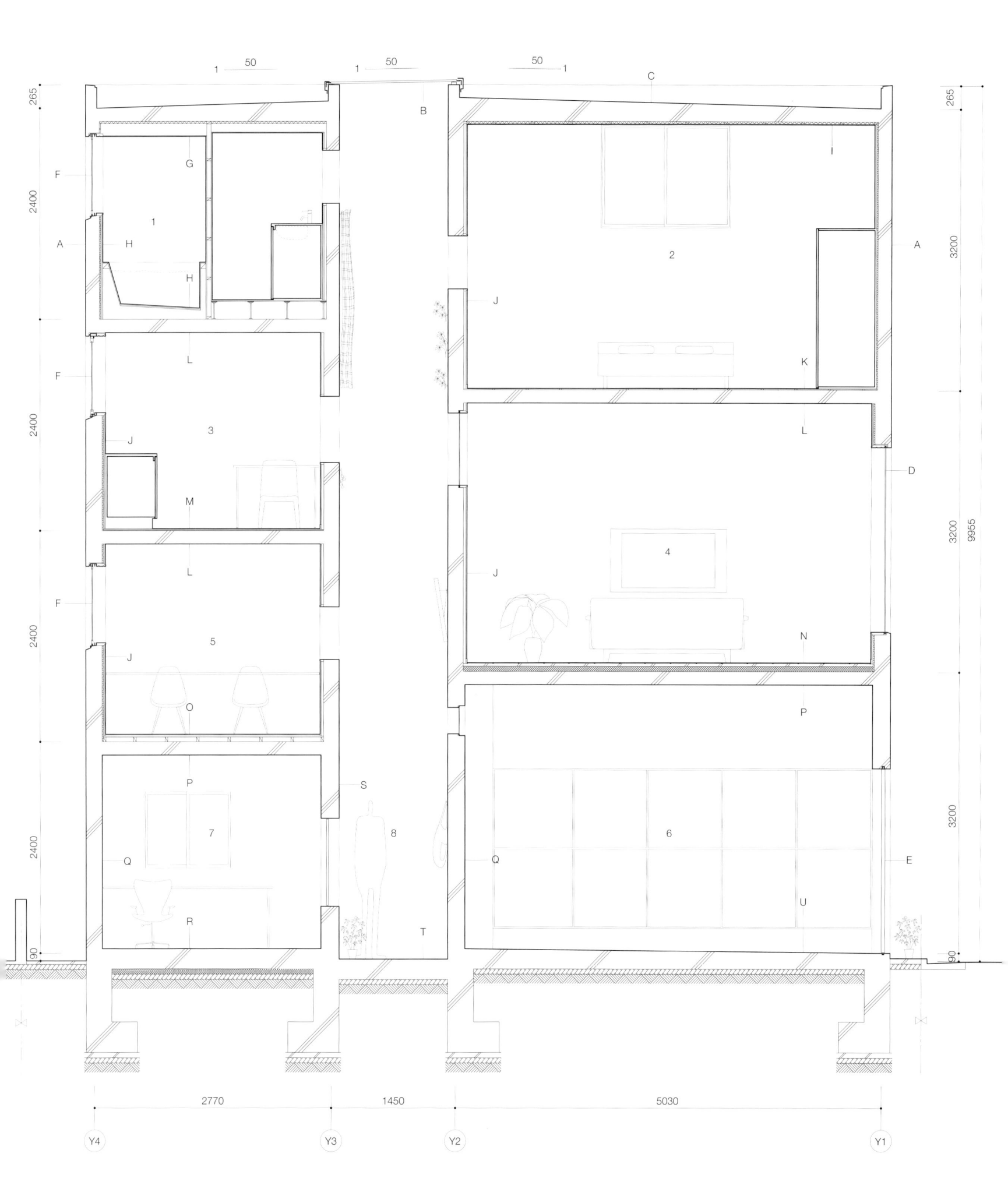

矩計図 1:50　　1:浴室　2:寝室　3:ダイニングキッチン　4:リビング　5:書斎　6:車庫　7:オフィス　8:ホール

47

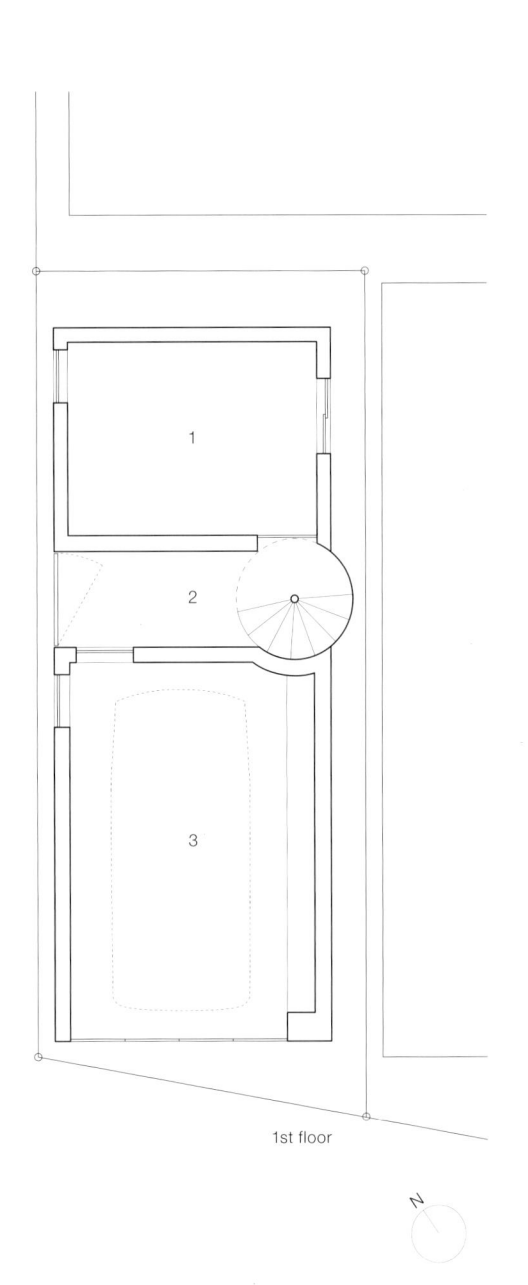

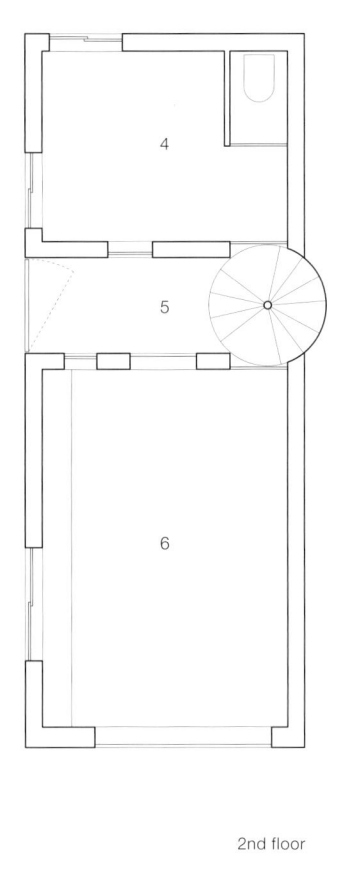

1st floor

2nd floor

48　　　　　　　　　　　　　　Plan 1:100　　　1: office 2: hall 3: garage 4: study room 5: void 6: living room 7: dining kitchen 8: bedroom 9: bathroom 10: skylight

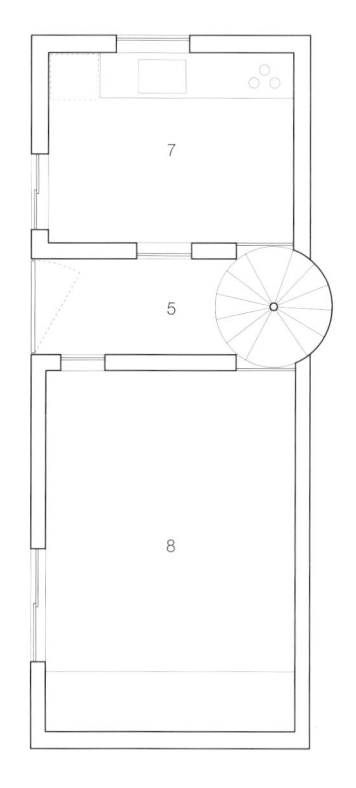

3rd floor 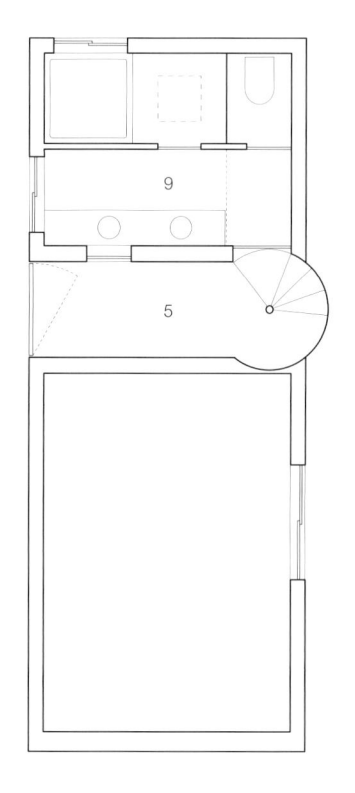	4th floor 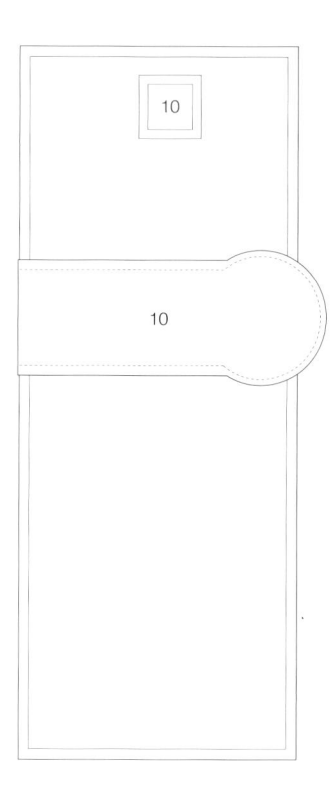	roof

平面図 1:100　　1:オフィス　2:ホール　3:車庫　4:書斎　5:吹抜け　6:リビング　7:ダイニングキッチン　8:寝室　9:風呂　10:トップライト

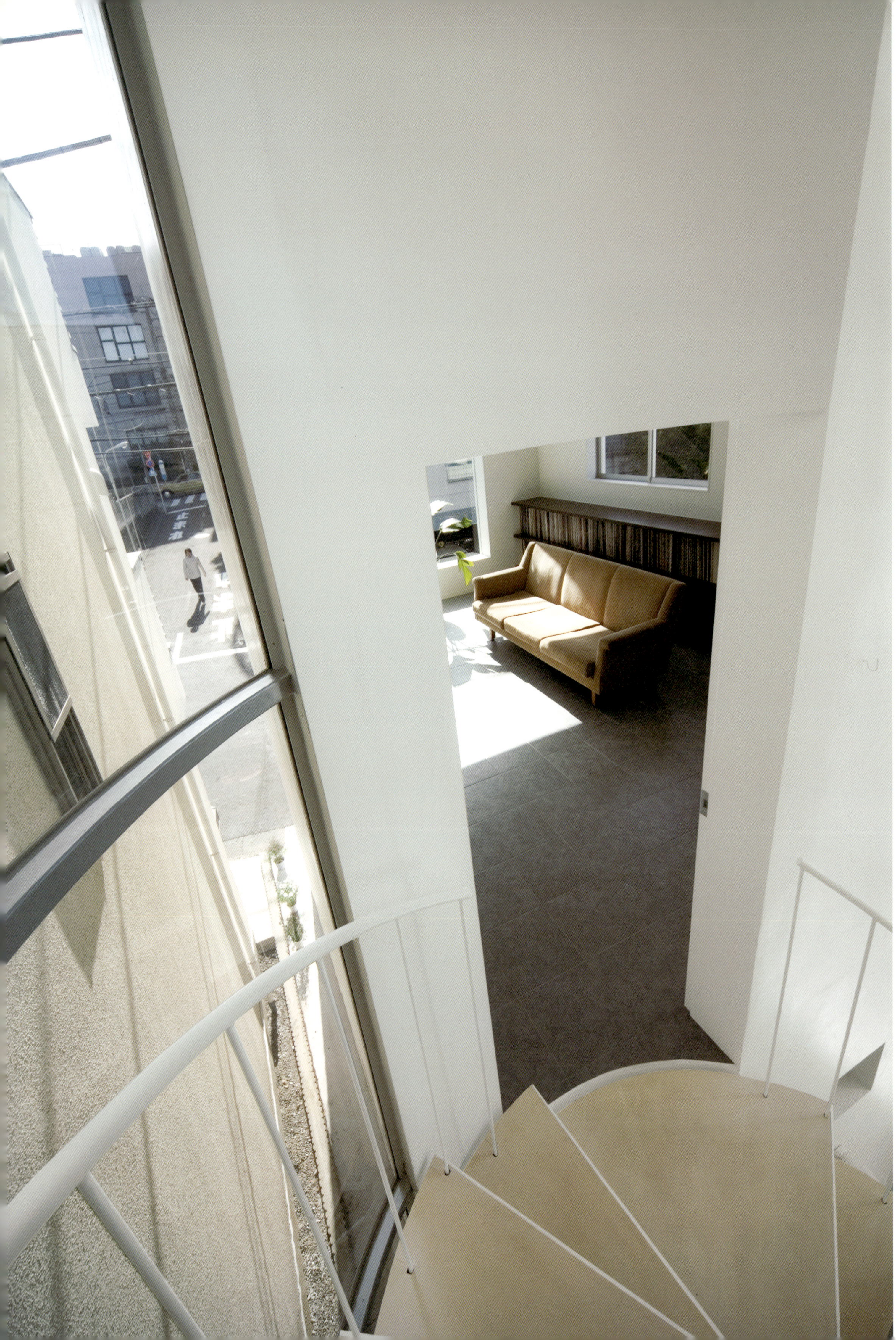

51

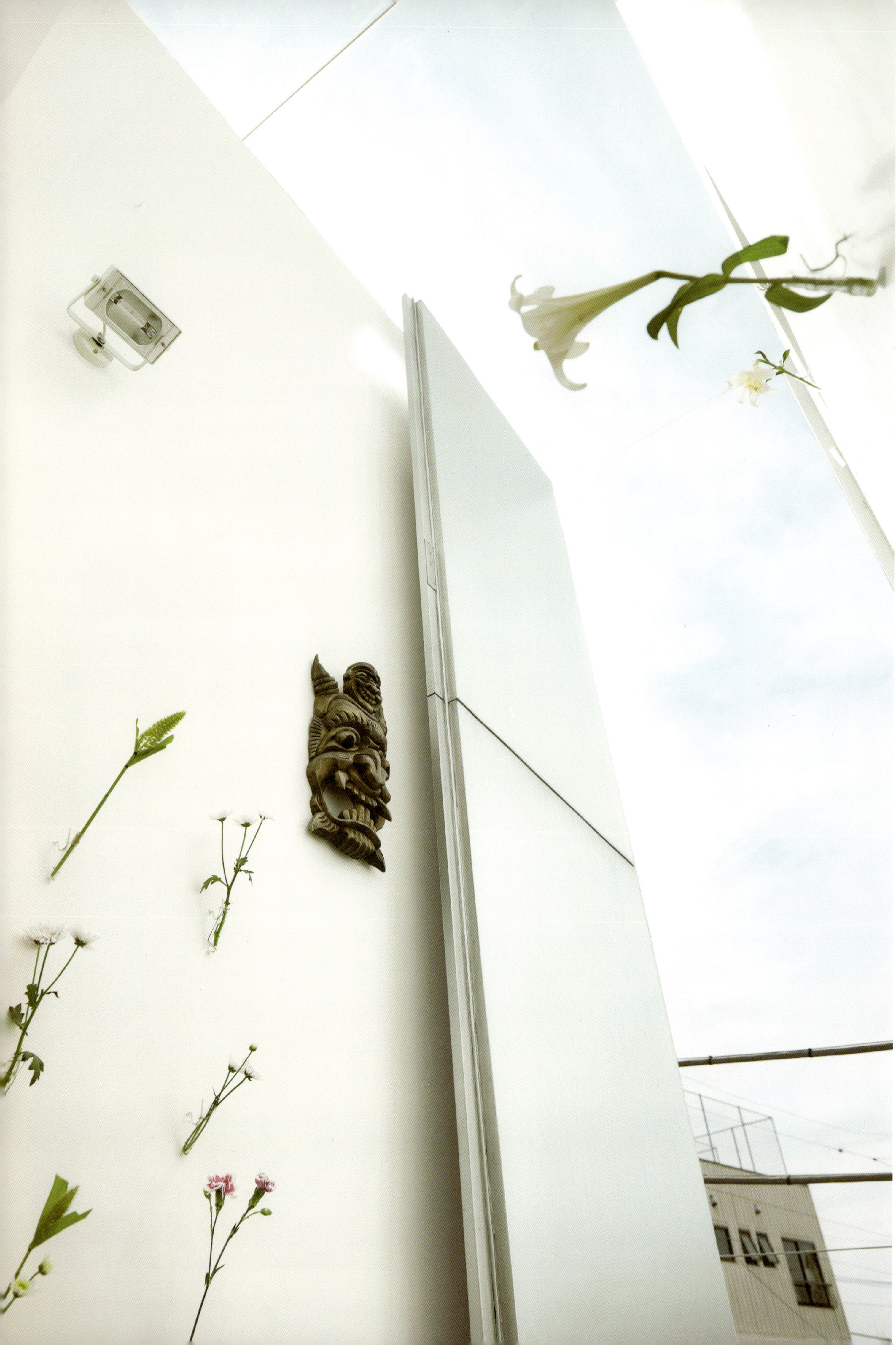

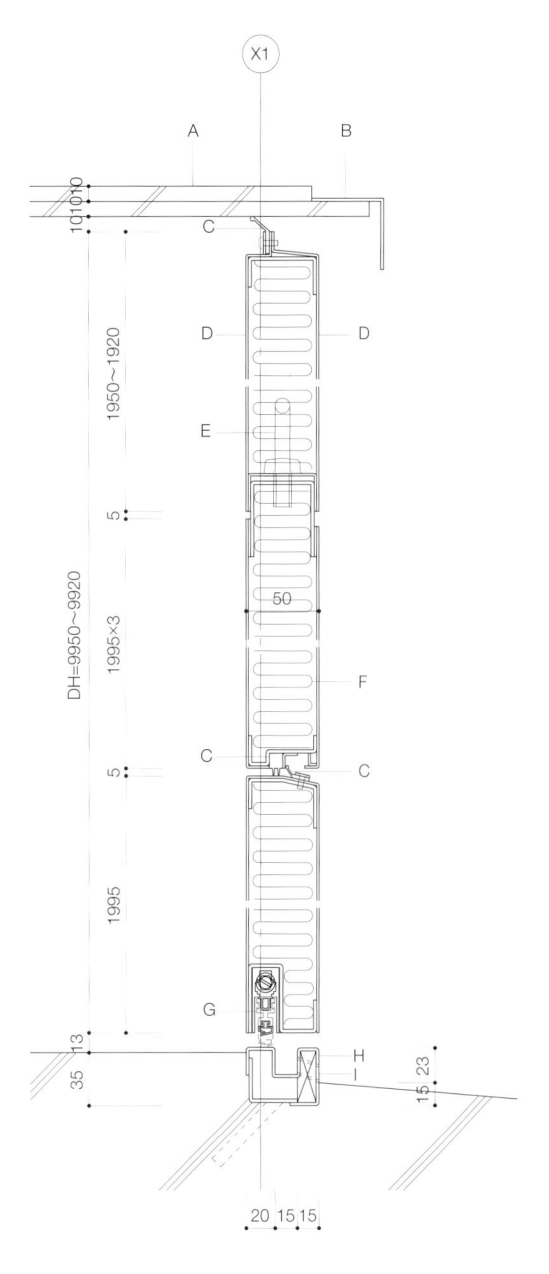

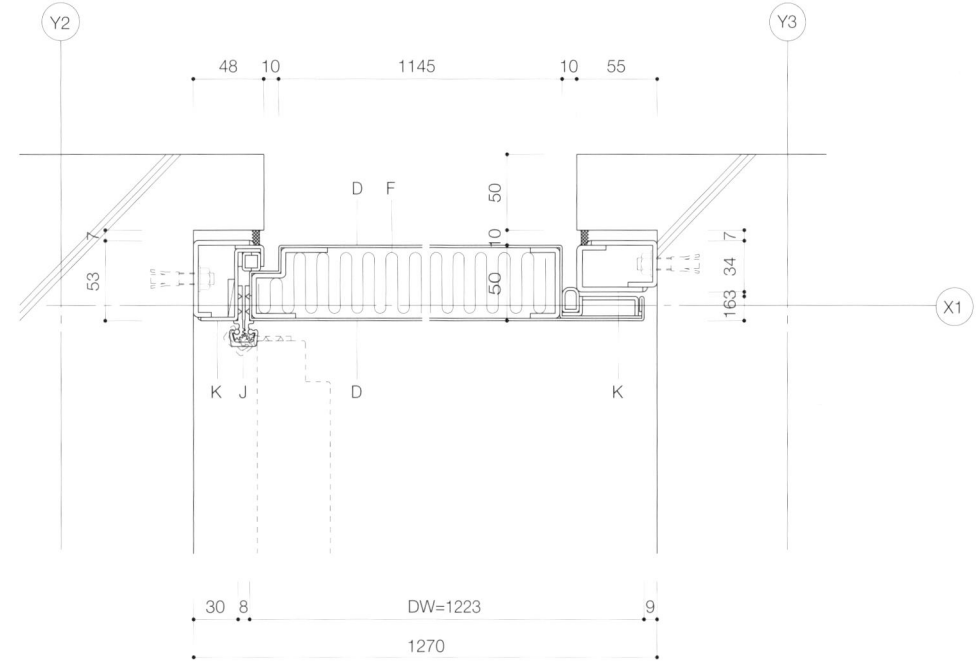

A—Skylight: Double reinforced glazing t=20mm (10+10mm), solar reflective film B—Skylight flashing: Acrylic angle 40×40mm t=2mm C—Rubber seal D—Door face: Steel plates t=2mm, polyurethane paint E—Door joint: Steel plates φ24mm F—Glasswool 24kg/m³ G—Air barrier H—Lower door frame: Stainless steel plates t=2mm I—Drain pipe: Stainless steel φ12mm K—Door jamb: Bent steel plates t=2.3mm, polyurethane paint J—Long hinge

A—トップライト：強化合わせガラス t=20mm（10＋10mm）熱線反射フィルム貼り B—トップライト水切り：アクリルアングル 40×40×2t C—ゴムパッキン D—ドア面材：St PL t=2mm UP E—ドアジョイント材：St φ24 F—グラスウール 24kg/m³ G—エアタイト H—ドア下枠：SUS PL t=2mm マゲ I—水抜きパイプ：SUS φ12 K—ドア縦枠：St PL t=2.3mm マゲ UP J—ロングヒンジ

Detail of entrance door 1:5　玄関ドア詳細図 1:5

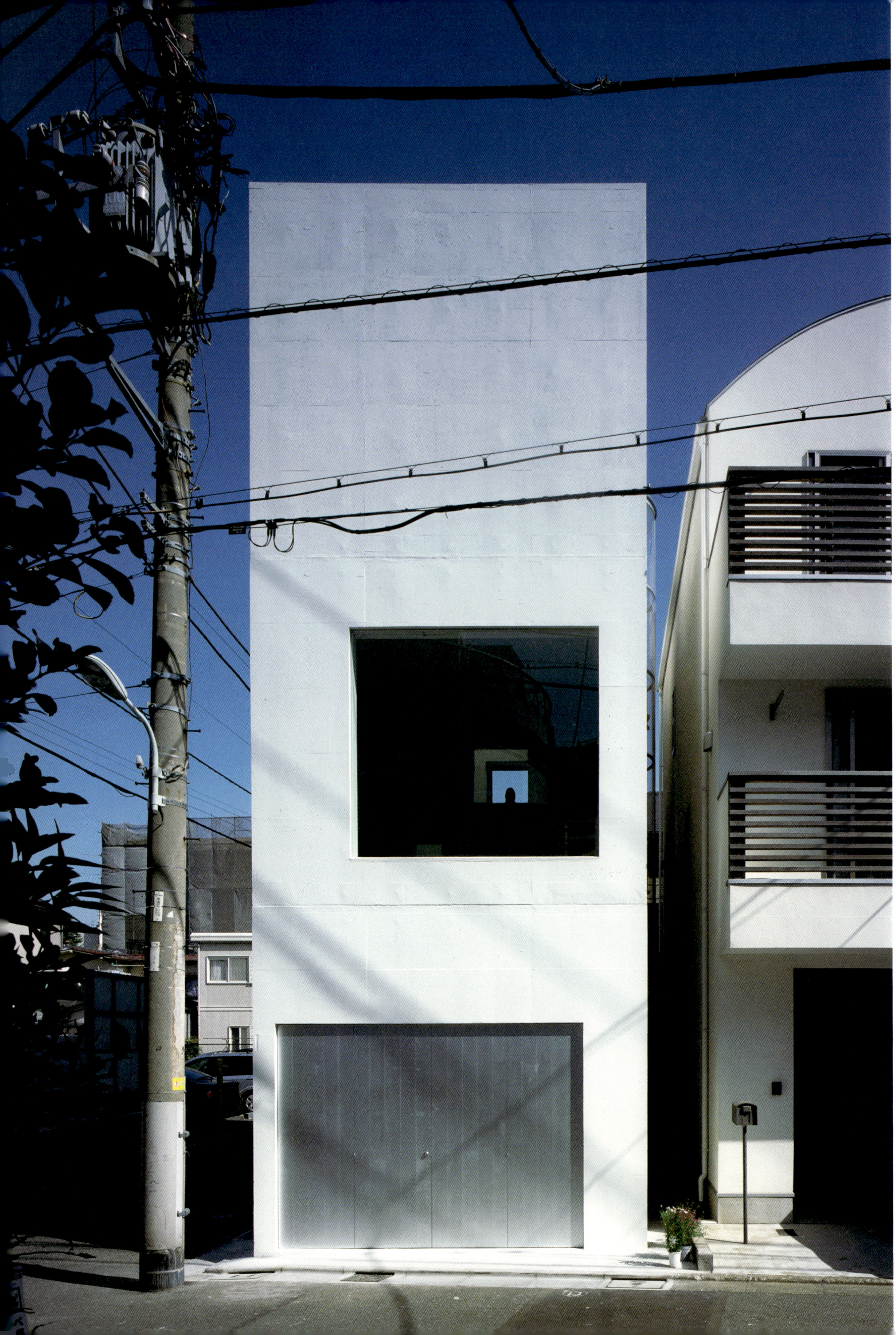

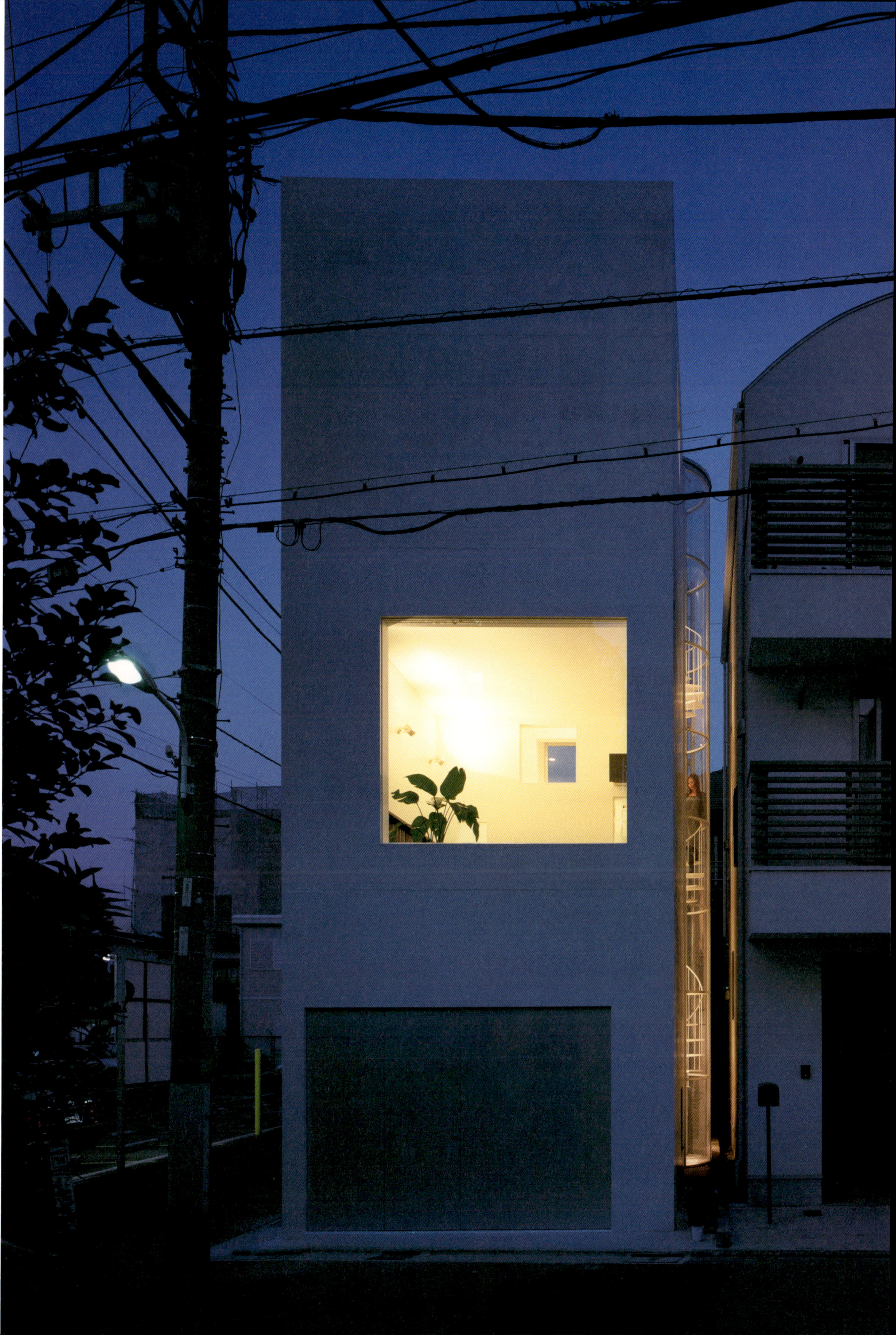

Site plan 1:1000　配置図 1:1000

House in Gotanda

Location: Shinagawa, Tokyo
Principal use: Residential
Site area: 48.27m^2
Building area: 33.64m^2
Total floor area: 105.15m^2
Number of stories: 4
Structure: Reinforced concrete

五反田の住宅

所在地：東京都品川区
主要用途：専用住宅
敷地面積：48.27m^2
建築面積：33.64m^2
延床面積：105.15m^2
規模：地上4階
構造：鉄筋コンクリート造

House in Komae | 狛江の住宅

This house, designed for a couple and their child, stands in a residential district in the center of Tokyo. It occupies a roughly 100-square-meter corner lot that is limited to 50 percent building coverage. In other words, more than half of the lot has to be set aside for a garden. But looking at the neighboring houses, I noticed that because they often didn't have enough space for a garden, the residents tended to block the roadside windows with curtains, giving the neighborhood a slightly dark atmosphere. It seemed necessary to reorganize the relationship between the building, the garden, and the road. I decided to create a building that occupied the entire lot, using half of the area for the living spaces and the other half for the garden, and make a private semi-basement space beneath the garden for the bedrooms and wet area. The garden, elevated one meter above ground level (a height of up to one meter is not subject to the coverage regulation), stands at the same height as the sofa in the living room. Lying in bed or in the bath in the semi-underground space, you can gaze up at the garden through a skylight. With a variety of openings and two staircases, the living room, garden, and bedrooms are loosely linked and gently combined. Furniture and other equipment can be installed in the garden in order to use the space as an outdoor living room. In addition, I thought this small, open space would add a little light to the densely populated residential district.

東京都内の住宅地に建つ、夫婦と子供1人のための住宅。敷地は100m^{2}ほどの角地で、建蔽率が50％と限られていた。つまり敷地の半分以上は庭になる。しかし近隣の住宅を見ると庭に十分な大きさがないため道路側の窓はカーテンで塞がれ、それが住宅地の印象を少し暗くしていた。建物／庭／道路の関係性を再編する必要性を感じた。敷地いっぱいに建物を建て、半分を居間、もう半分を庭、庭の下に寝室や水回りなどのプライベートな半地下の空間をつくる。地面より1m高い位置にある庭（高さ1mまでは建蔽率の対象外）はリビングのソファと同じ高さになる。半地下の空間ではベッドや浴槽に横たわり、トップライトを介して頭上の庭を眺める。いろいろな開口と2つの階段が、居間、庭、寝室の3つの空間を少しずつつなぎ、穏やかに混ぜ合わせていく。庭は家具や設備が設えられ、外のリビングとして使われる。さらにこの小さなオープンスペースのような空間が、密集した住宅地を少し明るくするようなものになればと考えた。

Site plan 1:1000　配置図 1:1000

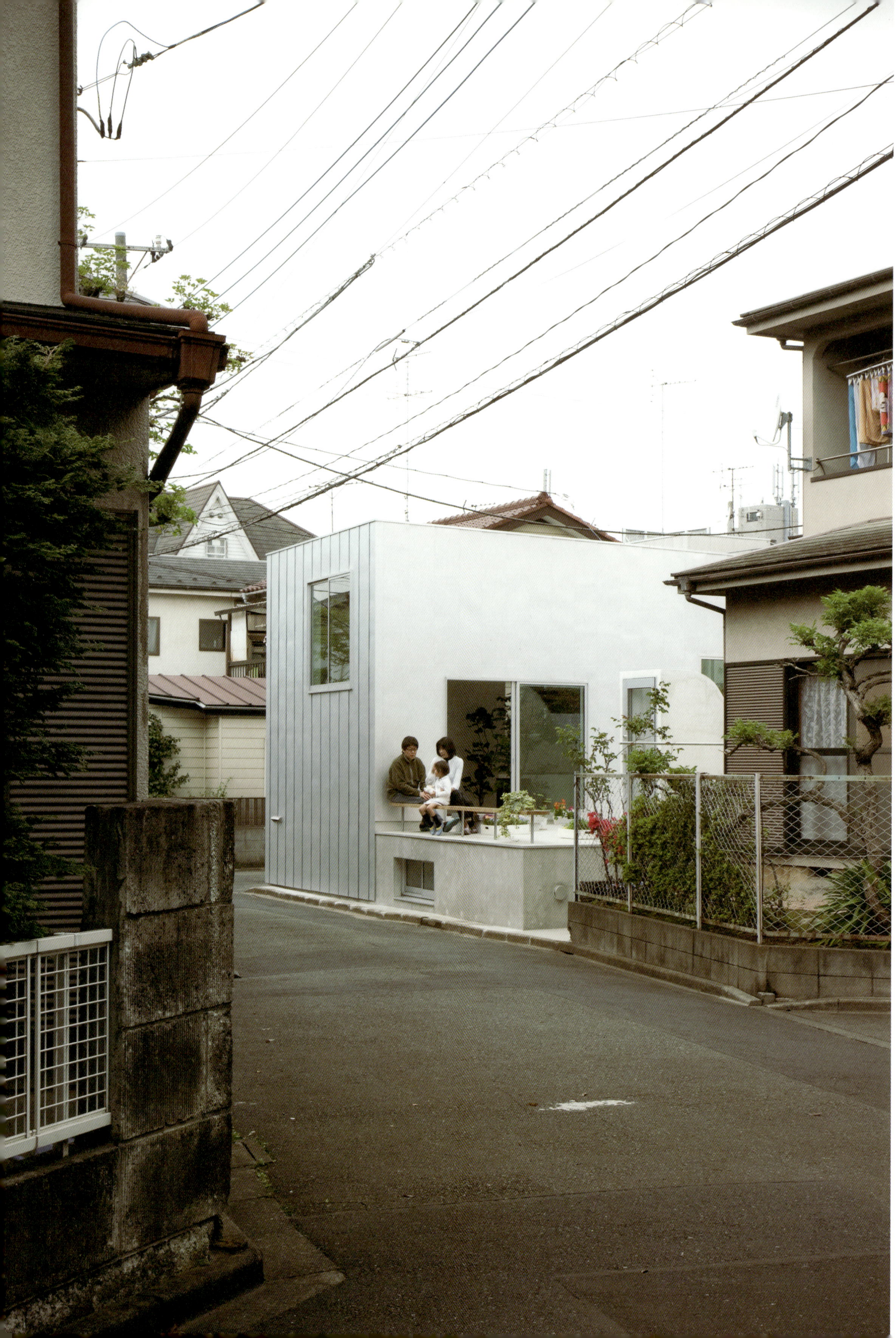

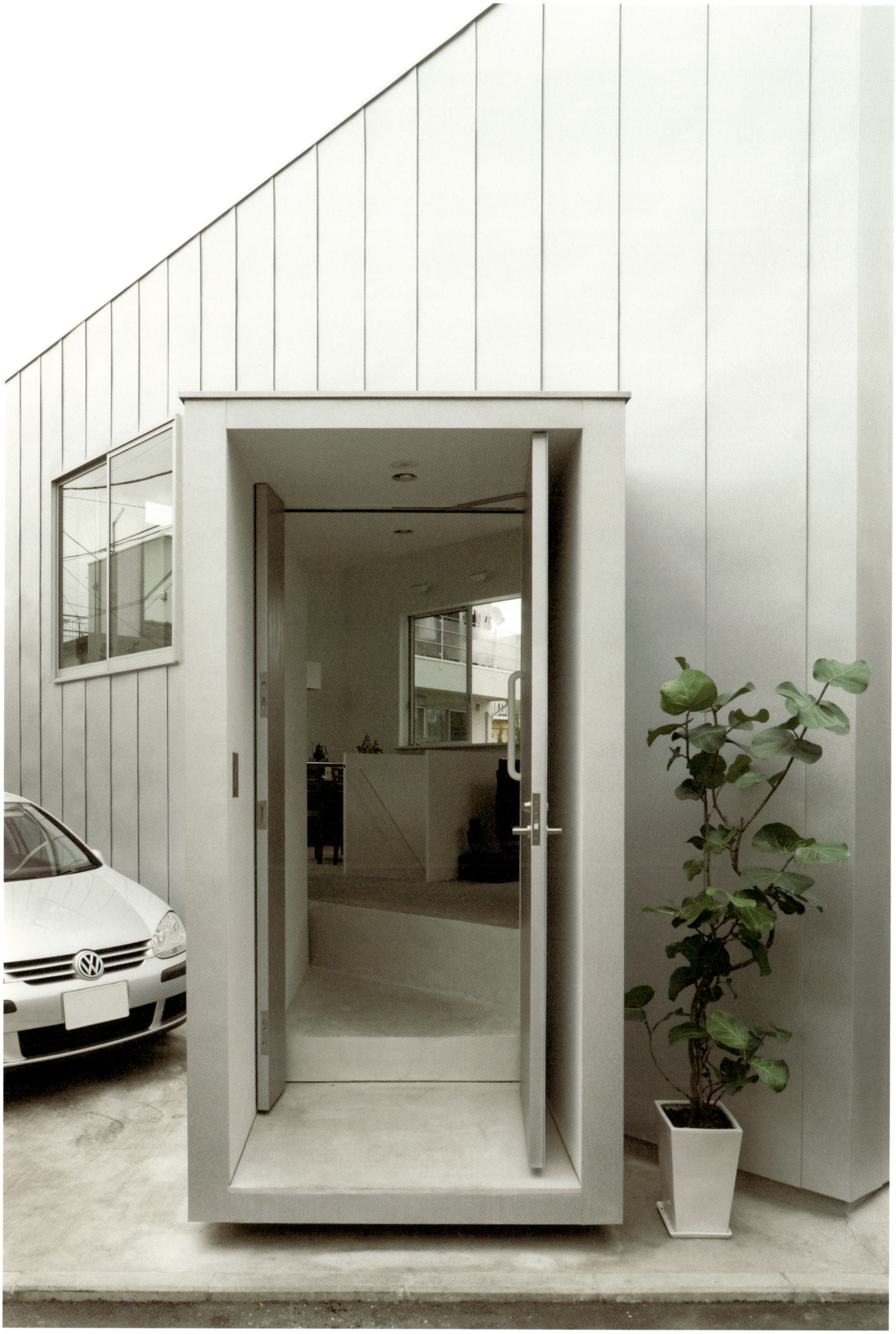

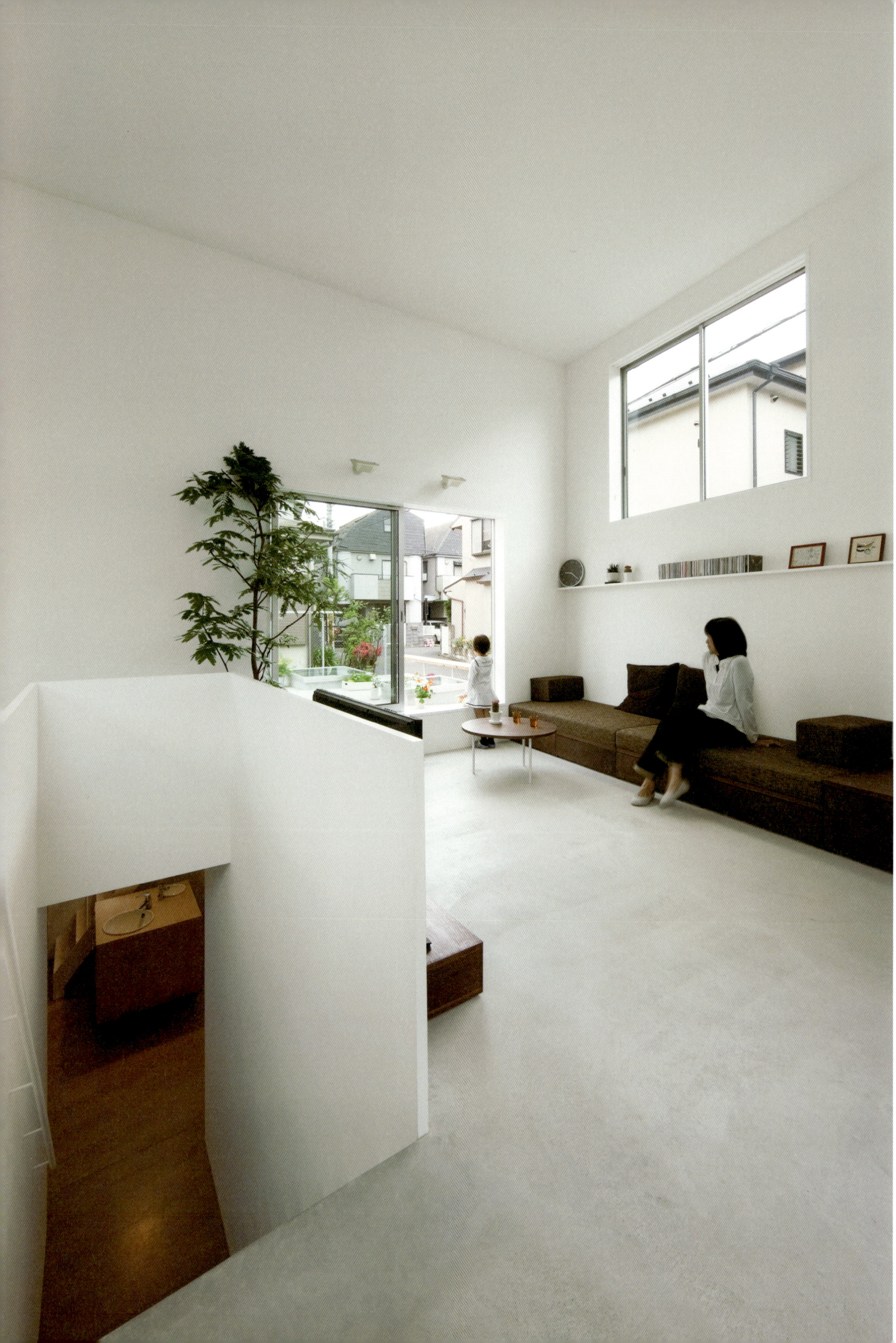

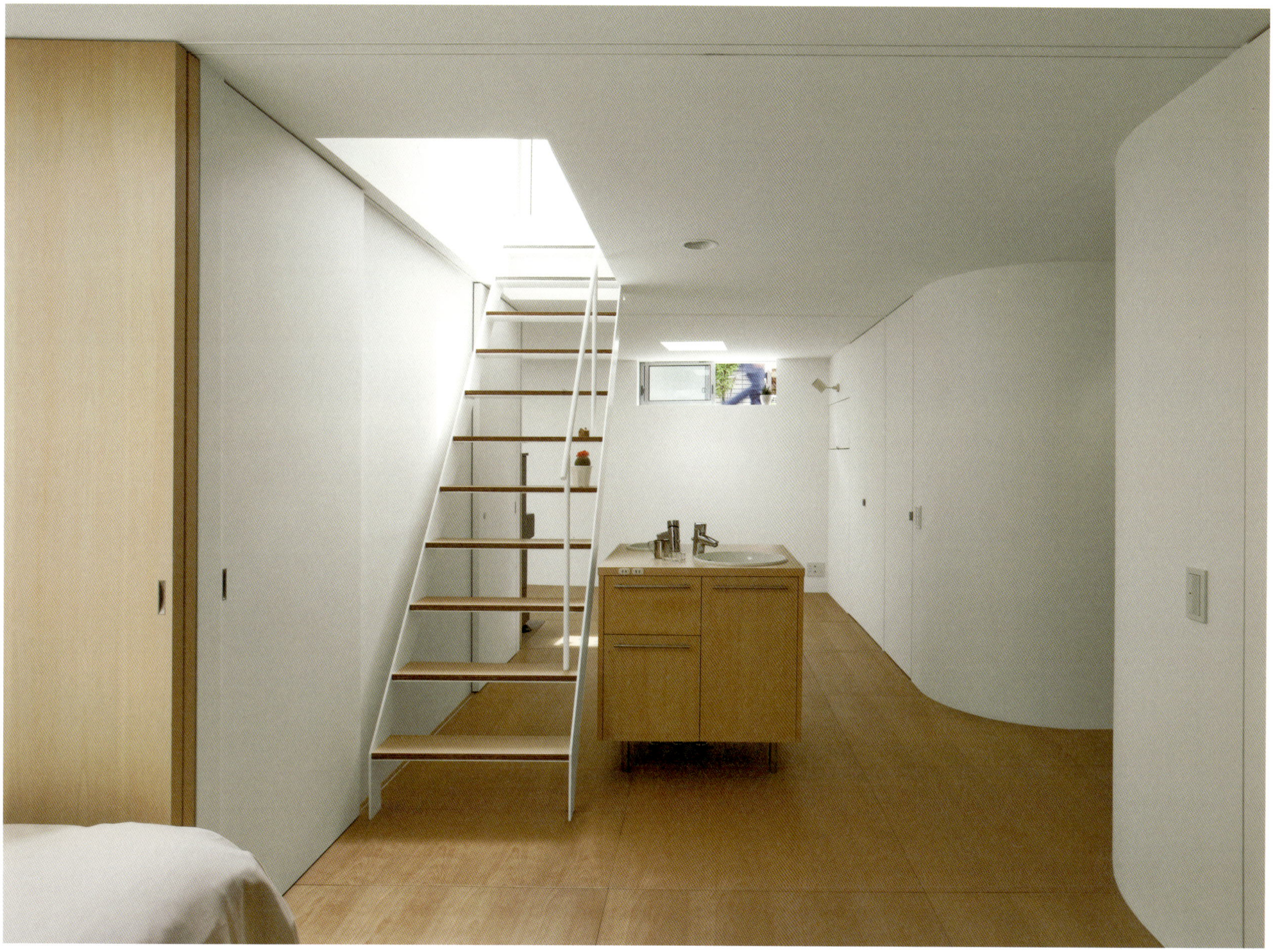

semi-underground floor

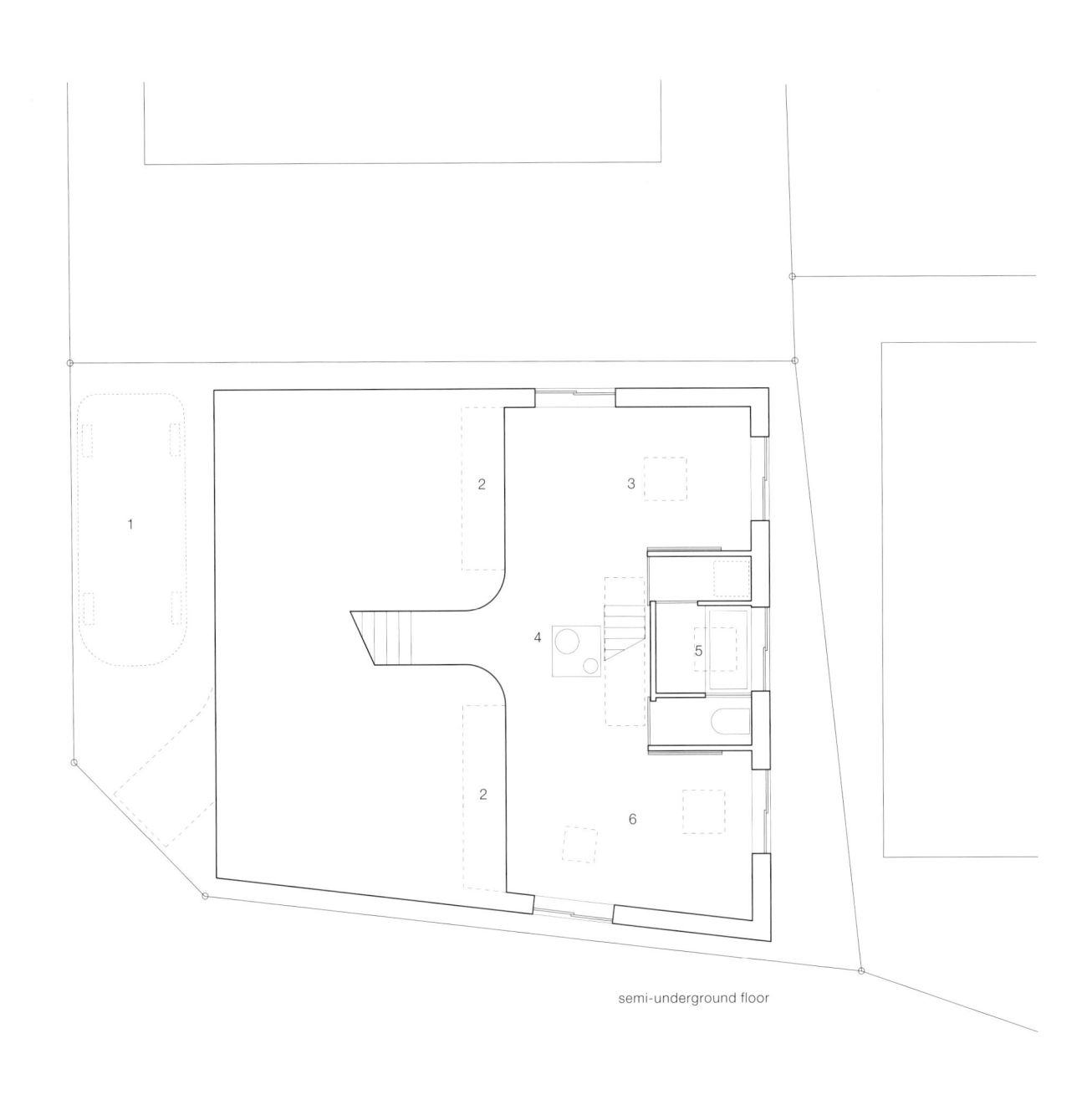

Plan 1:100   1: parking 2: closet 3: bedroom 4: washroom 5: bathroom 6: children's room 7: entrance 8: dining kitchen 9: living room 10: garden

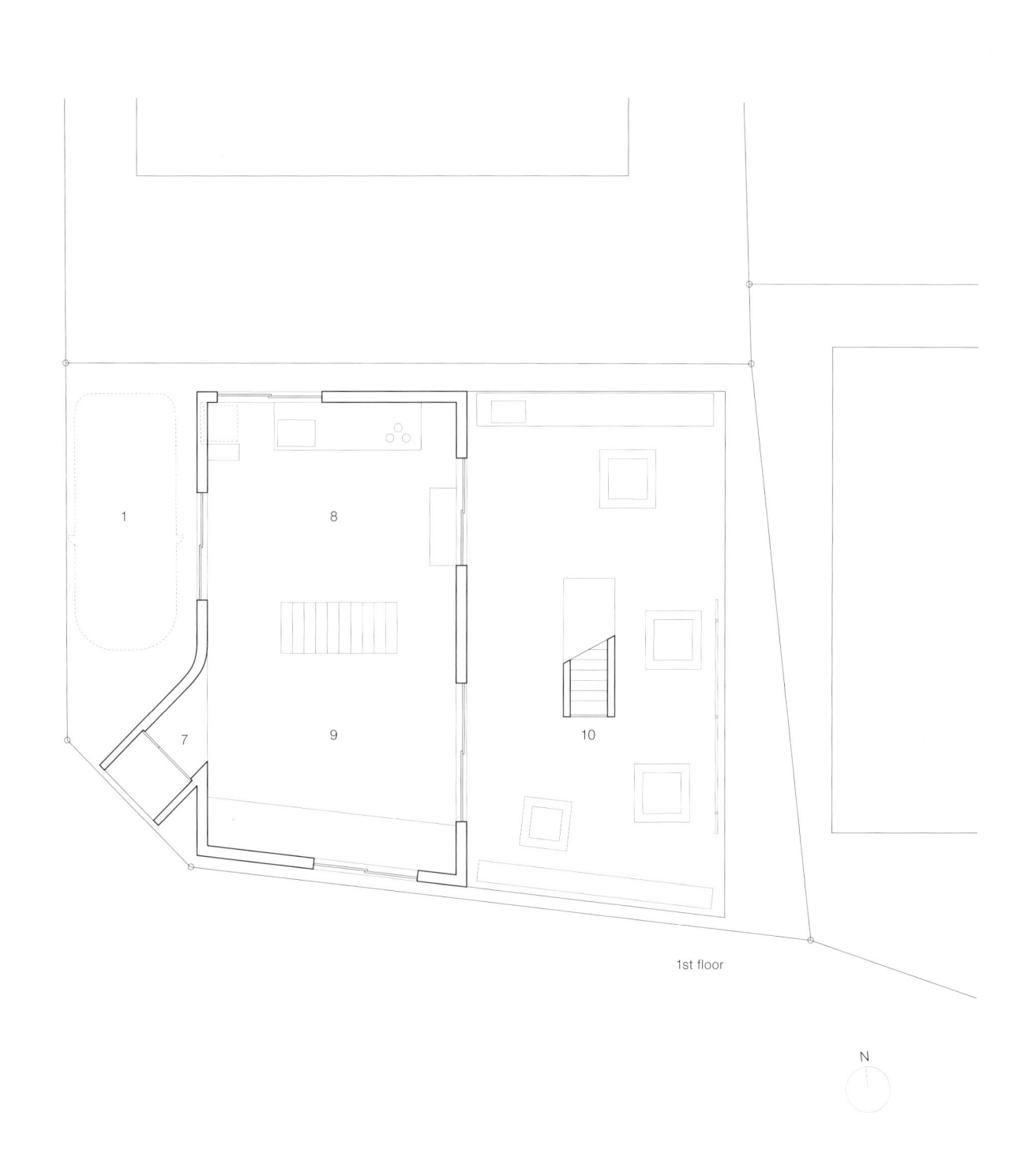

平面図 1:100　　1:駐車場　2:クロゼット　3:寝室　4:洗面室　5:浴室　6:子供室　7:玄関　8:ダイニングキッチン　9:リビング　10:庭

semi-underground floor

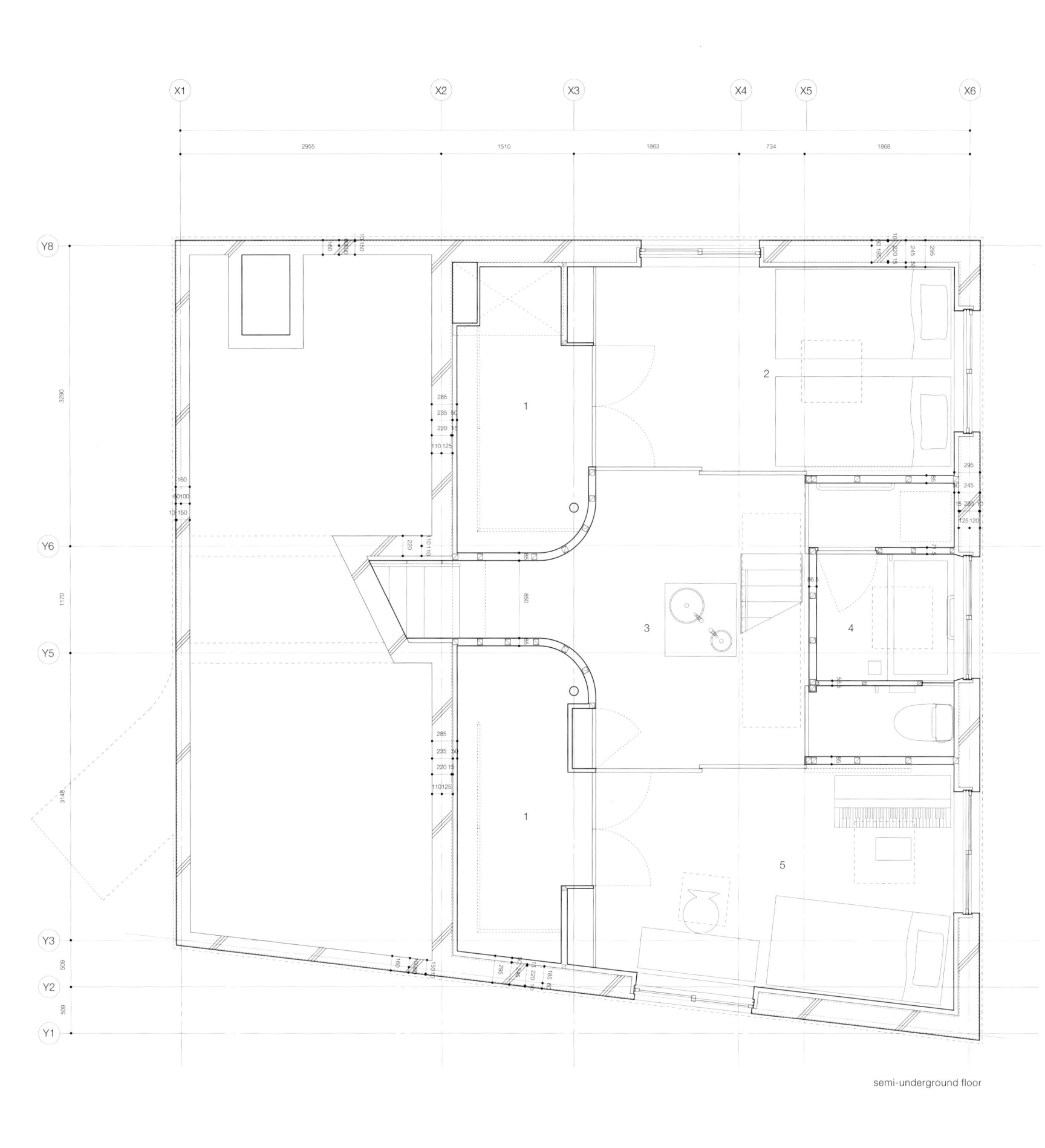

66 Plan detail 1:50   1: closet 2: bedroom 3: washroom 4: bathroom 5: children's room 6: entrance 7: dining kitchen 8: living room 9: garden

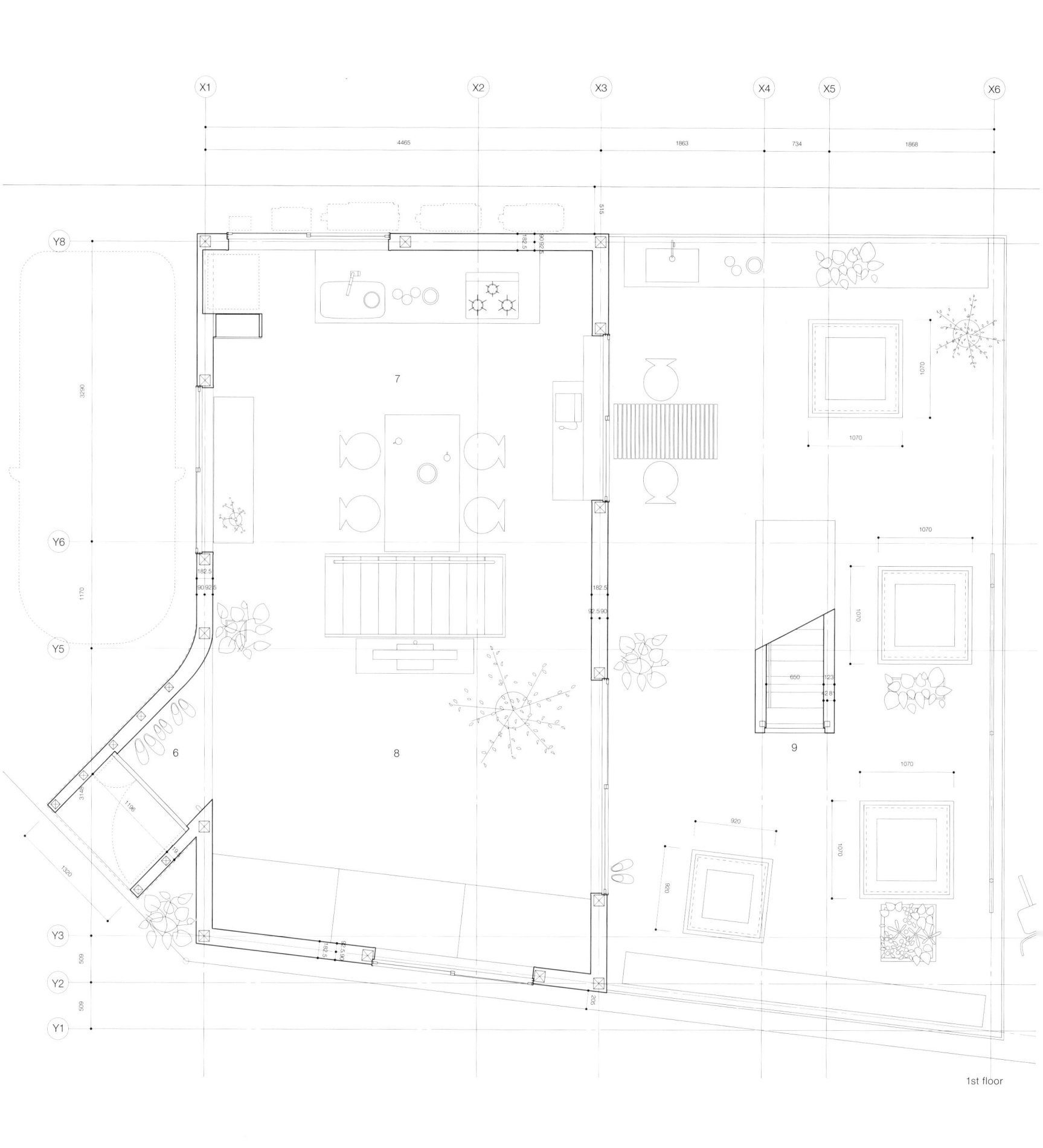

平面詳細図　1:50　　　1:クロゼット　2:寝室　3:洗面室　4:浴室　5:子供室　6:玄関　7:ダイニングキッチン　8:リビング　9:庭

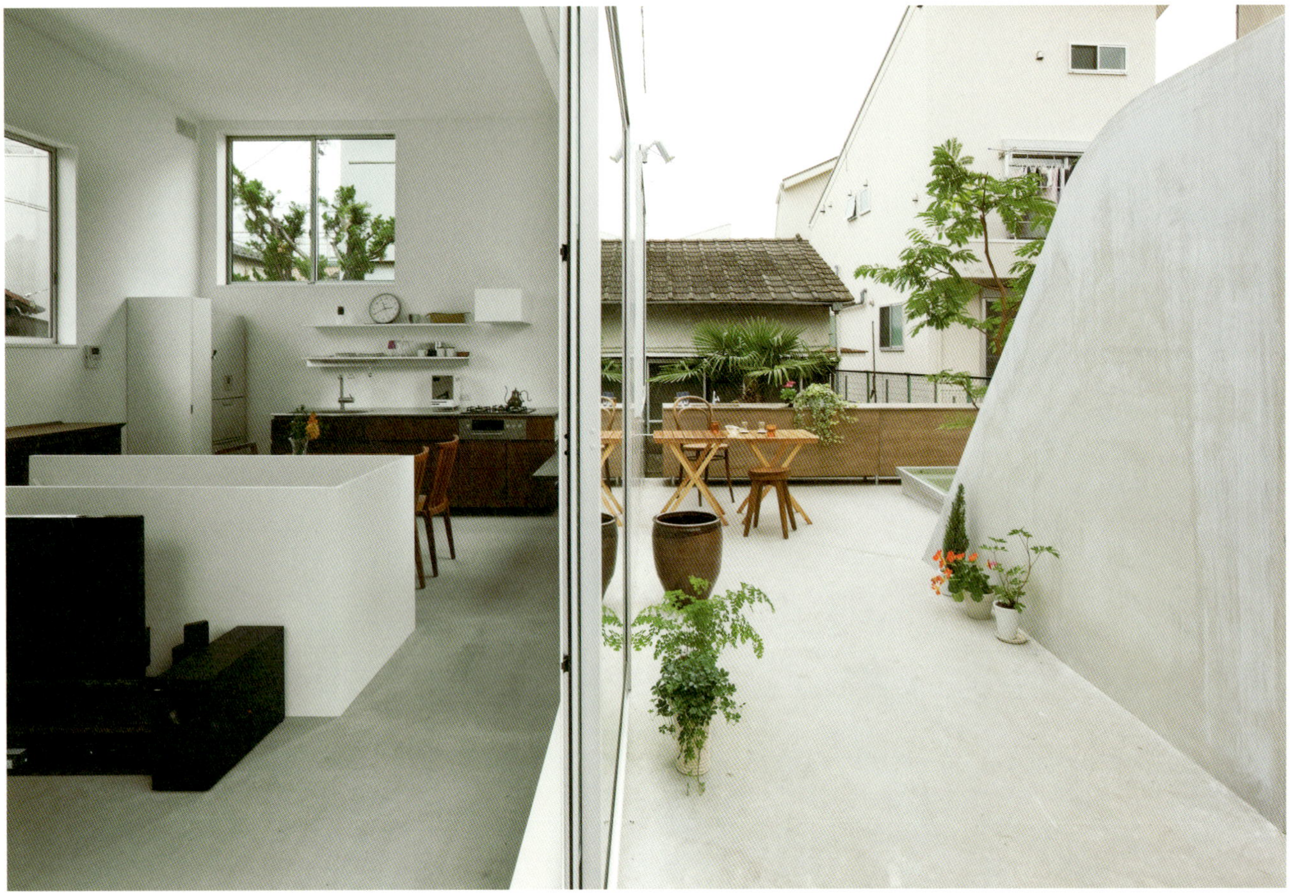

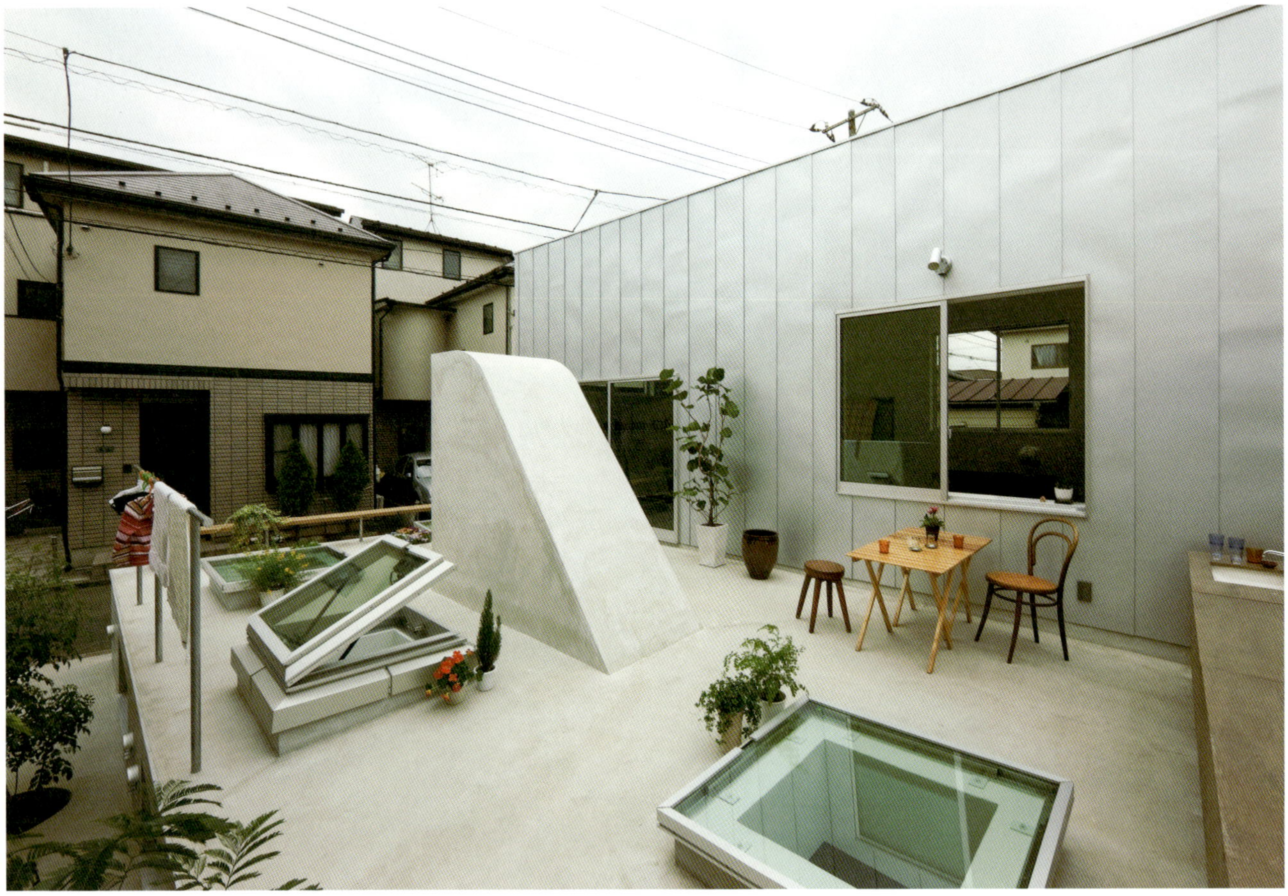

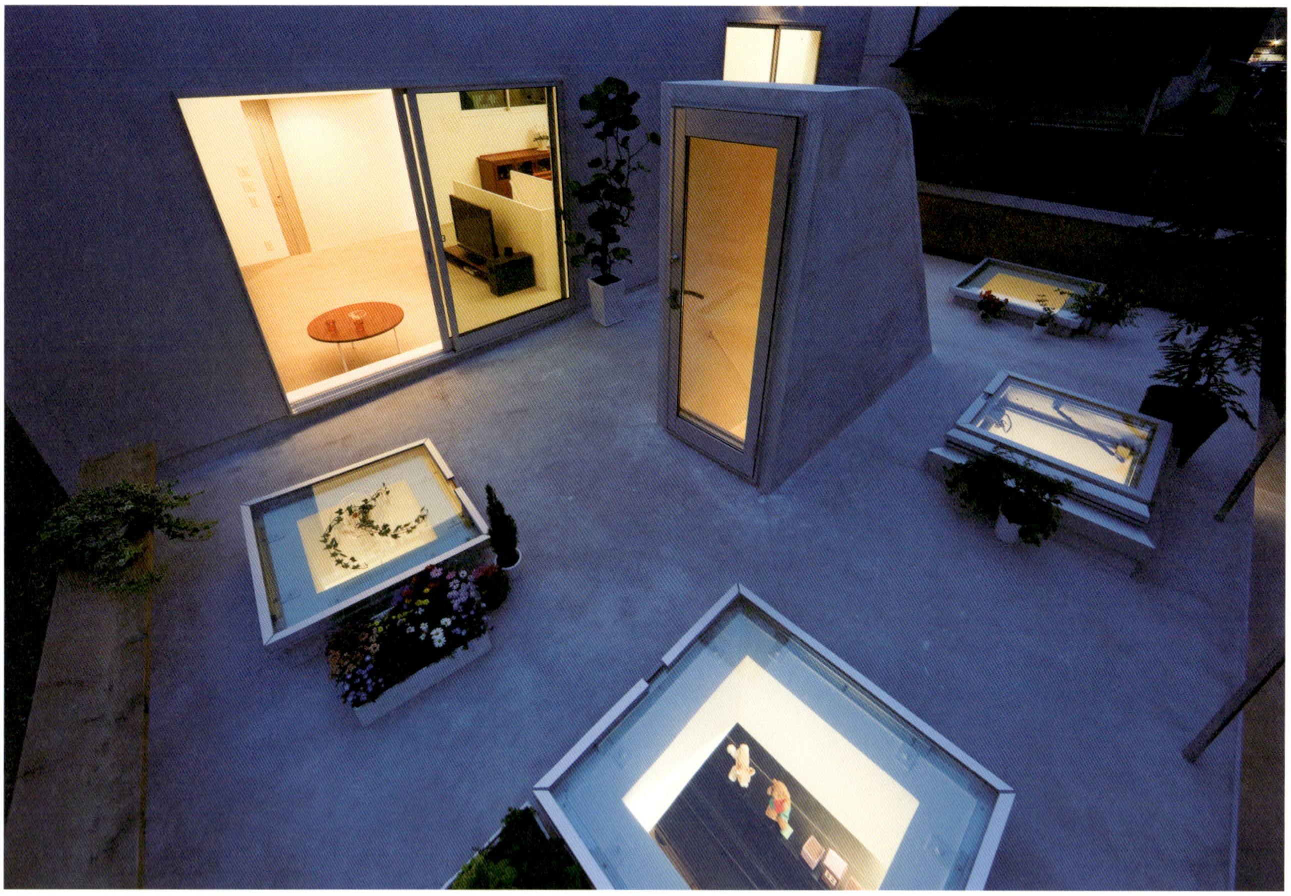

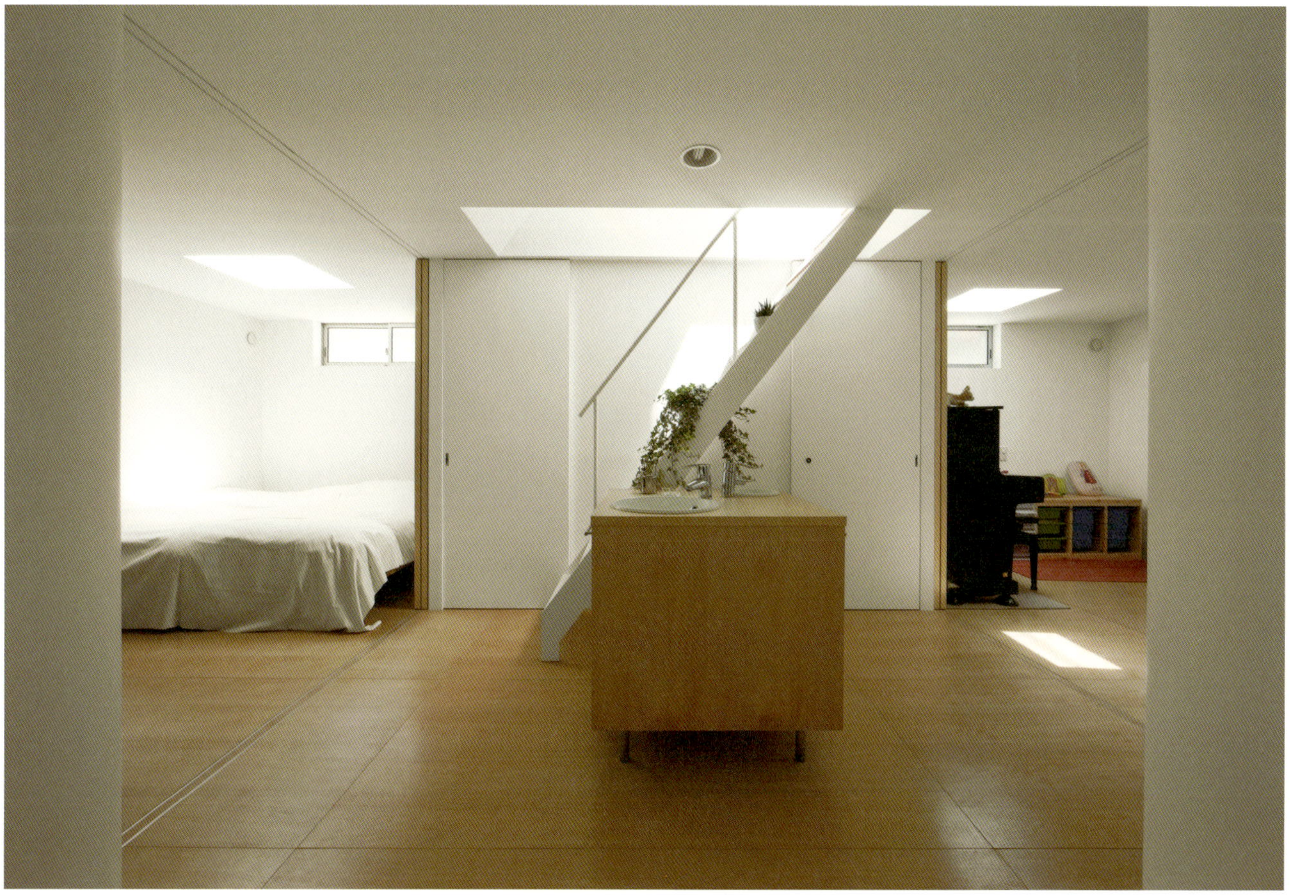

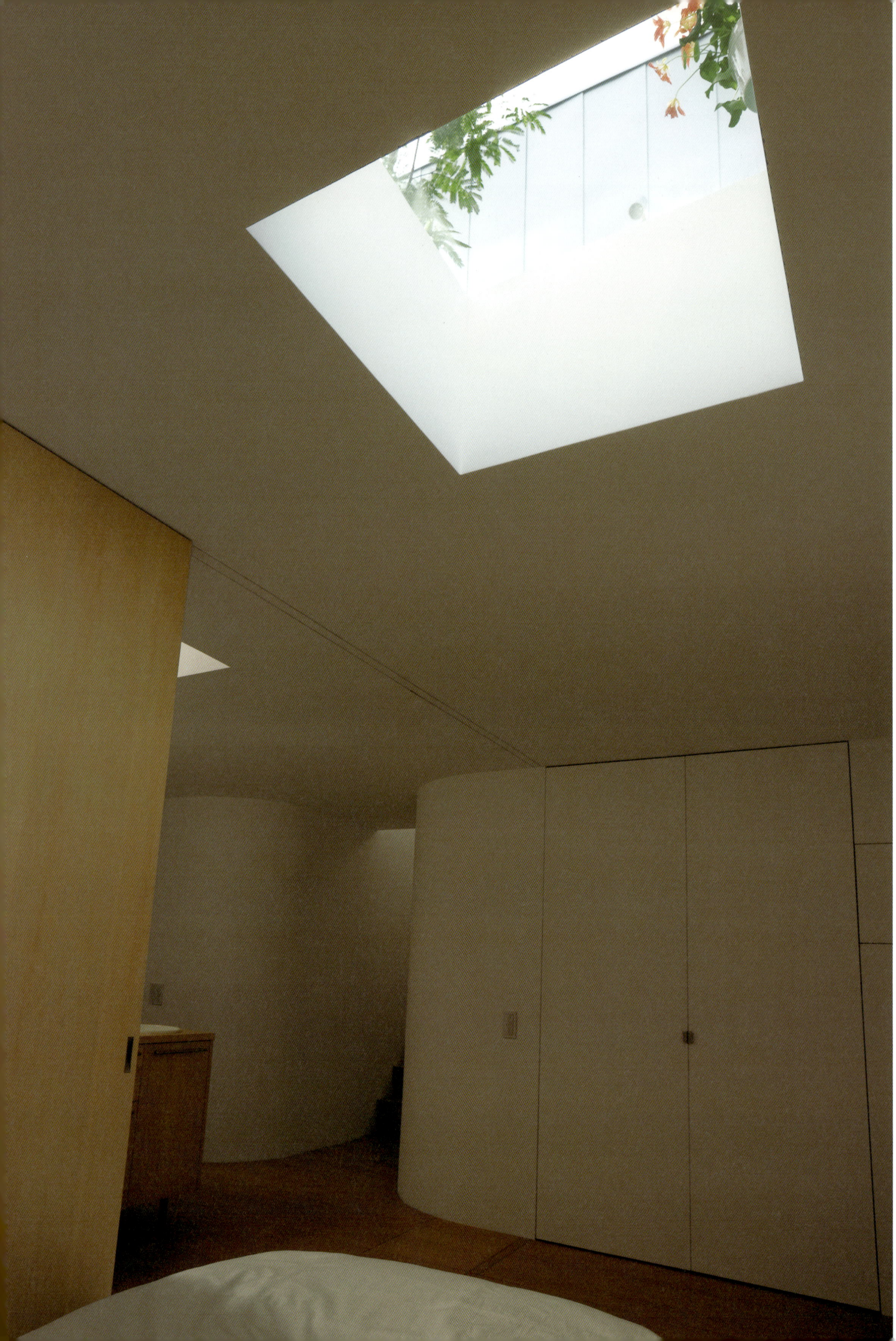

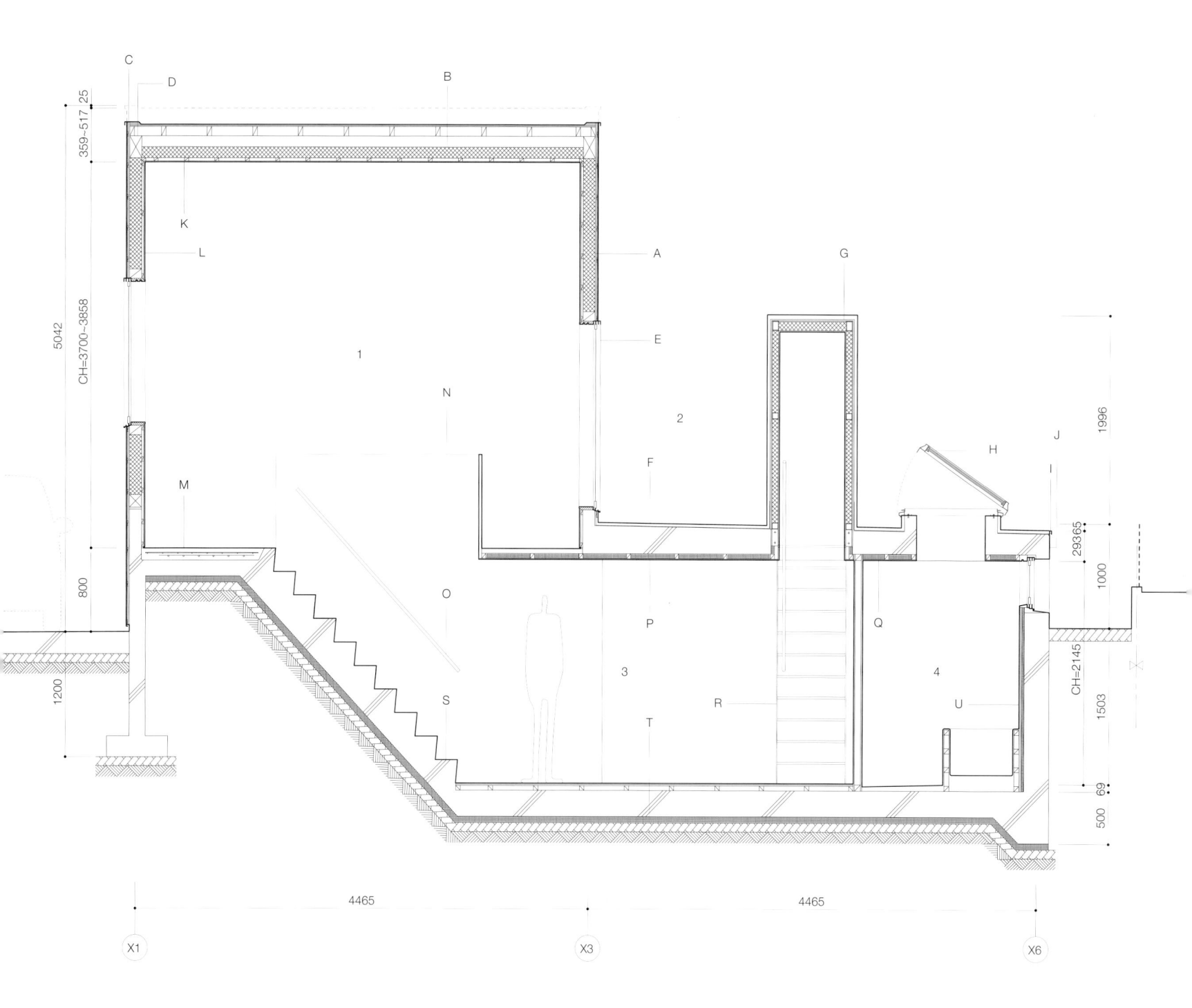

A—External walls: Seamed galvanized steel sheeting t=0.35mm, furring strips 10×40mm @300mm | Moisture permeable waterproof sheeting | Structural plywood t=12mm | Studs: 120×60mm @450mm | Insulation: Glasswool t=100mm (24kg/m³)　B—Roof: Polyvinyl chloride sheet waterproofing t=2mm | Waterproof plywood t=9+9mm | Purlin: 90×45mm @450mm | Beam: 210×90mm @900mm | Insulation: Glasswool t=100mm (24kg/m³)　C—Coping: Bent galvanized steel t=0.35mm　D—Girder: 210×120mm　E—Sliding window: Aluminum sash (low-e glass)　F—Floor: Concrete trowel finish t=30mm　G—Walls/roof: Waterproof mortar t=30mm, photocatalyst paint | Metal lath | Waterproof paper | Fiber reinforced cement panel t=12mm | Steel 60×60mm ×3.2mm | Insulation: Polyurethane foam t=50mm　H—Skylight: 600×600mm (low-e glass)　I—Flashing: Bent galvanized steel t=0.35mm　J—External Wall: Exposed concrete, photocatalyst paint　K—Ceiling: Plasterboard t=9mm, acrylic emulsion paint | Ceiling joist: 30×40mm @300mm　L—Wall: Plasterboard t=12.5mm, acrylic emulsion paint | Furring strips: 20×40mm @300mm　M—Floor: Concrete trowel finish t=70mm, wax | Metal lath | Floor heating copper pipe (copper plated) | Concrete slab t=150mm | Insulation: Styrofoam t=60mm | Polyethylene film sheeting t=0.2mm | Crushed stone t=60mm　N—Balustrade: Basswood lumber t=30mm, polyurethane paint　O—Balustrade: Steel pipe φ21mm, polyurethane paint　P—Ceiling: Plasterboard t=9mm, acrylic emulsion paint | Ceiling joist: 30×40mm @300mm | Insulation: Polyurethane spray t=50mm　Q—Ceiling: Waterproof plywood t=9mm, topcoat finish | Ceiling joist: 50×40mm @300mm | Insulation: Polyurethane foam t=50mm　R—Tread: Bent steel plates t=4.5mm, polyurethane paint | Cut string: Steel plates t=9mm, polyurethane paint | Balustrade: Steel pipe φ30mm, polyurethane paint　S—Stair tread/riser: Mended exposed concrete, water repellent paint　T—Floor: Birch plywood t=12mm, polyurethane paint | Structural plywood t=12mm | Floor joist: 45×45mm | Concrete slab t=250mm, reforming waterproof finish | Insulation: Styrofoam t=60mm | Polyethylene film sheeting t=0.2mm | Crushed stone t=60mm

A—外壁：ガルバリウム鋼板 t=0.35mm 縦ハゼ葺き | 断熱材：グラスウール t=100mm(24kg/m³) | 胴縁：10×40mm @300mm 透湿防水シート | 構造用合板 t=12mm | 間柱：120×60mm @450mm | 断熱材：グラスウール t=100mm(24kg/m³)　B—屋根：塩ビシート防水 t=2mm | 耐水合板 t=9+9mm | 母屋：90×45mm @450mm | 梁：210×90mm @900mm | 断熱材：グラスウール t=100mm(24kg/m³)　C—笠木：ガルバリウム鋼板 t=0.35mm マゲ　D—桁：210×120mm　E—引き違い窓：アルミサッシ既製品(Low-Eガラス)　F—床：コンクリート t=30mm 金ゴテ仕上げ　G—壁・屋根：防水モルタル t=30mm 光触媒塗料塗布 | メタルラス | 防水紙 | 繊維強化セメント板 t=12mm | St-□60×60mm ×3.2t | 断熱材：ウレタンフォーム t=50mm　H—トップブライト：アルミ既製品 600×600mm(Low-Eガラス)　I—水切り：ガルバリウム鋼板 t=0.35mm マゲ　J—外壁：コンクリート打放し 光触媒塗布　K—天井：プラスターボード t=9mm AEP 野縁：30×40mm @300mm　L—壁：プラスターボード t=12.5mm AEP | 胴縁：20×40mm @300mm　M—床：コンクリート t=70mm 金ゴテ仕上げWAX | メタルラス | 床暖房銅管(表面銅板付き) | コンクリートスラブ t=150mm | 断熱材：スタイロフォーム t=60mm | ポリエチレンフィルム t=0.2mm | 砕石 t=60mm　N—手摺：シナランバー t=30mm UP　O—手摺：Stパイプφ21mm UP　P—天井：プラスターボード t=9mm AEP | 野縁：30×40mm @300mm | 断熱材：ウレタンフォーム吹付け t=40mm　Q—天井：耐水合板 t=9mm トップコート仕上げ | 野縁：50×40mm @300mm | 断熱材：ウレタンフォーム t=50mm　R—踏み板：St PL t=4.5mm マゲ UP | ササラ：St PL t=9mm UP | 手摺：Stパイプφ30mm UP　S—階段踏面・蹴上：コンクリート打放し補修、撥水剤塗布　T—床：バーチ合板 t=12mm UP | 構造用合板 t=12mm | 根太：45×45mm | コンクリートスラブ t=250mm ザイペックス塗布 | 断熱材：スタイロフォーム t=60mm | ポリエチレンフィルム t=0.2mm | 砕石 t=60mm

Section 1:50　　1: dining kitchen　2: garden　3: washroom　4: bathroom　　矩計図 1:50　　1：ダイニングキッチン　2：庭　3：洗面室　4：浴室

Elevation 1:100　立面図 1:100

House in Komae

Location: Komae, Tokyo
Principal use: Residential
Site area: 108.99m^2
Building area: 39.61m^2
Total floor area: 86.70m^2
Number of stories: 1 plus 1 basement
Structure: Reinforced concrete+timber frame

狛江の住宅

所在地：東京都狛江市
主要用途：専用住宅
敷地面積：108.99m^2
建築面積：39.61m^2
延床面積：86.70m^2
規模：地下1階　地上1階
構造：鉄筋コンクリート造＋木造

Apartment in Nerima | 練馬のアパートメント

This rental apartment complex is located in the Tokyo metropolitan area. The lot abuts the street that runs in front of the station, and the complex stands on the border between an area of apartment buildings and one of houses. As the site is near an office district and a university, there was a need to create a few different kinds of units that could be used both by working people and students. For each dwelling, I designed a large terrace with approximately the same size as the interior that functions like a garden in a detached house. Moreover, by equipping the corner units with an L-shaped terrace, the long, narrow units with a long, narrow terrace, and the three-level maisonette units with a vertical, atrium-style terrace that extends through the three levels, I was also able to incorporate a semi-outdoor space with a unique form that reflects the interior characteristics of each dwelling. Rather than attaching a balcony to the building, I used the terraces to shape the interior and way of living in each unit through the strong individual qualities, such as form and brightness, in each space. These distinctive terraces also provide the residents with a view of the town below, the sky above, and an awareness of their neighbors' movements. They also offer them options in their daily lives such as whether to dine inside or outside on a particular day. The various movements in the residents' awareness and lives are also conveyed to the neighborhood via the exterior of the complex.

都内に建つ賃貸集合住宅。敷地は駅前通りに面しており、集合住宅エリアと住宅地の境界に建つ。オフィス街と大学のエリアの両方に近いため、社会人と学生の両方に入居してもらえるように住戸にいくつかのバリエーションをつくることなどが求められた。各住戸に、戸建て住宅の庭のように、インテリアと同じくらい大きなテラスを用意する。しかも角部屋の住戸にはL型テラス、細長い住戸には細長テラス、3層メゾネット住戸には3層吹抜けの縦長テラスといったように、各住戸の特徴となるような個性的な形をもった半屋外空間をインテリアに併置する。これらはいわゆるバルコニーのような建物に付属するものではなく、形や明るさなど空間の強い個性によって各住戸のインテリアや生活をかたちづくるものである。また個性的なテラスは、街を見下ろしたり、空を見上げたりと、住人の意識に動きを与える。あるいは今日は外で食事をしようか、内で食べようか、と生活のなかに選択肢を与える。こうした住人の意識や生活のなかのさまざまな動きが、集合住宅の外観として街にも表れている。

Elevation 1:200　　立面図 1:200

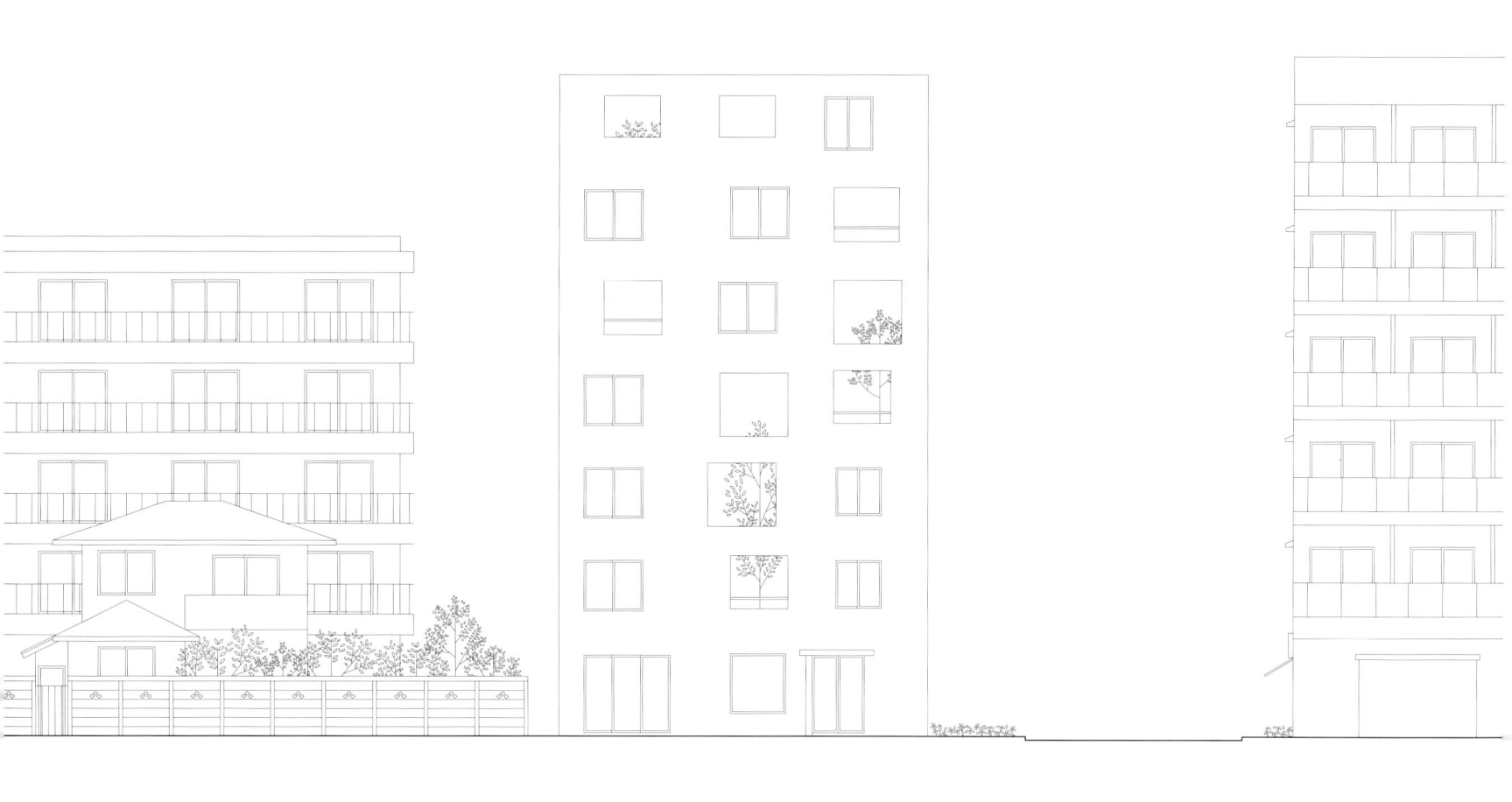

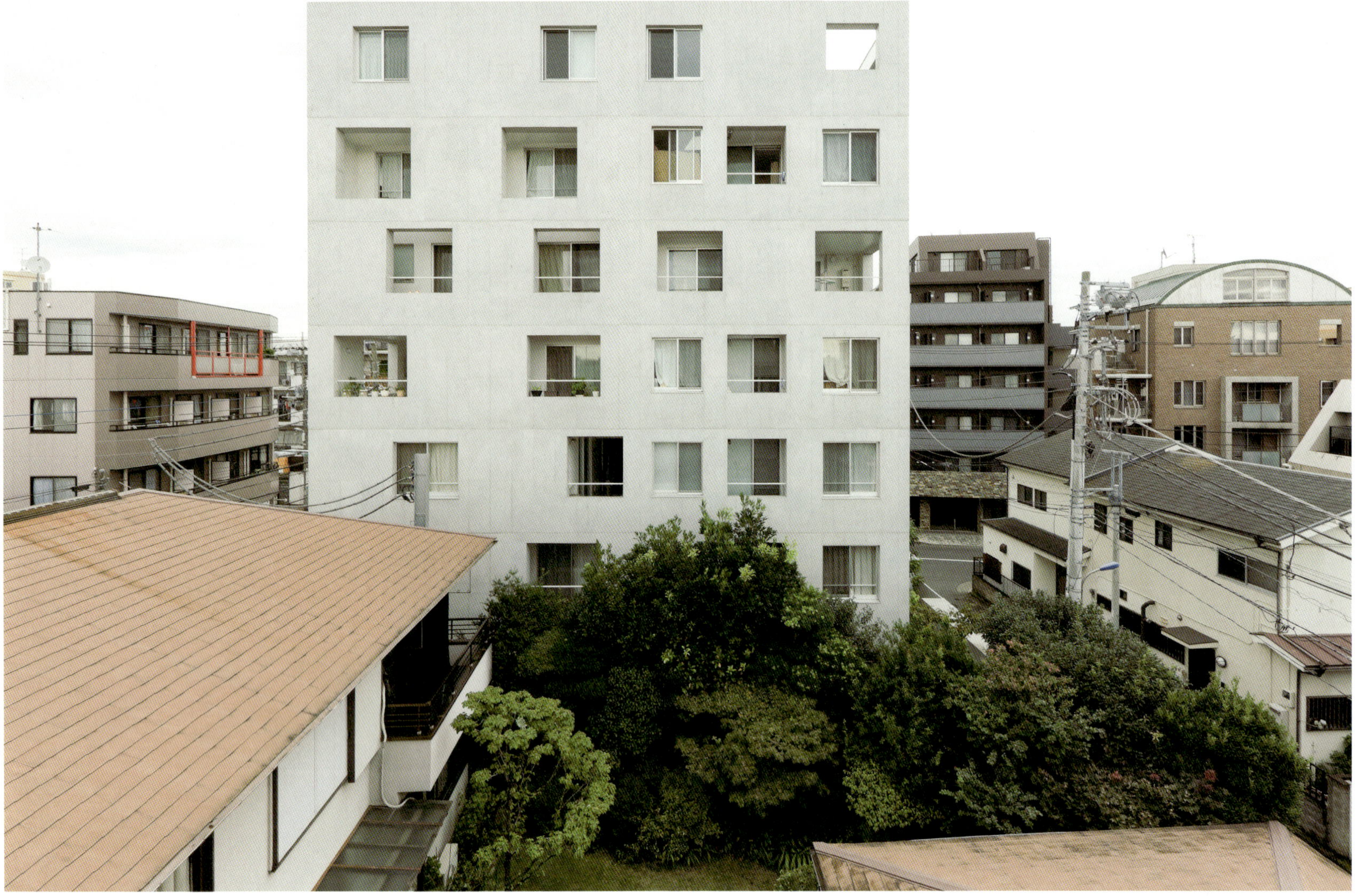

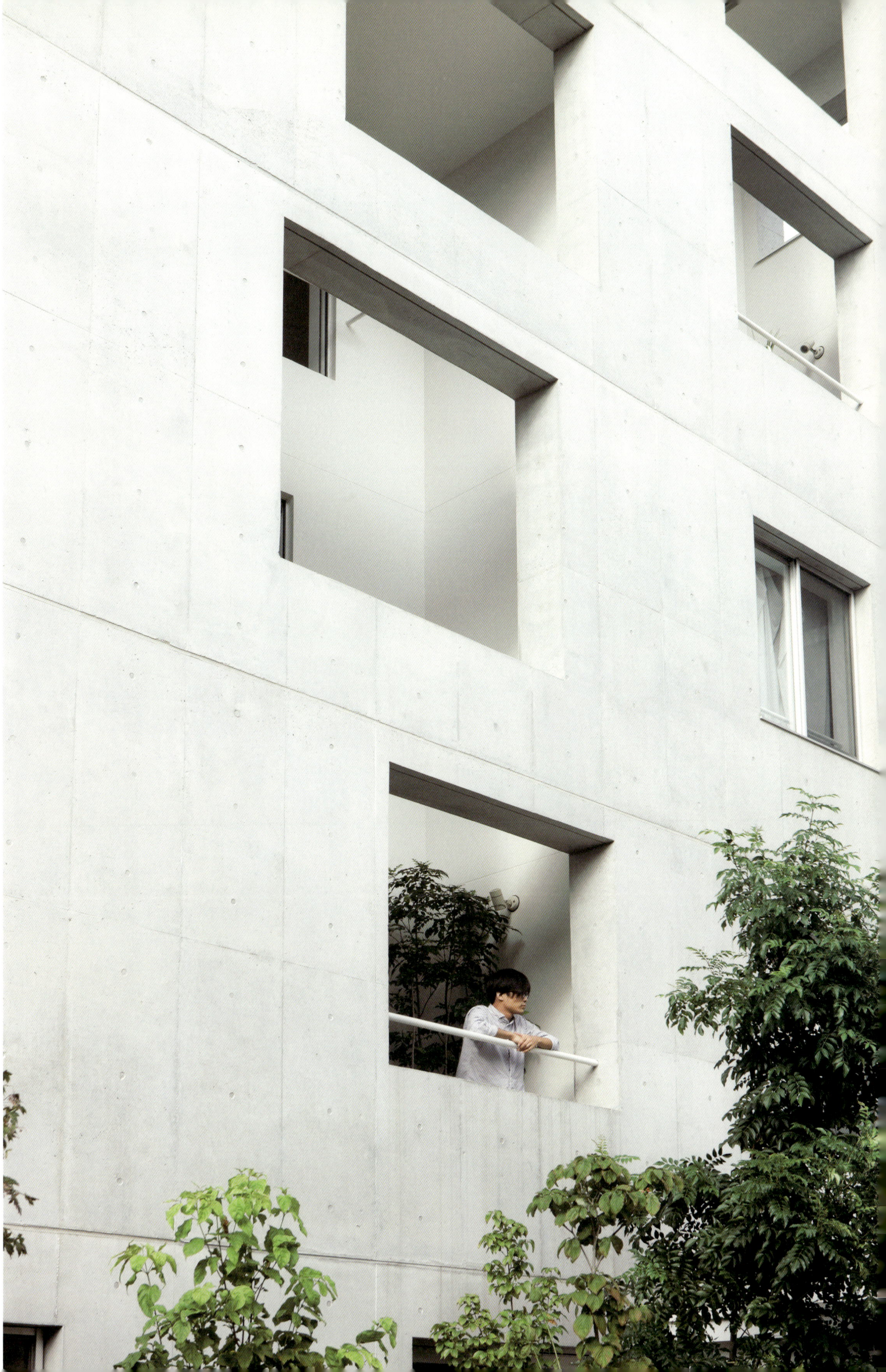

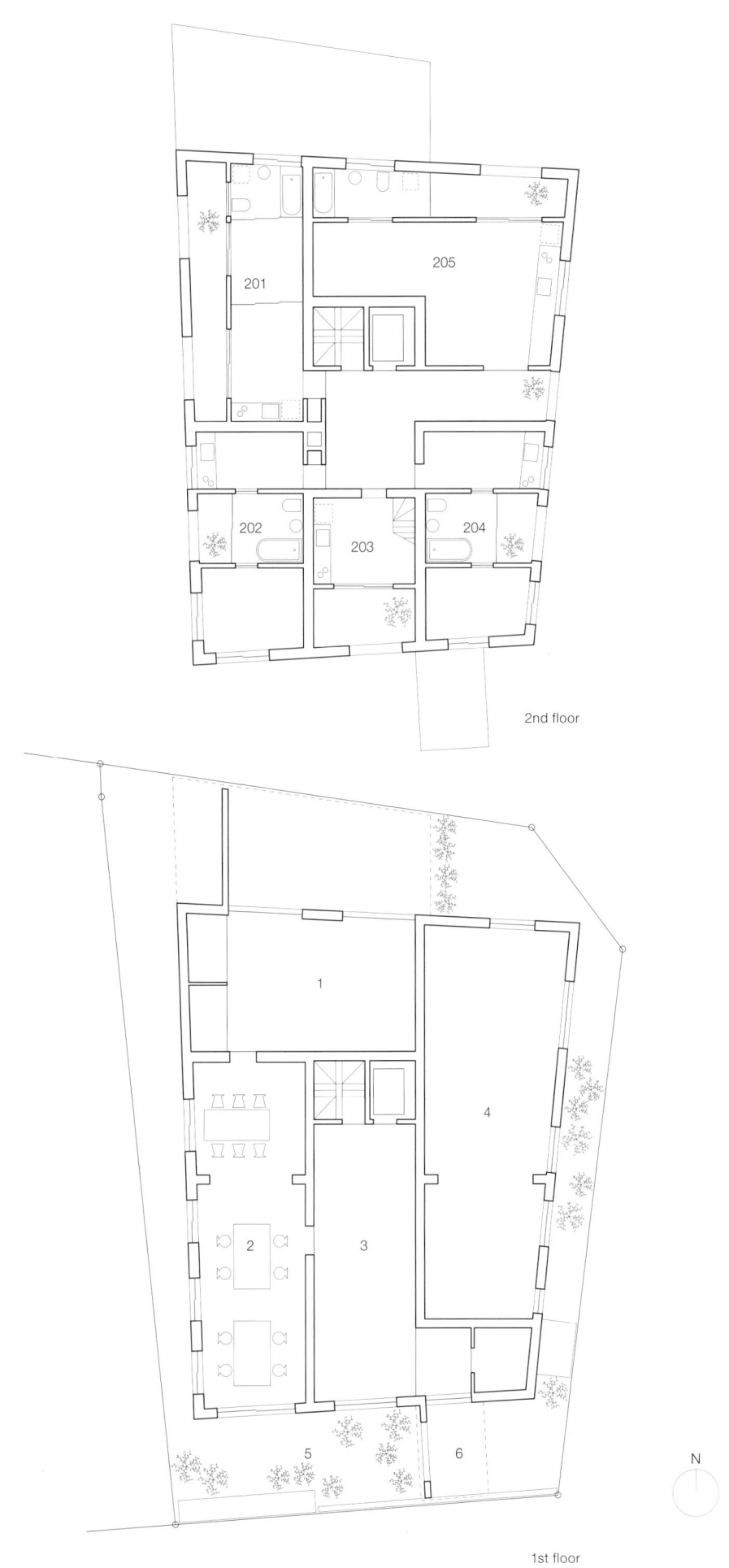

2nd floor

1st floor

78 Plan 1:200 1: garage 2: office 3: hall 4: shop 5: garden 6: approach

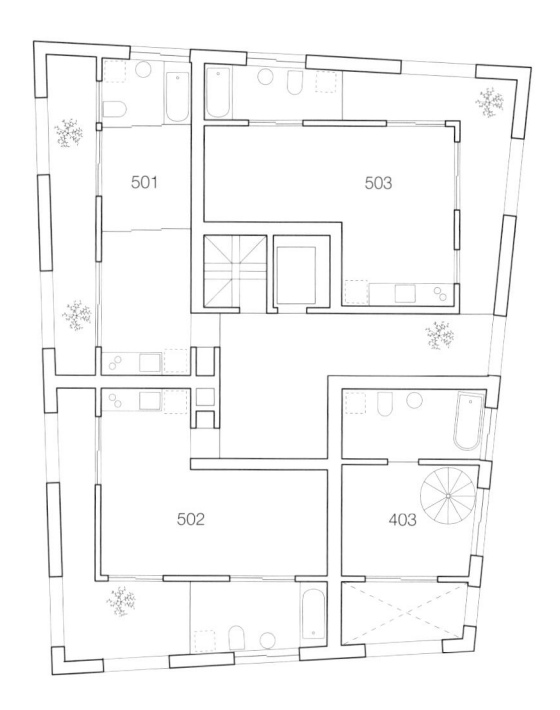

5th floor

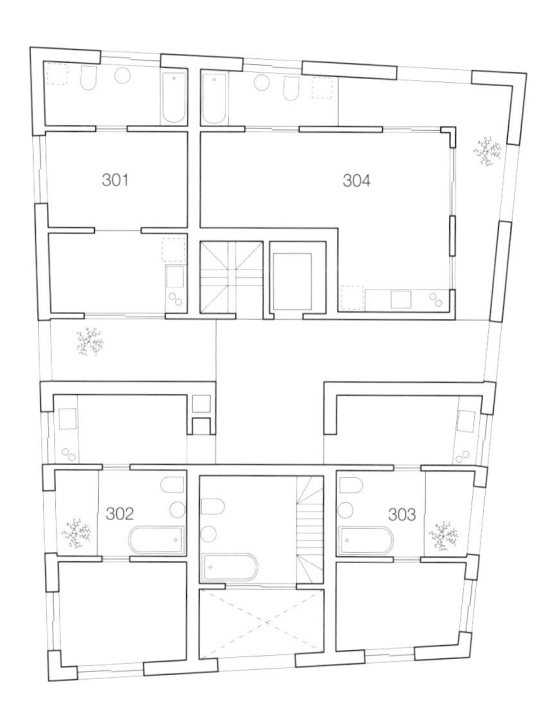

3rd floor

平面図　1:200　　1:駐車場　2:オフィス　3:ホール　4:ショップ　5:庭　6:アプローチ

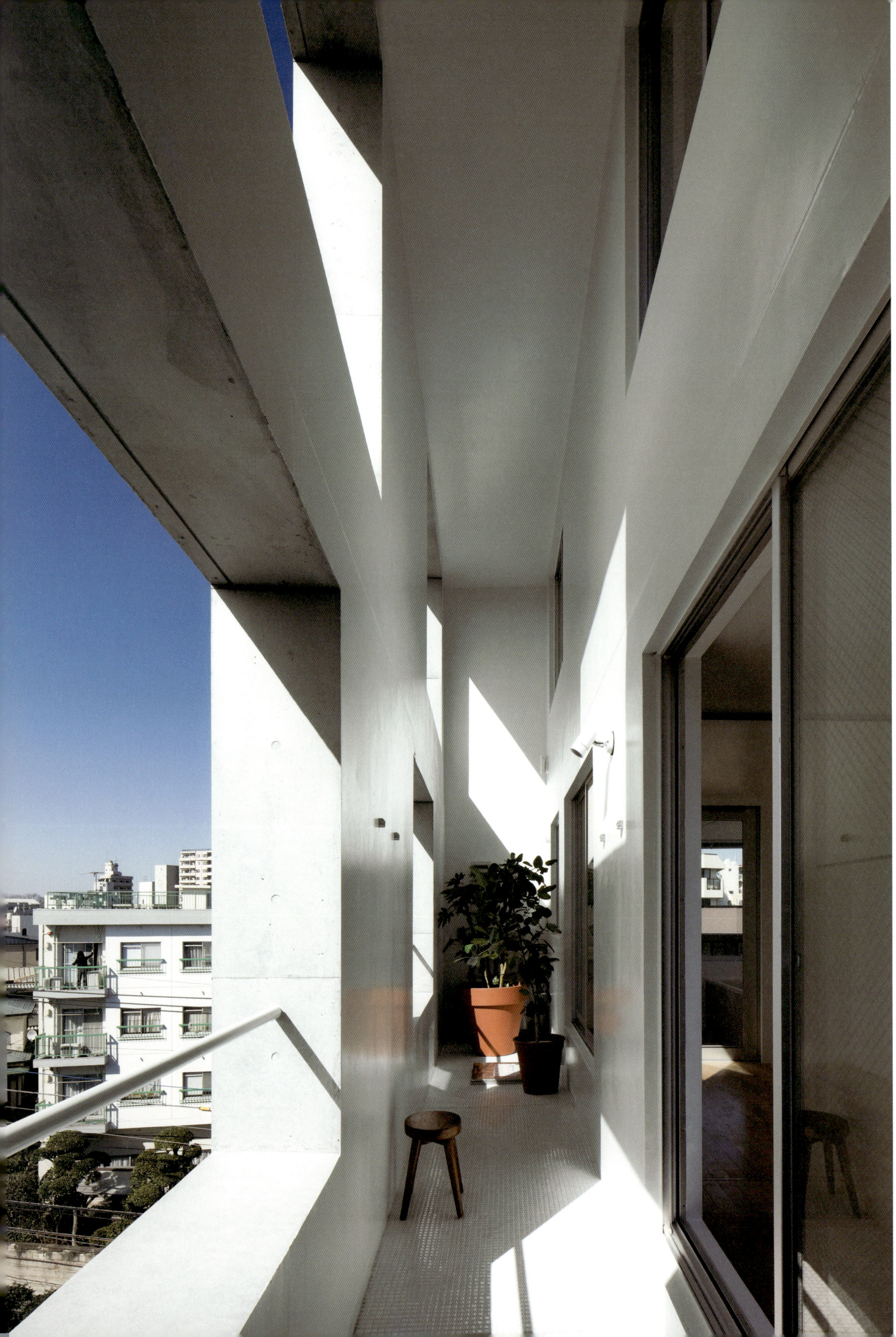

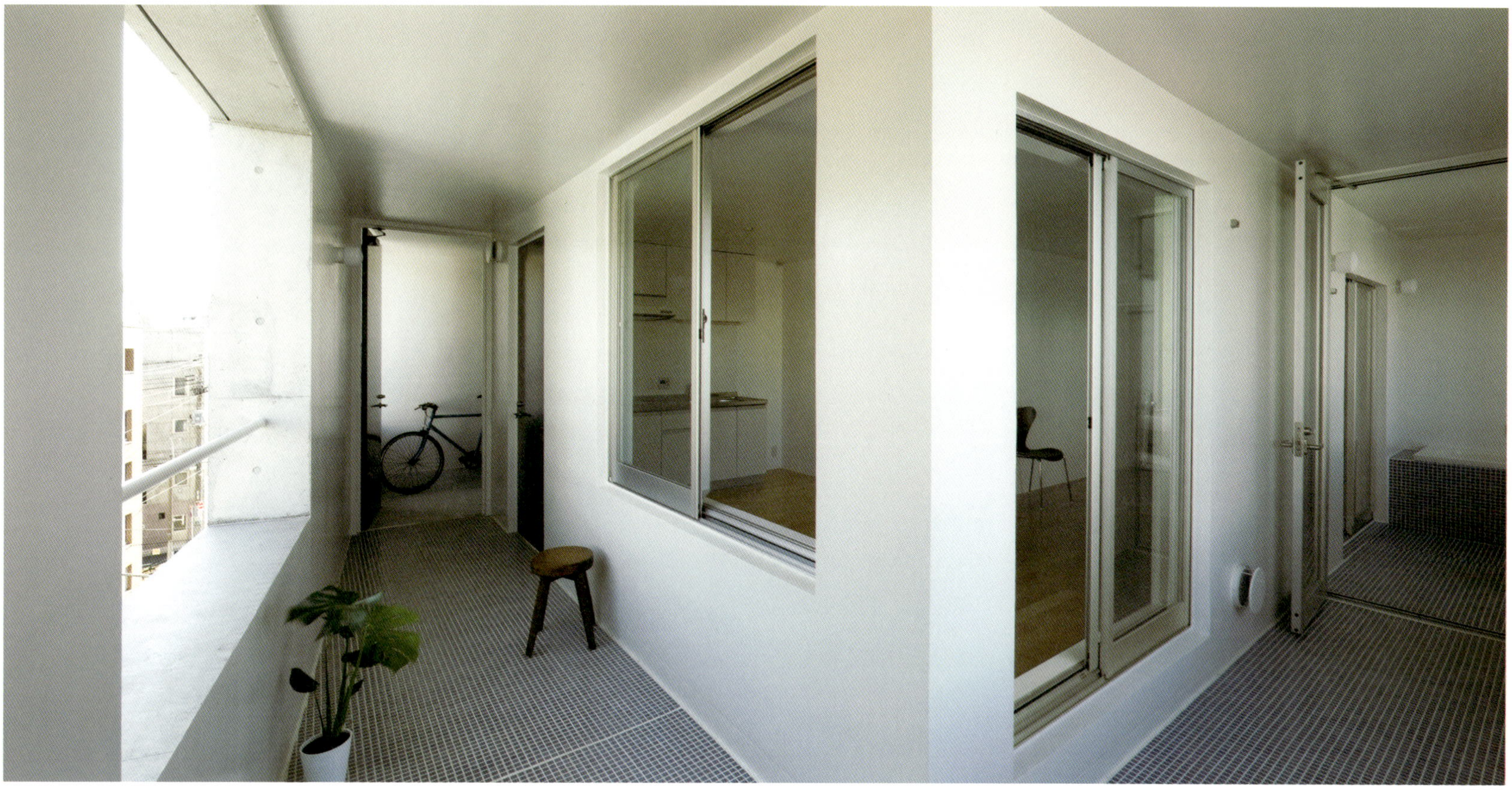

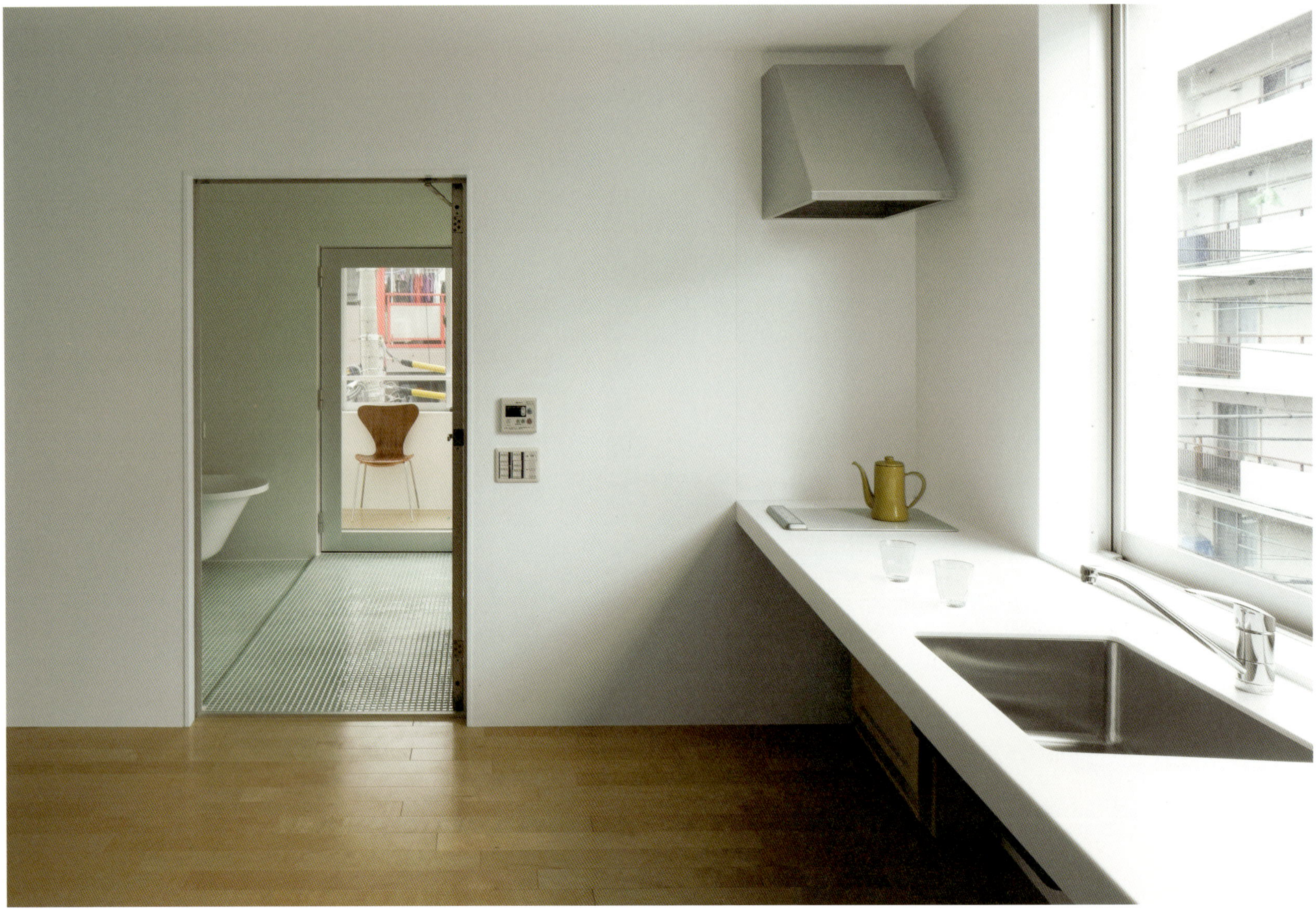

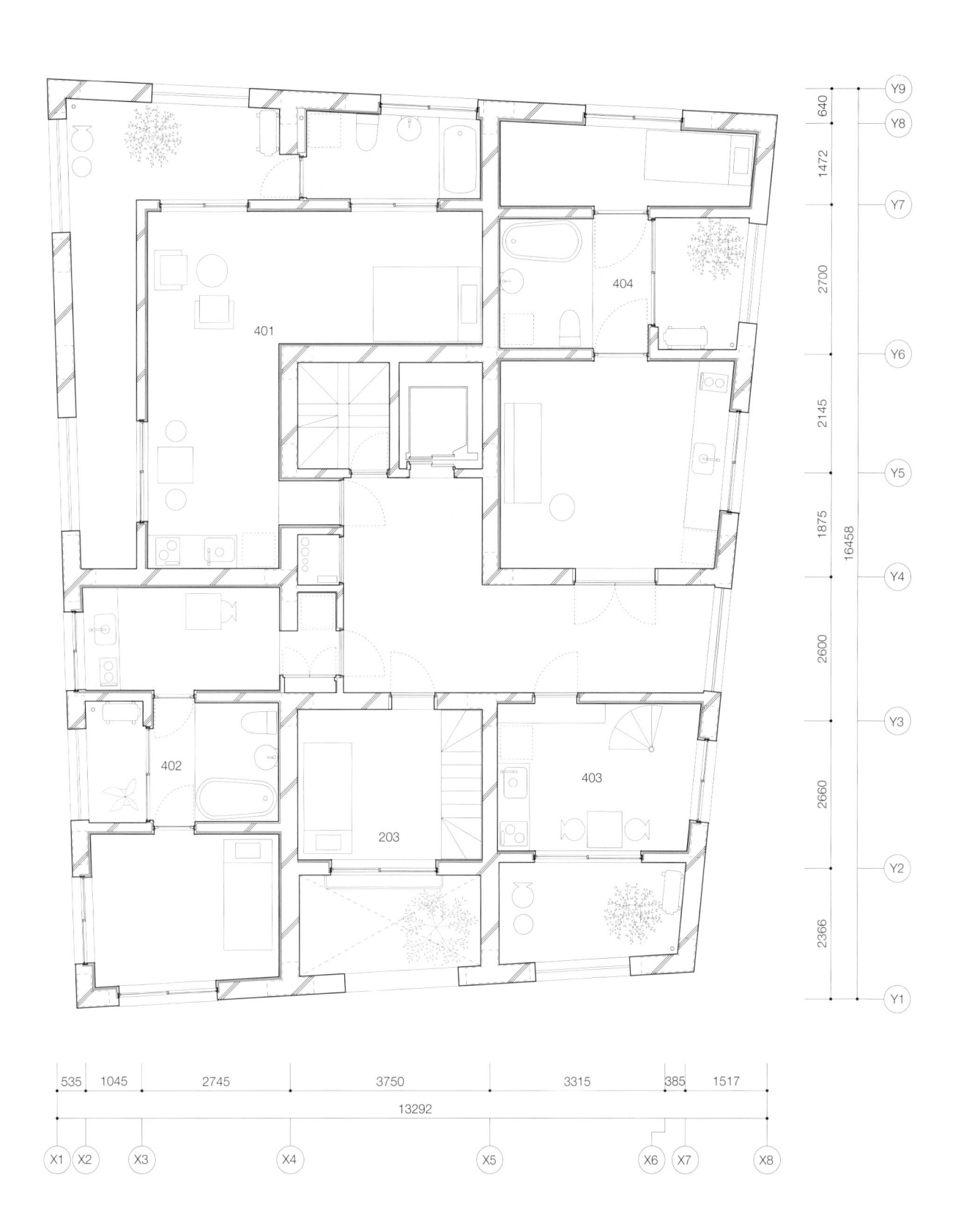

4th floor plan 1:100　4階平面図　1:100

Section 1:50   1: 502 bathroom   2: 502 bedroom   3: 203 terrace   4: 203 bedroom   5: 203 bathroom   6: 203 dinig kitchen   7: hall
矩計図 1:50   1:502浴室   2:502寝室   3:203テラス   4:203寝室   5:203浴室   6:203ダイニングキッチン   7:ホール

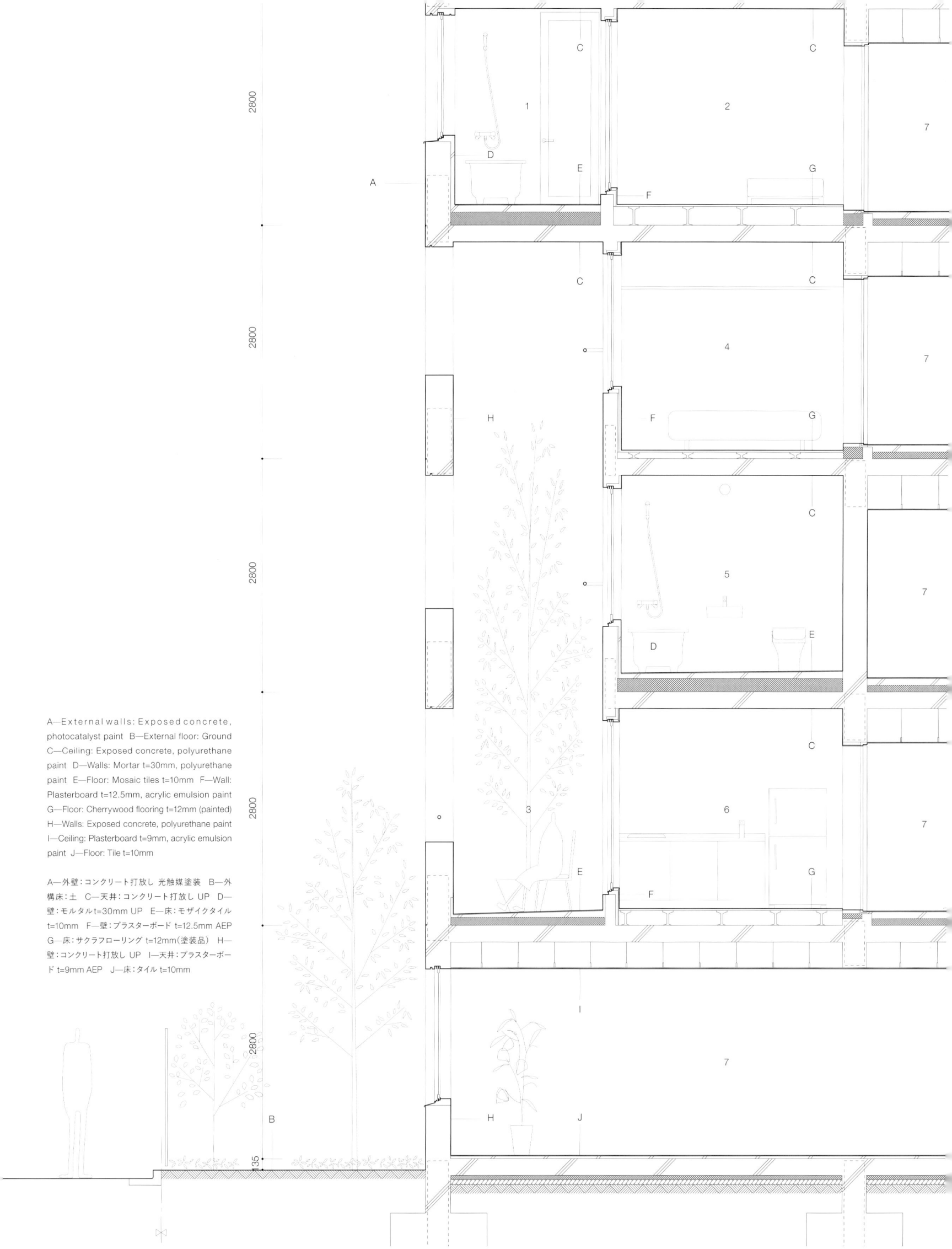

A—External walls: Exposed concrete, photocatalyst paint   B—External floor: Ground   C—Ceiling: Exposed concrete, polyurethane paint   D—Walls: Mortar t=30mm, polyurethane paint   E—Floor: Mosaic tiles t=10mm   F—Wall: Plasterboard t=12.5mm, acrylic emulsion paint   G—Floor: Cherrywood flooring t=12mm (painted)   H—Walls: Exposed concrete, polyurethane paint   I—Ceiling: Plasterboard t=9mm, acrylic emulsion paint   J—Floor: Tile t=10mm

A—外壁：コンクリート打放し 光触媒塗装　B—外構床：土　C—天井：コンクリート打放し UP　D—壁：モルタルt=30mm UP　E—床：モザイクタイル t=10mm　F—壁：プラスターボード t=12.5mm AEP　G—床：サクラフローリング t=12mm（塗装品）　H—壁：コンクリート打放し UP　I—天井：プラスターボード t=9mm AEP　J—床：タイル t=10mm

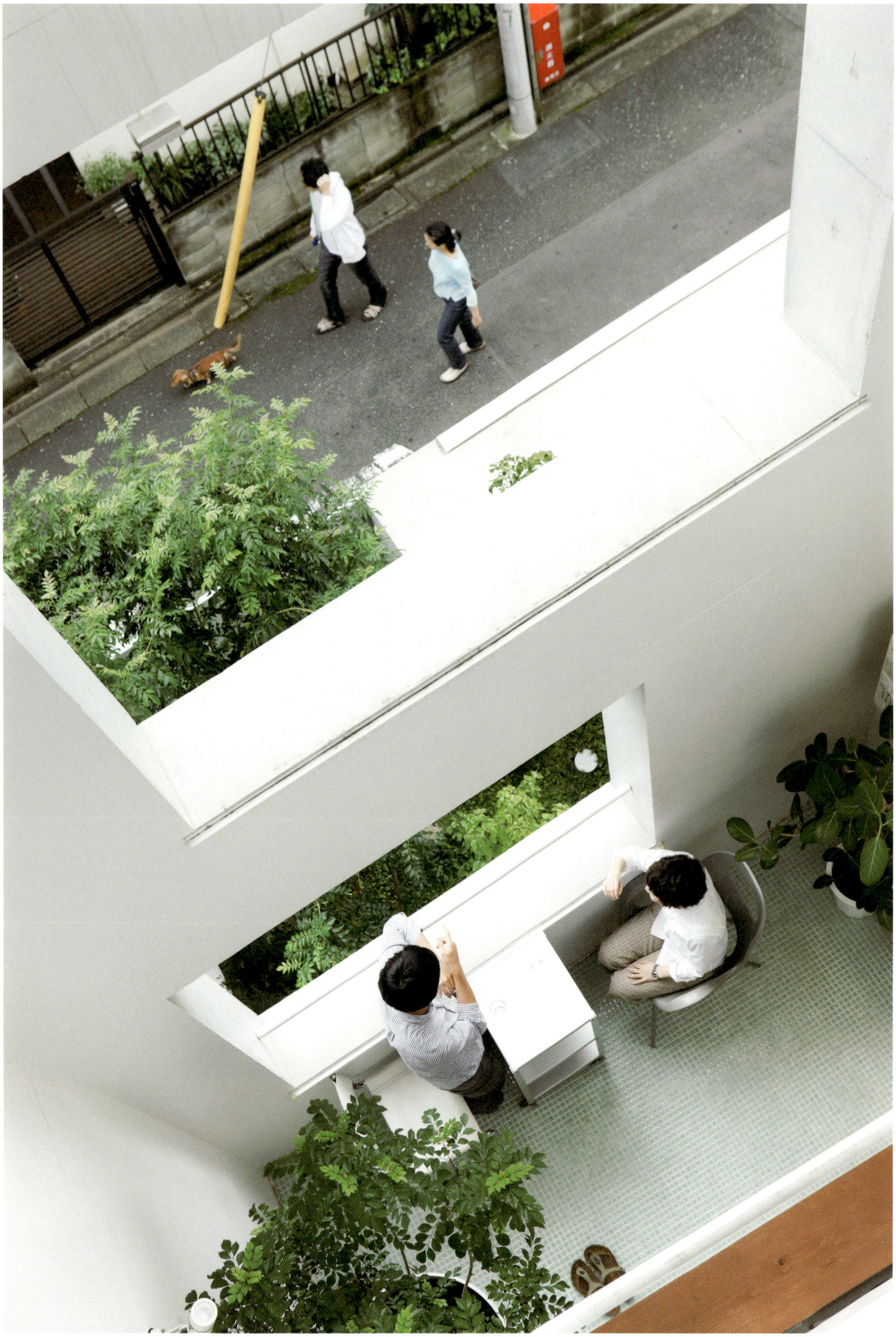

Site plan 1:1000　配置図　1:1000

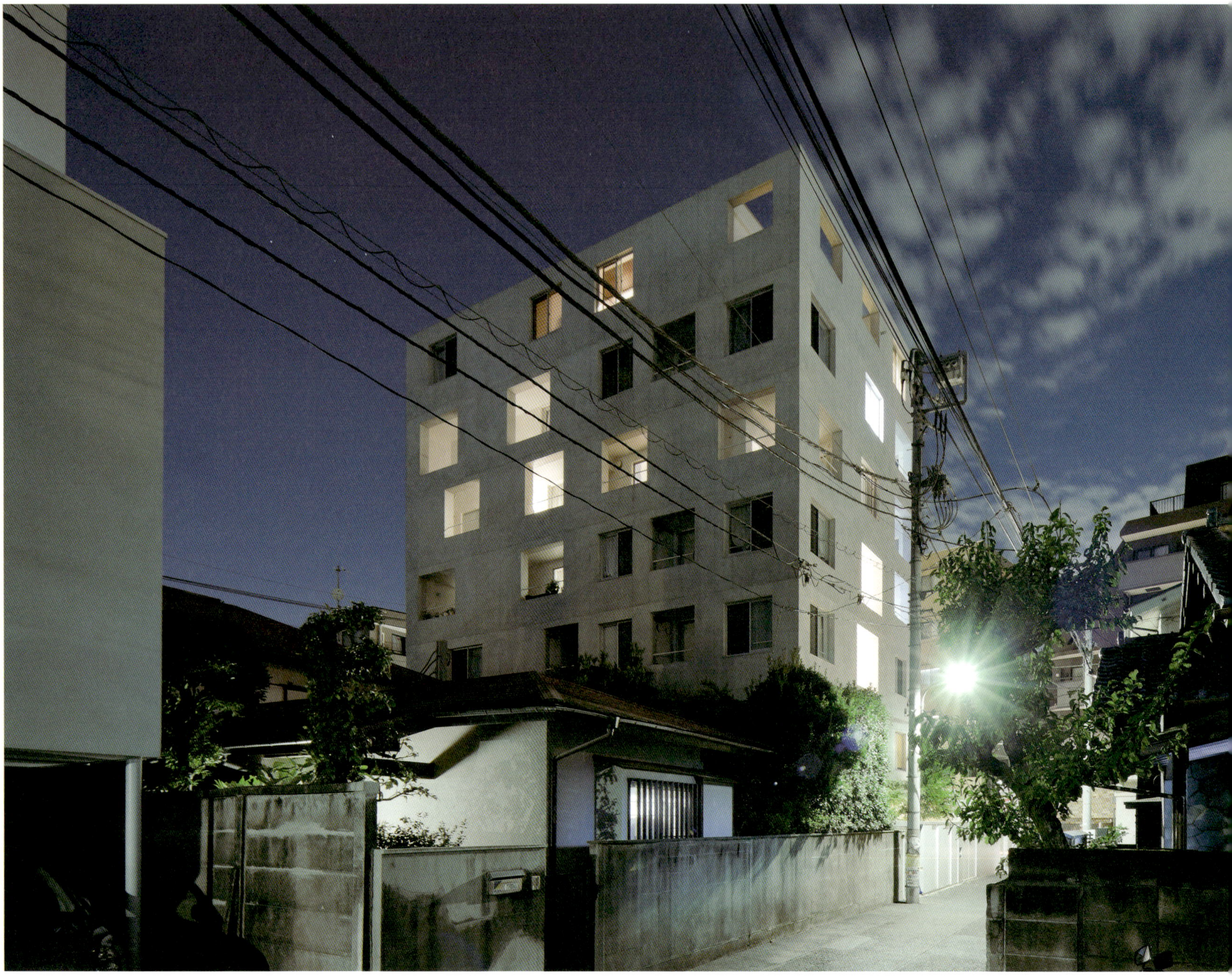

Apartment in Nerima

Location: Nerima, Tokyo
Principal use: Residential, shop, office
Site area: 352.22m^2
Building area: 223.58m^2
Total floor area: 1,054.27m^2
Number of stories: 7
Structure: Reinforced concrete

練馬のアパートメント

所在地：東京都練馬区
主要用途：共同住宅　店舗　事務所
敷地面積：352.22m^2
建築面積：223.58m^2
延床面積：1,054.27m^2
規模：地上7階
構造：鉄筋コンクリート造

Pilotis in a Forest | 森のピロティ

This weekend house was built in a densely vegetated forest in Kita-Karuizawa. The project called for a compact indoor space and a terrace to enjoy barbecues and other events. Doing my best to leave the trees undisturbed, I decided to create a group of pilotis in the forest. By making them tall enough so that even when you are in the bottom section of the house, you can see the trunks of the tall trees, I used the forest as the building's walls. Placing a large bench and table outside, and hanging a hammock between the trees, everyone can relax in the forest. In contrast, I created an aerial living room in the small attic-like space with 1.8-meter-high beams at the lowest point. By making the scale of the room one size smaller than normal, and a lower than normal dining table and chairs, I attempted to convey the sense that the natural environment outside is larger and closer. The large windows face Mt. Asama and the glass floor below the table gives you an even stronger sense of height. In good weather, you can relax under the pilotis in the middle of the forest, and after the sun goes down, sleep outside among the towering trees. I anticipated that these huge pilotis would provide a variety of links between the forest and the people.

木々が高密に生い茂る北軽井沢の森のなかに建つ週末住宅。コンパクトな室内空間とバーベキューが楽しめるテラスなどが求められた。既存の樹木をできる限りそのまま残して、森のなかに巨大なピロティをつくる。建物の下にいても高木の幹まで見えるくらいにピロティを十分に高くして、壁面を森につくってもらう。大きなベンチとテーブルを置き、柱間にはハンモックを吊るし、森に囲まれてみんなで寛ぐ。またそれとは対照的に上空の居室は低いところで梁下高さ1.8mの小屋裏のような空間にする。ダイニングテーブルや椅子なども通常より低くして部屋のスケールを一回り小さくすることで、外の森の環境がより大きく、近く感じられるようにした。大窓は浅間山に向け、さらにテーブル下のガラス床を介して自分がいる場所の高さを感じることができる。過ごしやすい季節にはピロティに下りて森に囲まれてのんびり寛ぎ、また日が暮れたら上って木の傍で眠る。この巨大なピロティが、森と人間のさまざまな関わり合いを提供することを期待した。

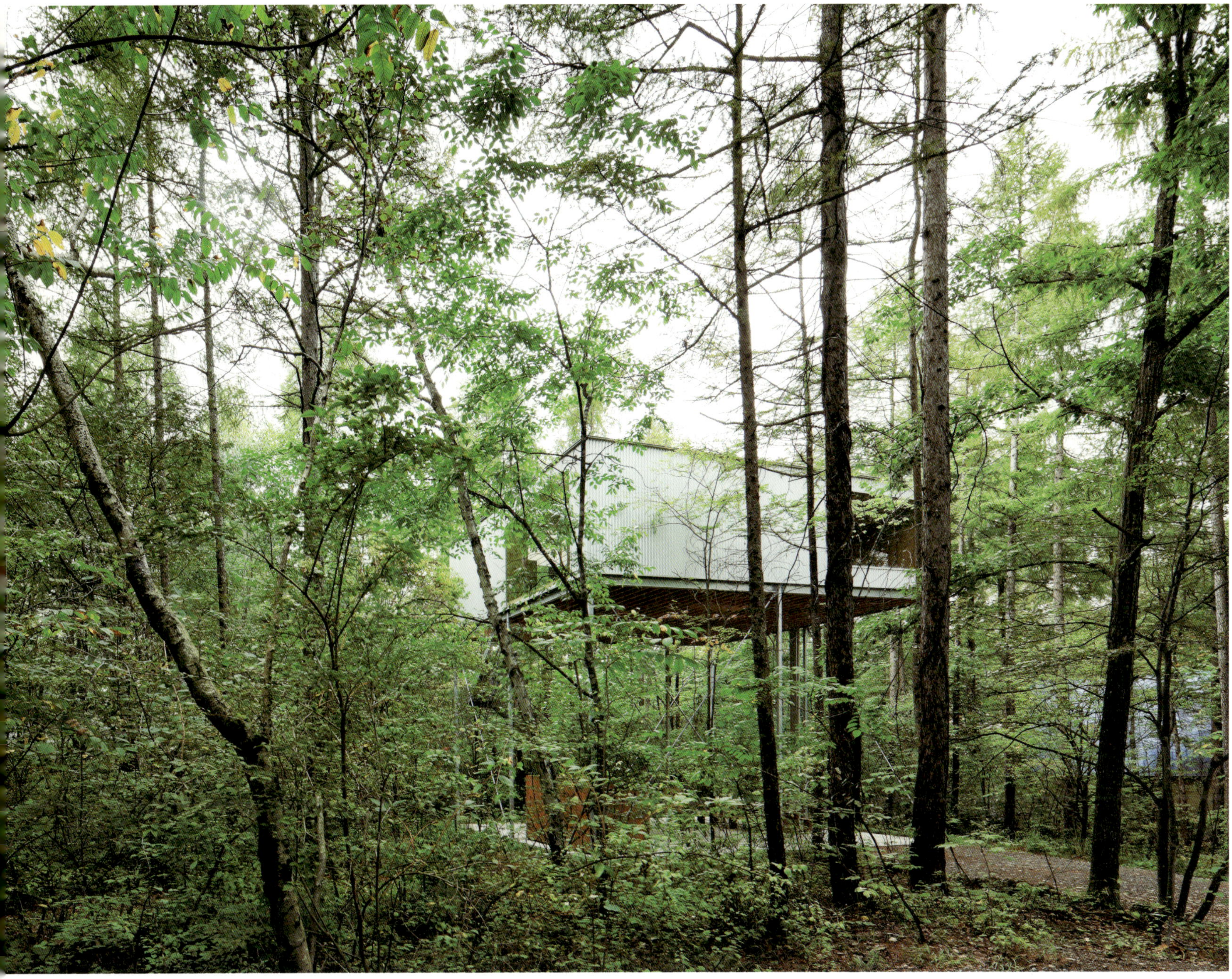

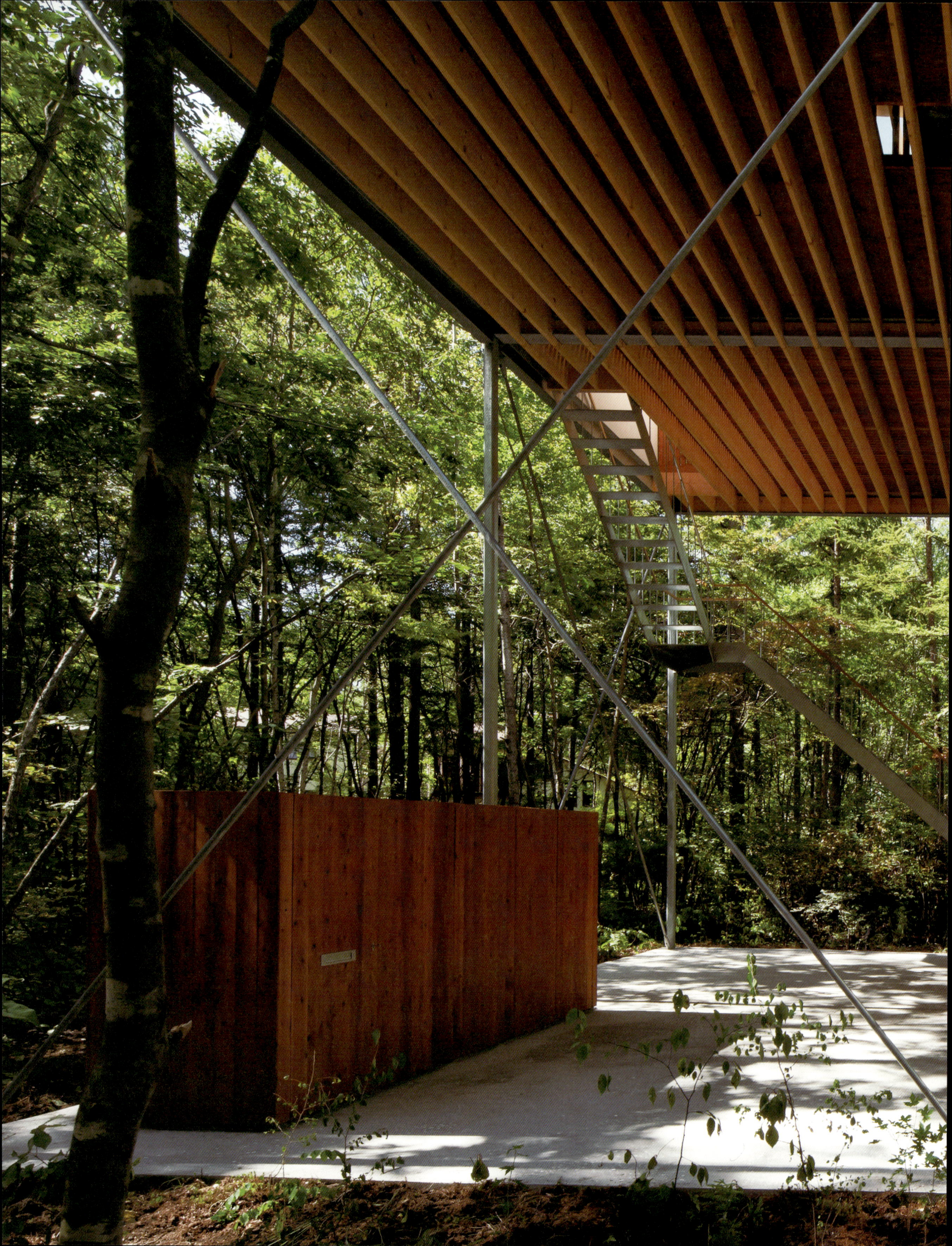

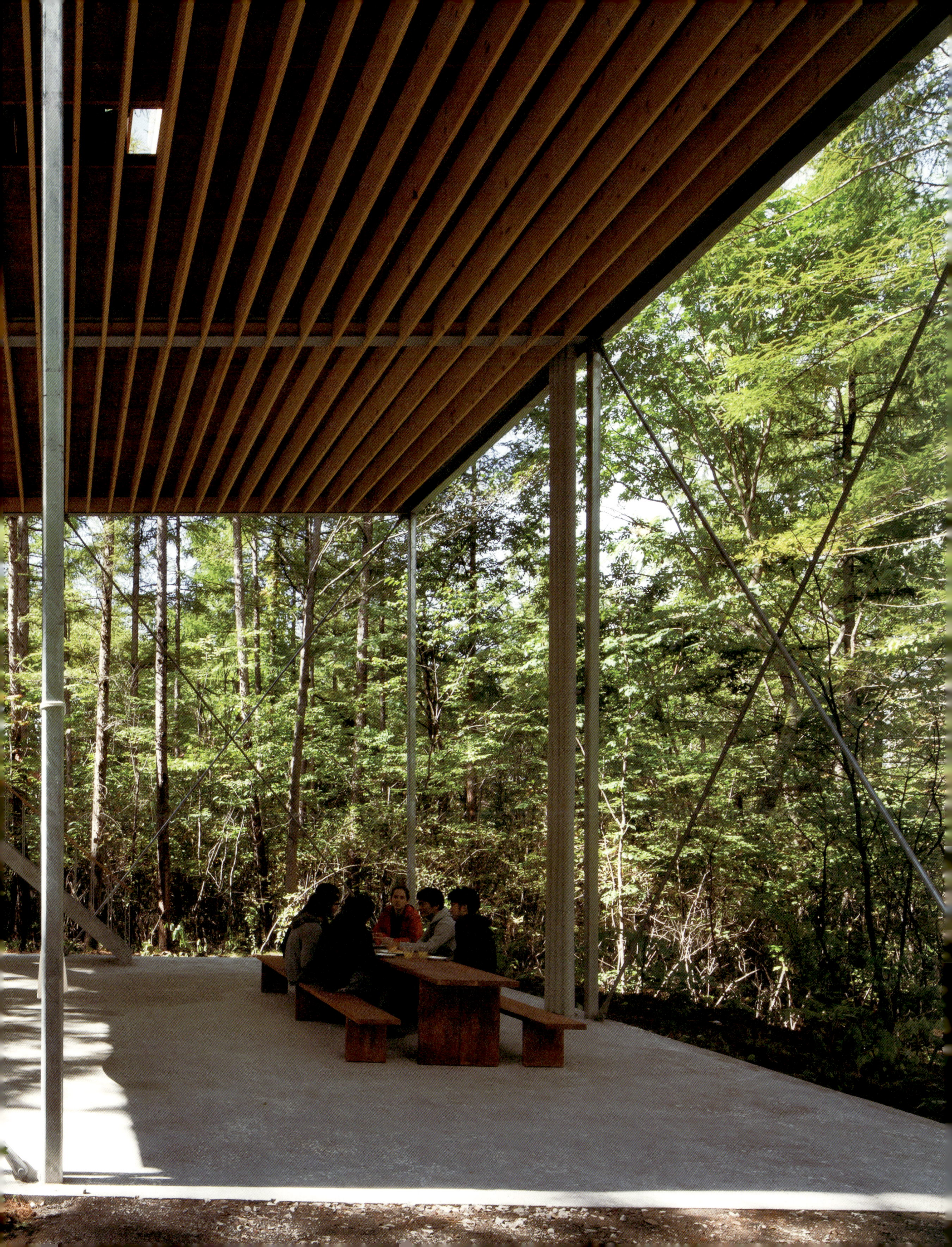

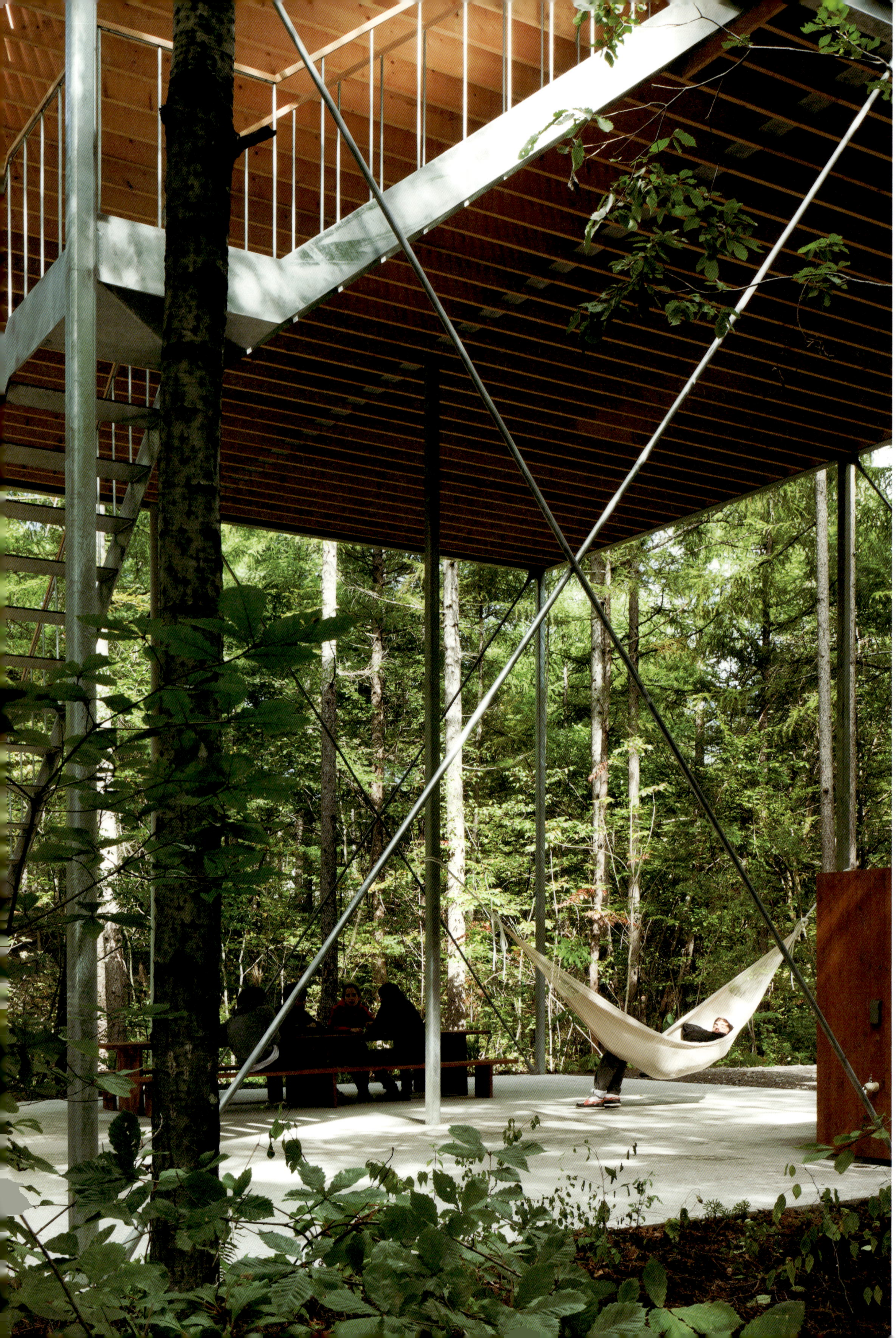

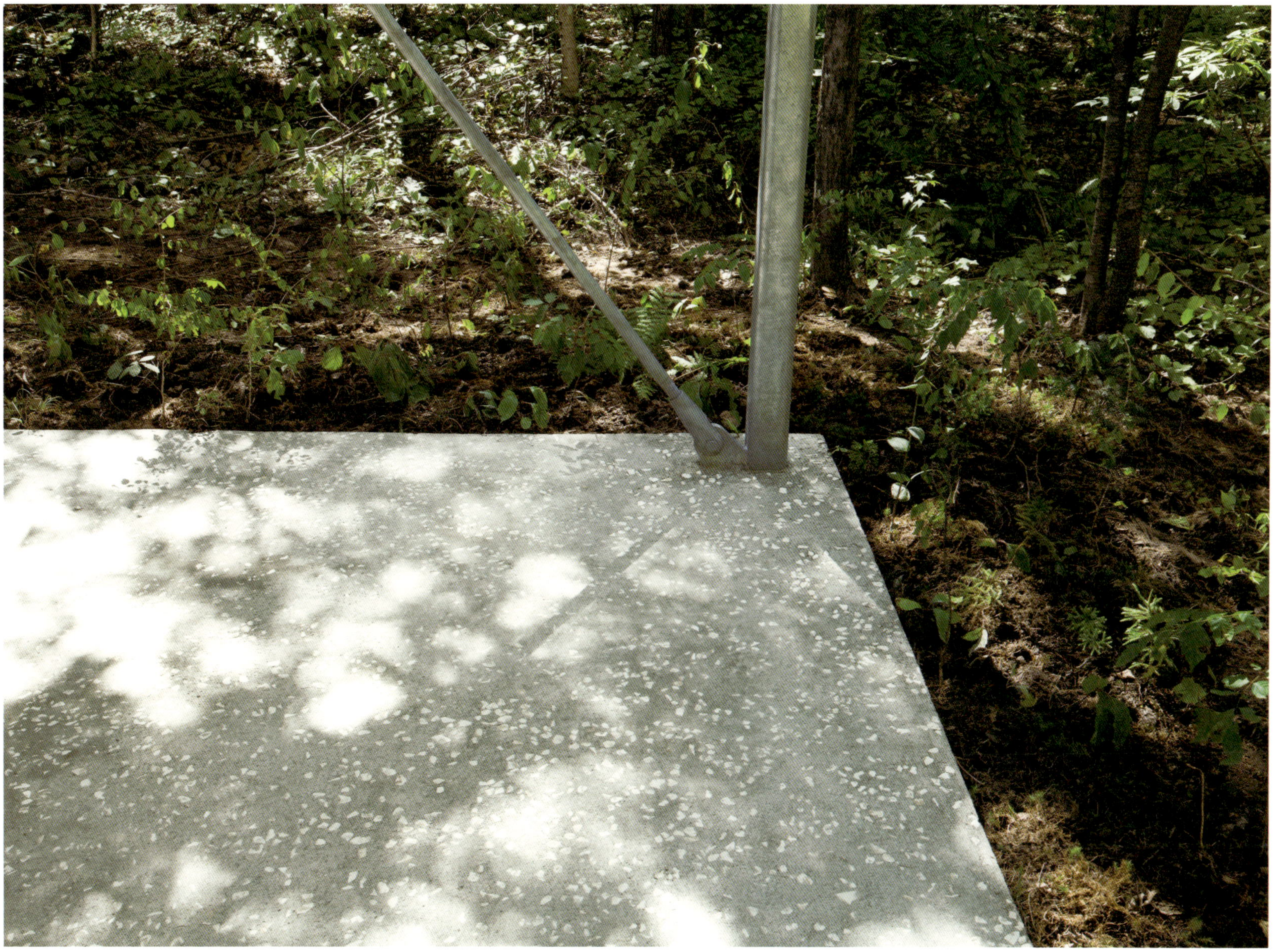

1

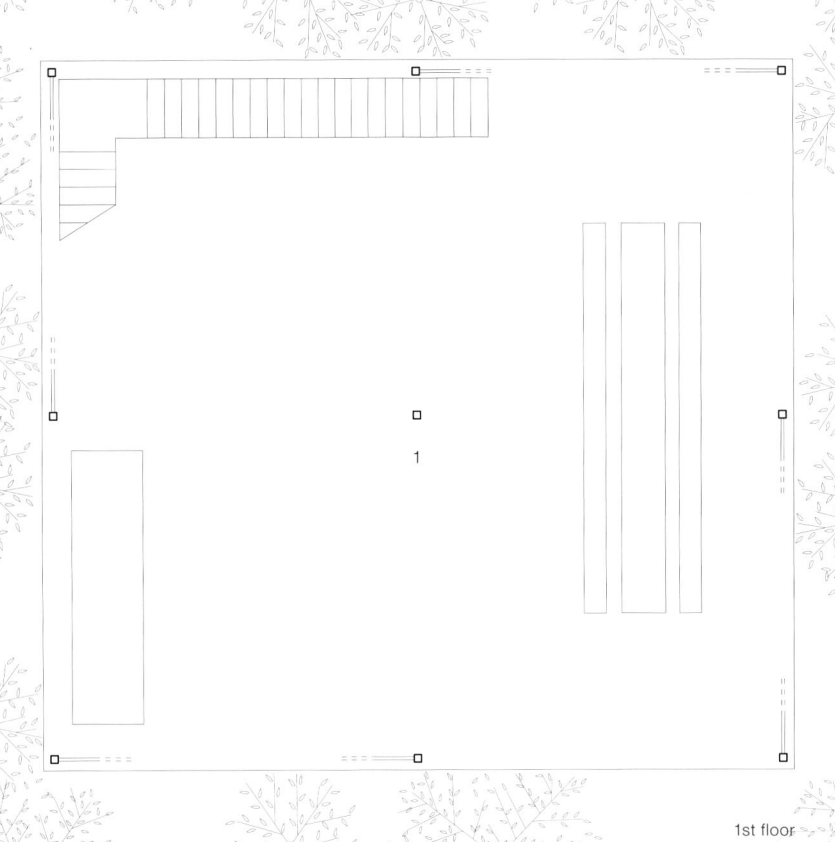

1st floor

Plan 1:100   1: plaza 2: terrace 3: entrance 4: dining room 5: guest room 6: bathroom 7: bedroom

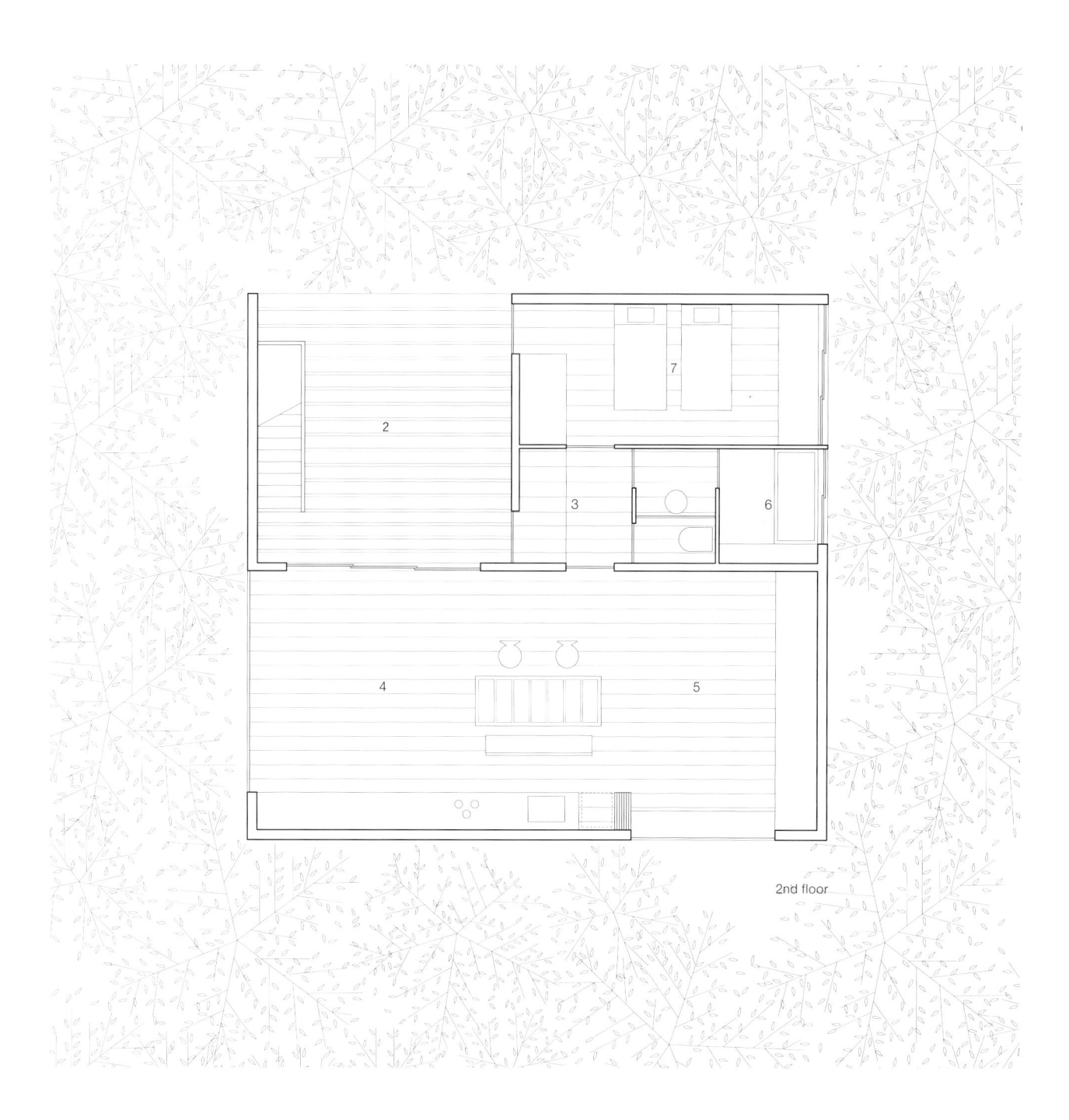

2nd floor

平面図 1:100　　1:広場　2:テラス　3:玄関　4:食堂　5:客室　6:浴室　7:寝室

A—External walls: Corrugated galvanized steel sheeting t=0.4mm | Furring strips: 40×20mm @303mm | Moisture permeable waterproof sheeting | Structural plywood t=12mm | Glasswool t=100mm (24kg/m³) B—Roof: Galvanized steel sheeting t=0.4mm S&W method | Asphalt roofing t=2mm | Structural plywood t=12mm | Seizing board t=12mm | Insulation: Styrofoam t=45mm | Joist: 45 ×45mm @455mm C—Skylight: Double glazing t=20mm (6+8A+6mm) D—Beam: 105×240mm E—Ceiling: Lauan structural plywood t=12mm, oil stain clear lacquer finish F—Batten: 2"×12" @303mm G—Fixed window: Double glazing t=28mm (10+A8+10mm) H—Floor: Solid oak flooring t=15mm, oil paint wipe finish | Structural plywood t=12mm | Hot water floor heating mat t=12mm | Rafter: 45 ×45mm @900mm | Styrofoam t=45mm I—Glass floor: Double reinforced glass t=8+8mm J—Walls: Structural plywood t=9mm, lauan plywood t=5.5mm, oil stain clear laquear finish K—Ceiling: Lauan plywood t=24mm, xyladecor finish L—Batten: 2"×12" @303mm, xyladecor finish M—Beam: H-section steel 125×250×6×9mm, hot dip zinc N—Stair tread/riser (tread depth=192.5mm, rise hight=235mm, riser=20mm): Steel plates t=12mm, hot dip zinc Stringer: Steel plates w=200mm t=12mm, hot dip zinc | Balustrade post: Steel rod 13mm @235mm, hot dip zinc O—Columun: Steel 100×100mm, hot dip zinc P—Brace: SNR490 1-M32 | Folk end: PIN1-M32+G.PL-22 (SN490A) Q—Floor: Concrete slab t=180mm, exposed aggregate finish t=70mm | Underlaying concrete t=50mm | Crushed stone t=50mm

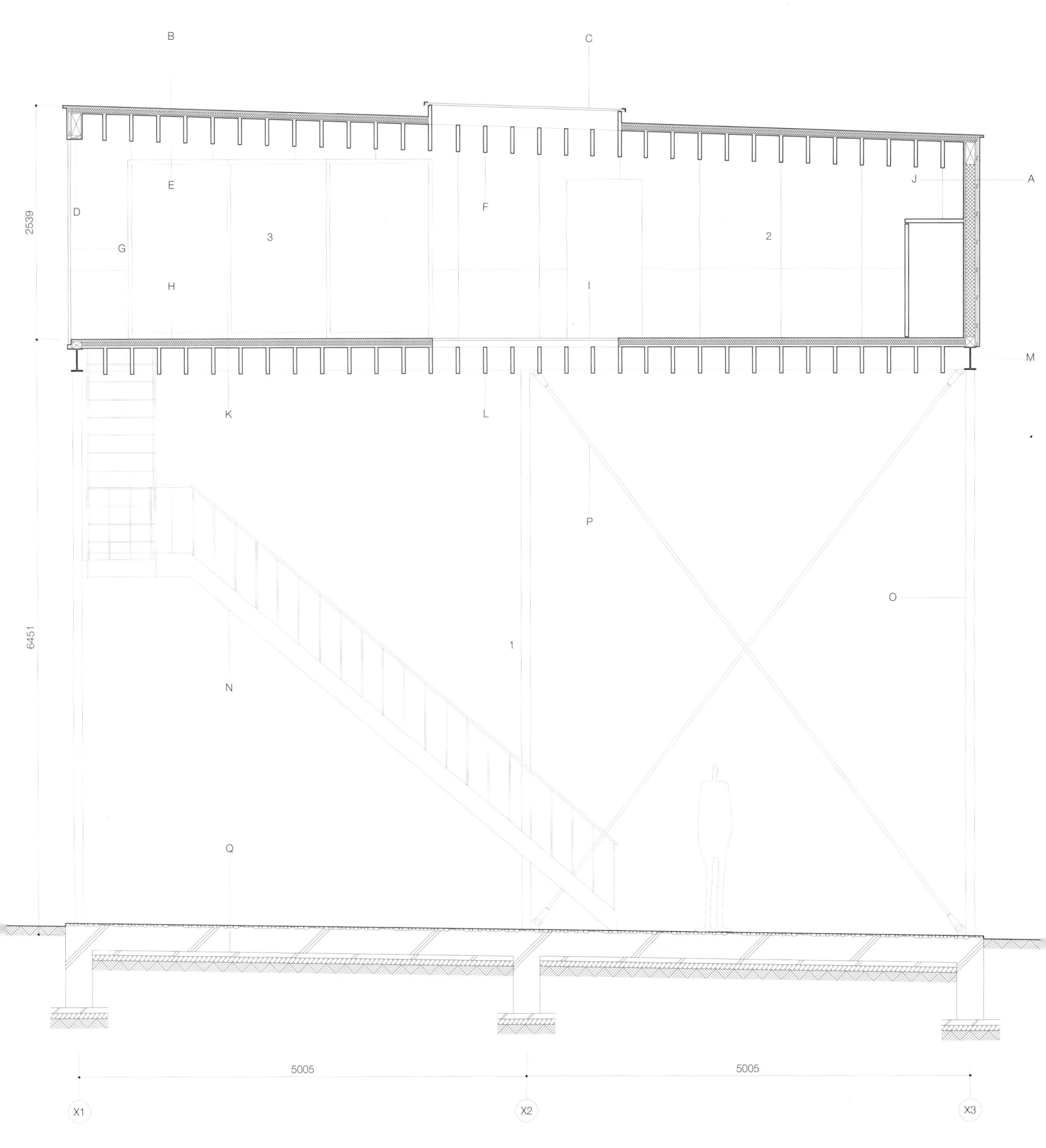

A—外壁：ガルバリウム鋼板 t=0.4mm 中波葺き｜胴縁：40×20mm @303mm｜透湿防水シート｜構造用合板 t=12mm｜グラスウール t=100mm（24kg/m³）　B—屋根：ガルバリウム鋼板 t=0.4mm S&W工法｜アスファルトルーフィング t=2mm｜構造用合板 t=12mm｜シージングボード t=12mm｜断熱材：スタイロフォーム t=45mm｜根太：45×45mm @455mm　C—トップライト：ペアガラス t=20mm（6mm+8A+6mm）　D—梁：105×240mm　E—天井：ラワン構造用合板 t=12mm OSCL　F—小梁：2"×12" @303mm　G—はめ殺し窓：ペアガラス t=28mm（10mm+9A+10mm）　H—床：ナラ無垢フローリング t=15mm OP拭き取り｜構造用合板 t=12mm｜温水床暖房パネル t=12mm｜根太：45×45mm @900mm｜スタイロフォーム t=45mm　I—ガラス床：強化合わせガラス t=16mm（8+8mm）　J—壁：構造用合板 t=9mmの上ラワン合板 t=5.5mm OSCL　K—天井：ラワン合板 t=24mm キシラデコール塗装　L—小梁：2"×12" @303mm キシラデコール塗装　M—大梁：St H-125×250×6×9mm 亜鉛ドブヅケ　N—階段踏み板（蹴上192.5mm 踏面235mm 蹴込み20mm）：St PL t=12mm 亜鉛ドブヅケ｜ササラ：St PL t=12mm 亜鉛ドブヅケ｜手摺子：St ロッド φ13mm @235mm 亜鉛ドブヅケ　O—柱：St-□100×100mm t=12mm 亜鉛ドブヅケ　P—ブレース：SNR490 1-M32｜フォークエンド：PIN1-M32＋G.PL-22(SN490A)　Q—土間床：コンクリートスラブ t=180mmの上コンクリート洗い出し仕上げ t=70mm｜捨てコンクリート t=50mm｜砕石 t=50mm

Section 1:50　　1: plaza 2: guest room 3: dining room　　矩計図 1:50　　1:広場　2:客室　3:食堂

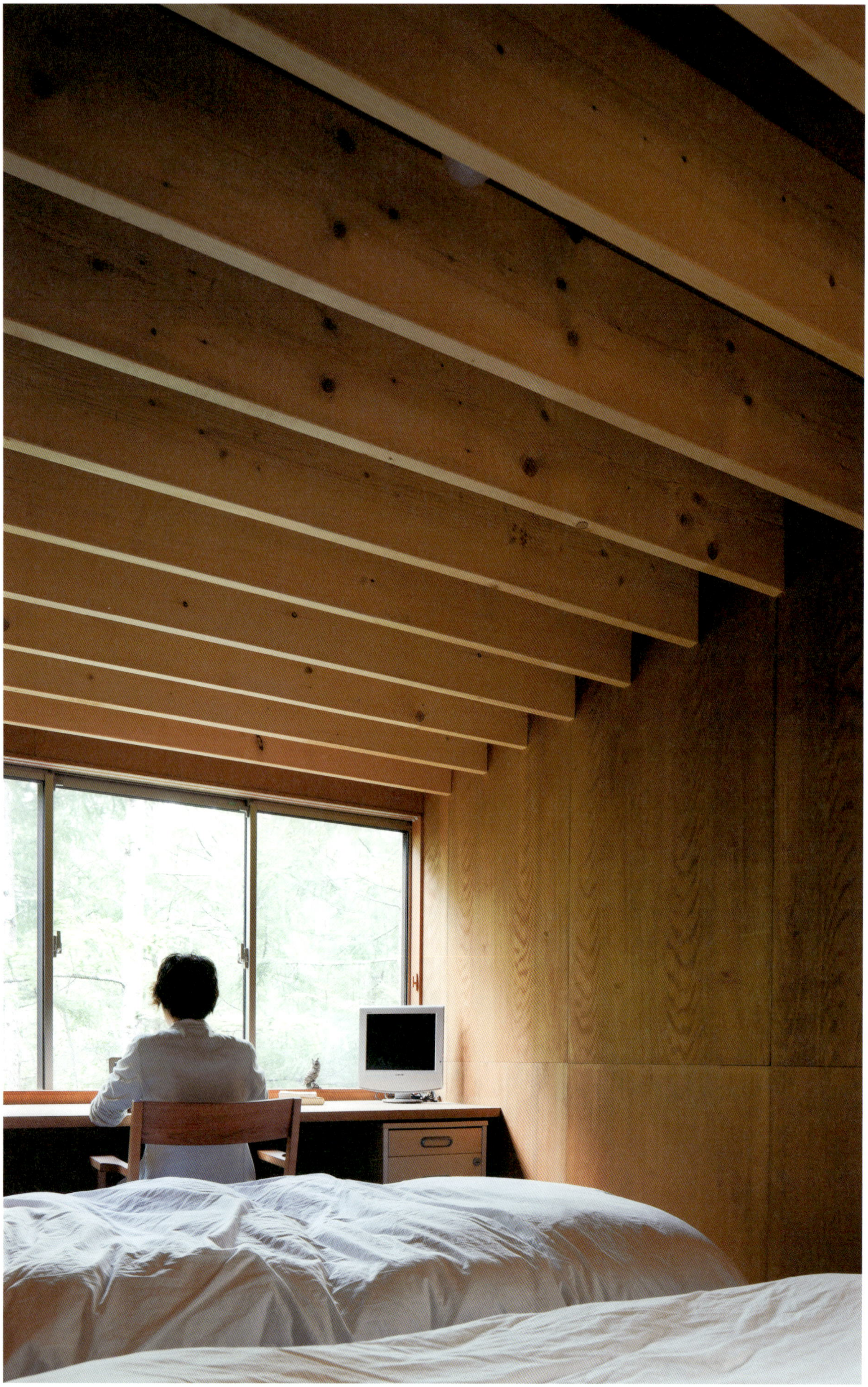

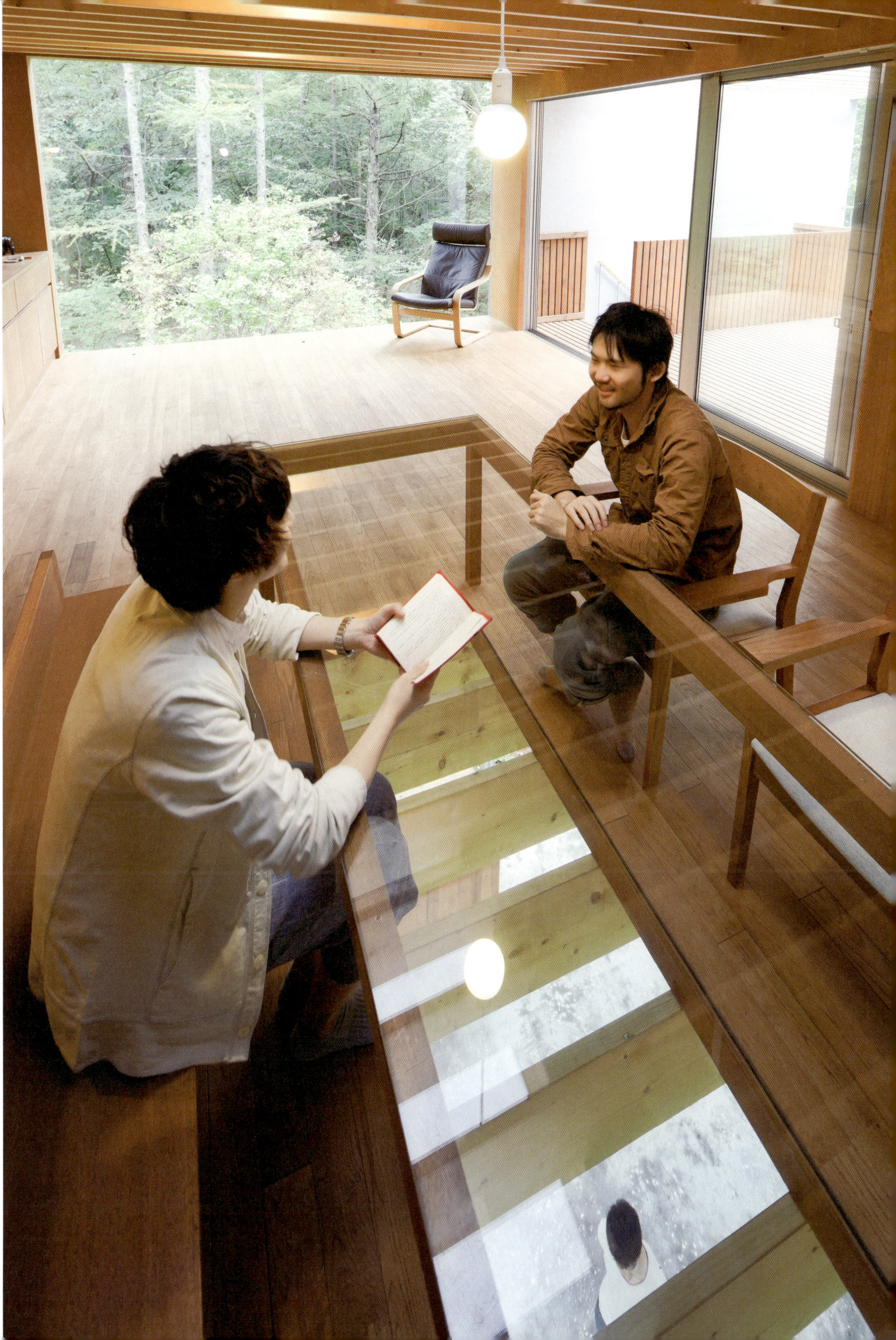

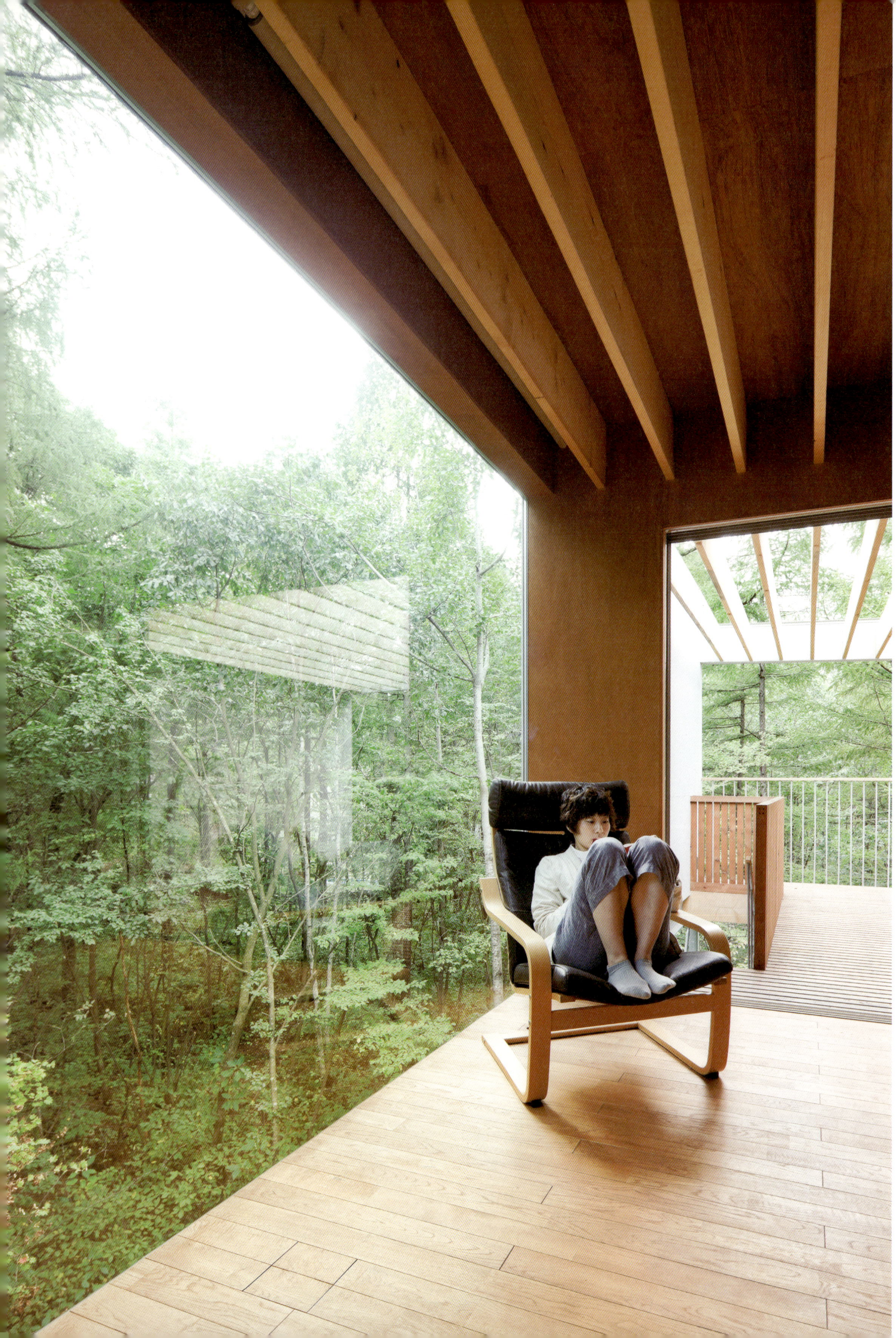

補充注文カード

貴店名

年　月　日

部数　書名　発行所　著者

TOTO出版

Go Hasegawa Works

長谷川豪作品集

長谷川豪

ISBN978-4-88706-323-5

C3052 ¥3400E

定価＝
本体3,400円+税

9784887063235

Site plan 1:1000　配置図　1:1000

Pilotis in a Forest

Location: Tsumagoi, Azuma-gun, Gunma
Principal use: Residential (resort)
Site area: 3,524.51m^2
Building area: 91.09m^2
Total floor area: 77.22m^2
Number of stories: 2
Structure: Steel frame+timber frame

森のピロティ

所在地：群馬県吾妻群嬬恋村
主要用途：別荘
敷地面積：3,524.51m^2
建築面積：91.09m^2
延床面積：77.22m^2
規模：地上2階
構造：鉄骨造＋木造

Townhouse in Asakusa | 浅草の町家

This house was built in a densely populated area that retains a traditional atmosphere. It occupies a corner lot in an area that is lined with houses (with a height of about three stories) that stand shoulder to shoulder with small factories. I decided to position the house so that it would take up the entire area, and dared to create a four-floor structure with a nine-meter-high volume in spite of being surrounded by houses with three floors. The ceiling height on each floor is 1.9 meters, but to eliminate any sense of discomfort, I made holes in the floor of each level. In some cases, this meant creating a huge hole in the center, and in others, I gave the floor a constricted form by making two holes in it. The large hole creates an area of light and shadow in various places on the same level as well as on the floor below while also connecting the entire space. Moreover, due to the holes and the windows in the exterior walls, and by altering the adjustable skylights, you can look down diagonally at the neighborhood from the upper floors, and look up at the windows from the lower floors. This four-story building with 1.9-meter ceilings condenses your vertical sense of distance, and creates a close connection between the upper and lower floors. In this house, I set out to realize a bright, complex environment in which the five floor areas are organically linked by means of the large hole.

下町情緒が残る密集地に建つ住宅。敷地は角地で、3階建て程度の高さの戸建て住宅や町工場が肩を寄せ合って建ち並ぶエリアにある。敷地いっぱいに建物を配置して、周りと同等の3階建ての建物高さ（9m）のヴォリュームのなかを思い切って4階建てにした。各階の天井高は1.9mになるが、窮屈さを払拭するために各床に大きな穴をあけていった。床の中央に巨大な穴をあけたり、2つの穴をあけてくびれた形の床にしたりする。床の大きな穴は、その階にあちら側とこちら側を、下階に光と影の領域をつくり、さらに空間全体をつなげていく。また床の穴、外壁の窓、トップライトの位置を連動させて、上階から斜め下方向に街を見下ろしたり、下階から上階の窓を見上げたりできるようにした。天井高1.9mの4階建ては、垂直方向の距離感を圧縮し、上下階の関係性を濃密にする。大きな穴によって各床が他の全ての床と有機的に関係づいた、5枚の床がつくりだす複雑で明るい環境を目指した。

Site plan 1:1000　配置図 1:1000

A—Roof: Concrete trowel finish, reforming waterproofing B—External walls (north/east): Exposed concrete C—External walls (south/west): Exposed concrete, mortar mending, lysine spray finish D—Balustrade: Glass t=8mm, shatter-proof sheeting E—Ceiling: Exposed concrete partially mended F—Skylight: Double glazing (reinforced glass t=8mm+A8+wire figured glass t=6.8mm) G—Skylight frame: Aluminum L-angle 100×100×5mm, polyurethane paint H—Walls: Exposed concrete, polyurethane paint I—Waist-high walls: Trowel mortar t=30mm, polyurethane paint | Insulation: Styrofoam t=30mm J—Floor: Trowel mortar t=40mm | Insulation: Styrofoam t=30mm, concrete trowel finish, reforming waterproofing K—Walls: Exposed concrete partially mended L—Ceiling: Exposed concrete partially mended M—Sliding door: Basswood plywood flush t=21mm, polyurethane paint N—Plasterboard t=12.5mm (with gypsum lining), acrylic emulsion paint | Insulation: Polyurethane spray t=15mm O—Bookshelves/desk: Lauan plywood t=18mm, oil stain clear lacquer finish P—Floor: Concrete trowel finish, wax Q—Floor: P tile 305×305mm t=2mm R—Ceiling: Fiber reinforced cement panel t=9mm S—Skylight: Polycarbonate t=5mm T—Floor: Concrete trowel finish U—Floor: Myanmar teak flooring t=12mm | Plywood underlayment t=12mm | Floor heading panel t=9mm | Plywood underlayment t=12mm | Leveling mortar t=15mm | Concrete slab t=100mm | Insulation: Styrofoam t=30mm | Polyethylene film sheeting t=0.2mm | Crushed stone t=60mm

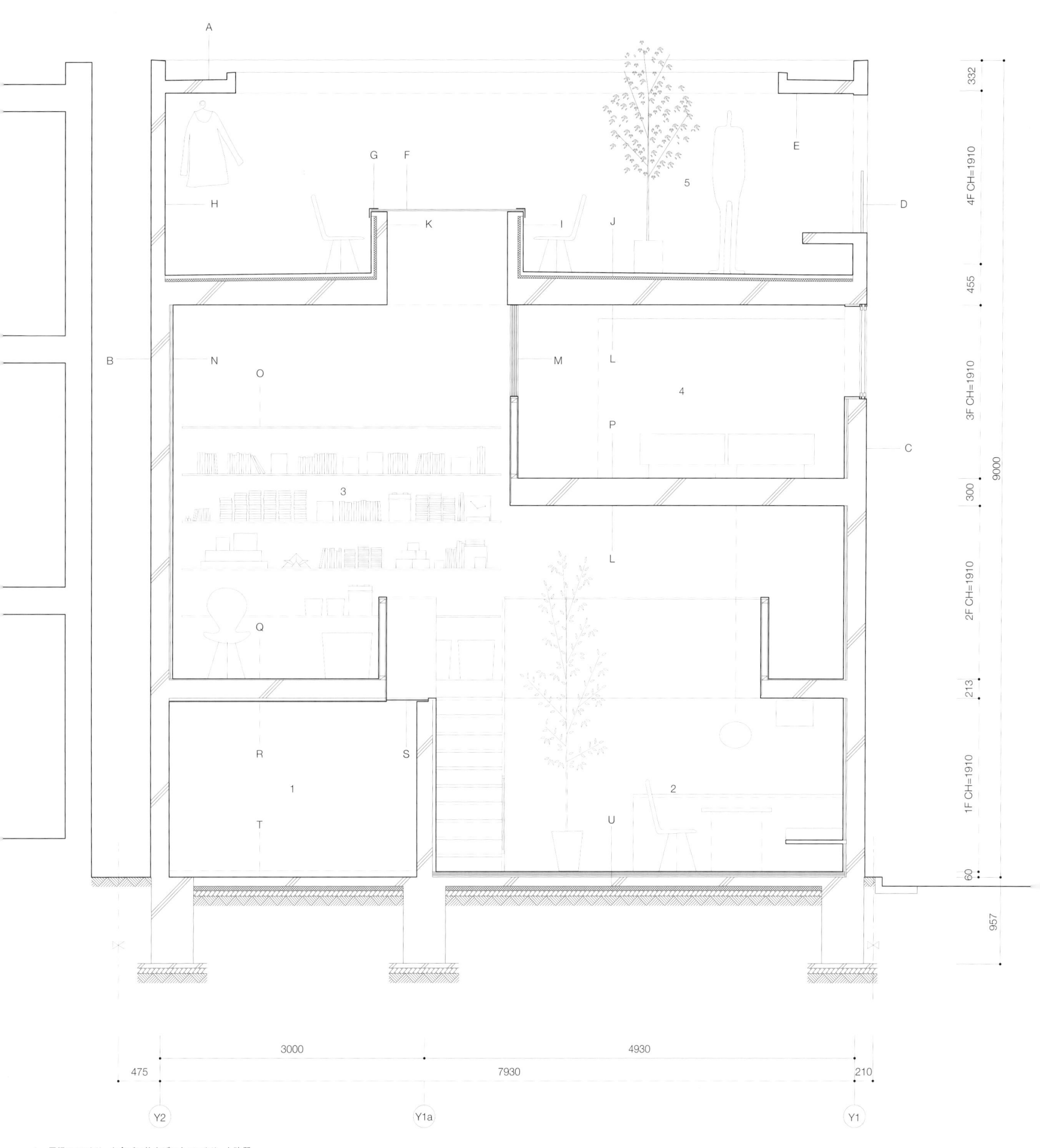

A—屋根：コンクリート金ゴテ仕上げの上コンクリート改質剤塗布　B—外壁（北・東）：コンクリート打放し　C—外壁（南・西）：コンクリート打放し モルタル補修の上リシン吹付　D—手摺：フロートガラス t=8mm 飛散防止フィルム貼り　E—天井：コンクリート打放し 部分補修　F—トップライト：ペアガラス t=22.8mm（強化ガラス t=8mm+A8+網入りガラス t=6.8mm）　G—トップライト枠：Al L-100×100×5mm UP　H—壁：コンクリート打放し UP　I—腰壁：モルタル t=30mm 金ゴテ仕上げ UP｜断熱材：スタイロフォーム t=30mm　J—床：モルタル t=40mm 金ゴテ仕上げ｜断熱材：スタイロフォーム t=30mm｜コンクリート金ゴテの上コンクリート改質剤塗布　K—立上壁：コンクリート打放し UP　L—天井：コンクリート打放し部分補修　M—引き戸：シナフラッシュ t=21mm UP　N—プラスターボード t=12.5mm（GL貼り）AEP｜断熱材：ウレタンフォーム吹付 t=15mm　O—本棚・机：ラワン合板 t=18mm OSCL　P—床：コンクリート金ゴテ仕上げ WAX　Q—床：Pタイル（305角）t=2mm　R—天井：繊維強化セメント板 t=9mm　S—トップライト：ポリカーボネート t=5mm　T—床：コンクリート金ゴテ仕上げ　U—床：ミャンマーチークフローリング t=12mm｜捨て張り合板 t=12mm｜床暖房パネル t=9mm｜捨て張り合板 t=12mm｜レベリングモルタル t=15mm｜コンクリートスラブ t=100mm｜断熱材：スタイロフォーム t=30mm｜ポリエチレンフィルム t=0.2mm｜砕石 t=60

矩計図 1:50　1：車庫　2：リビング　3：プレイルーム　4：寝室　5：テラス

109

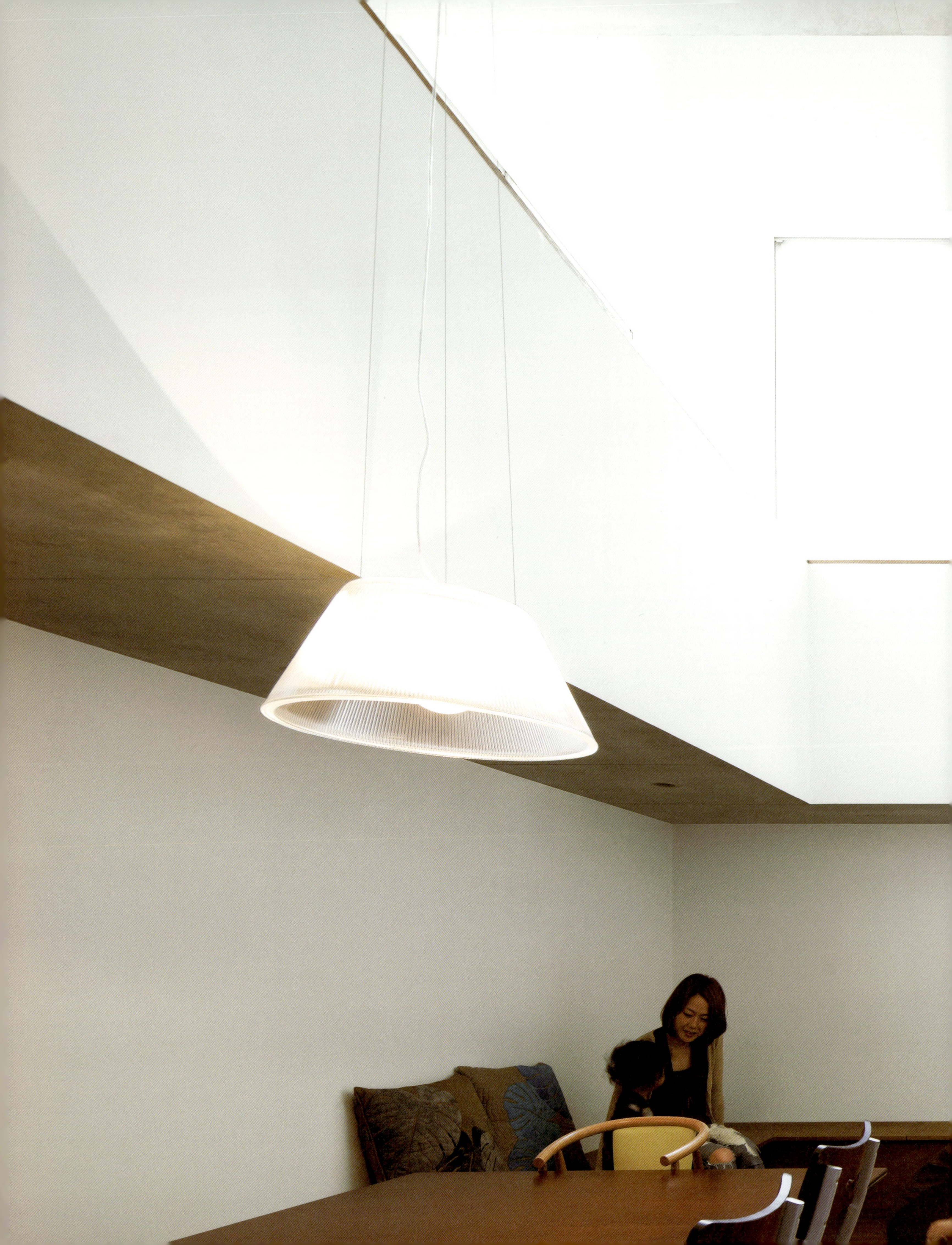

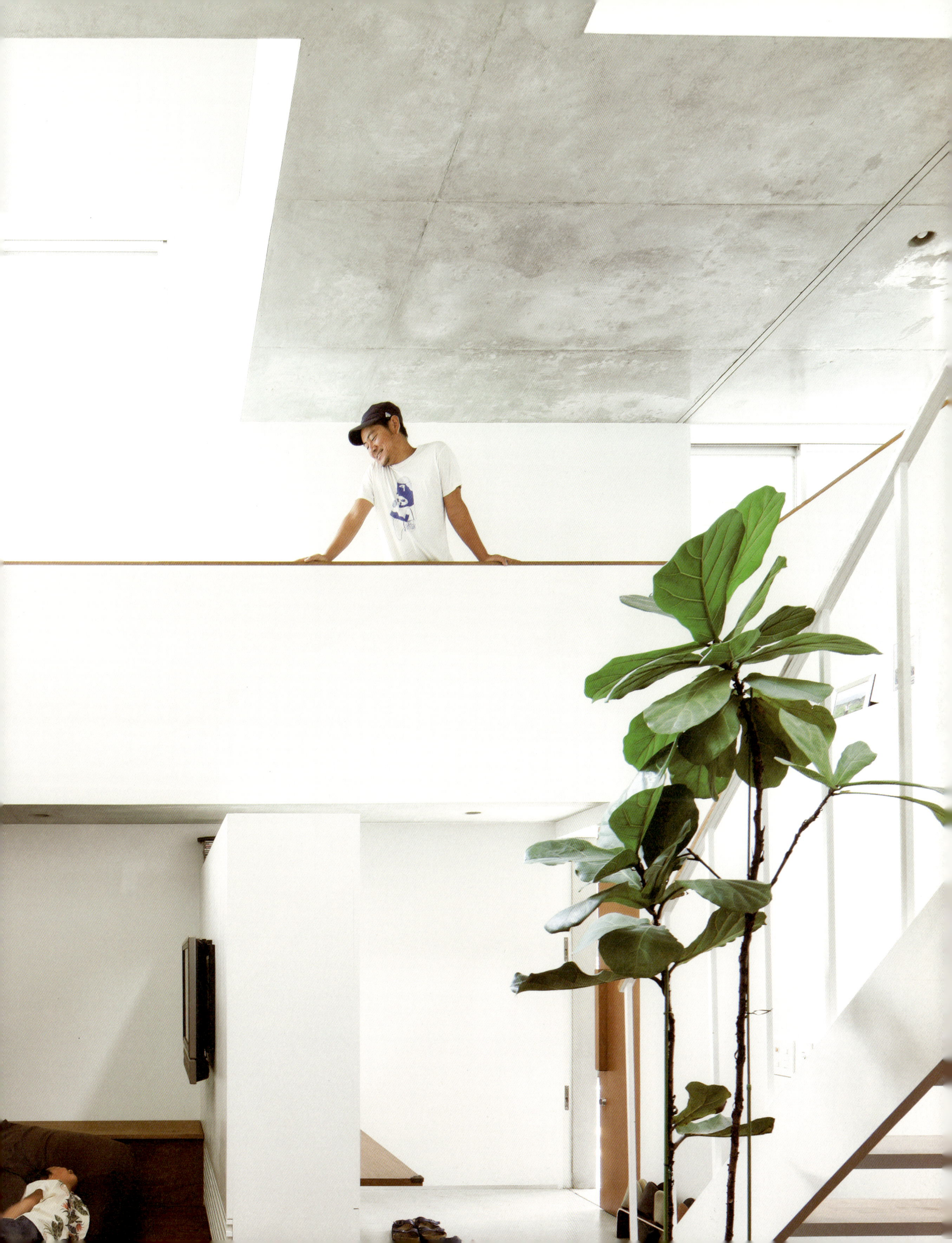

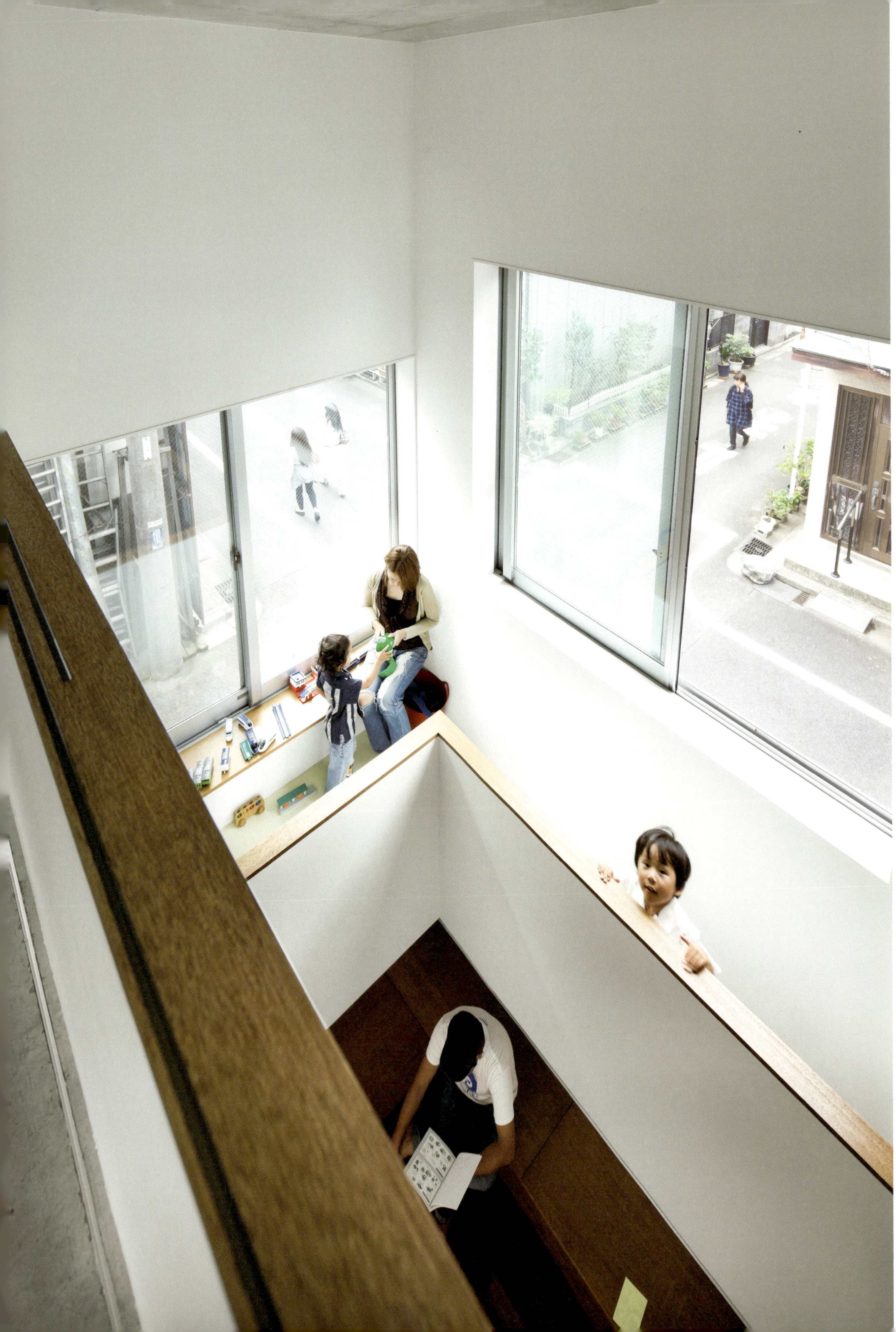

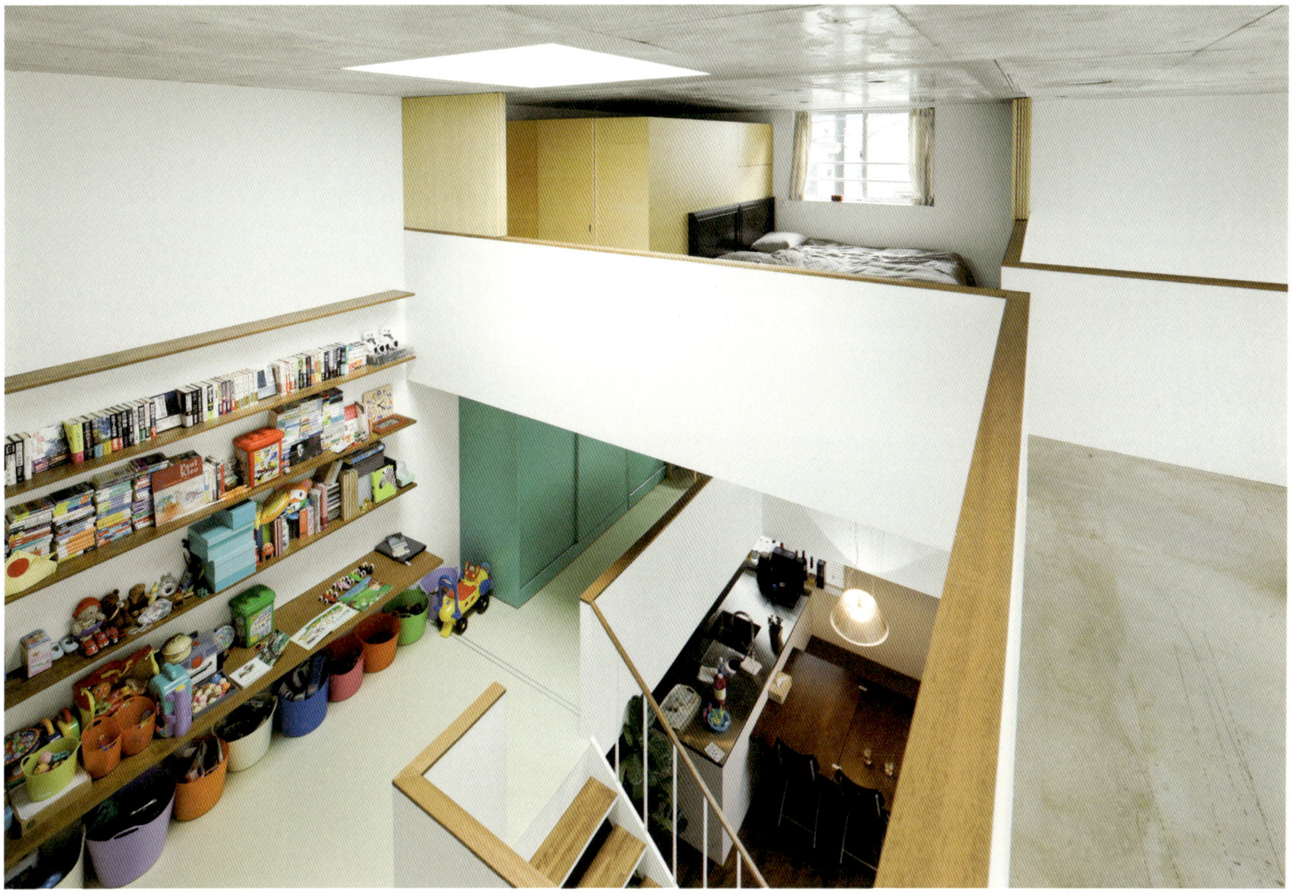

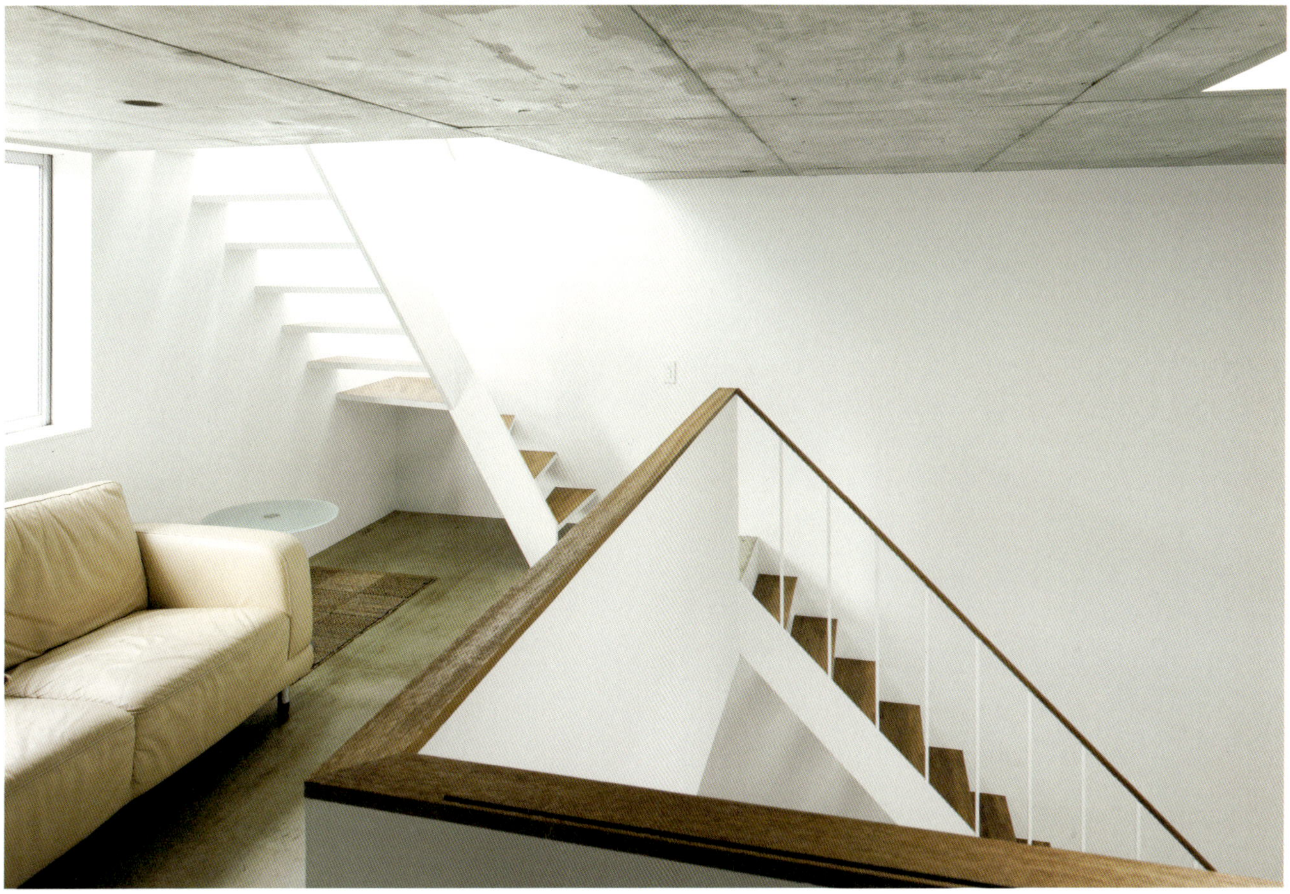

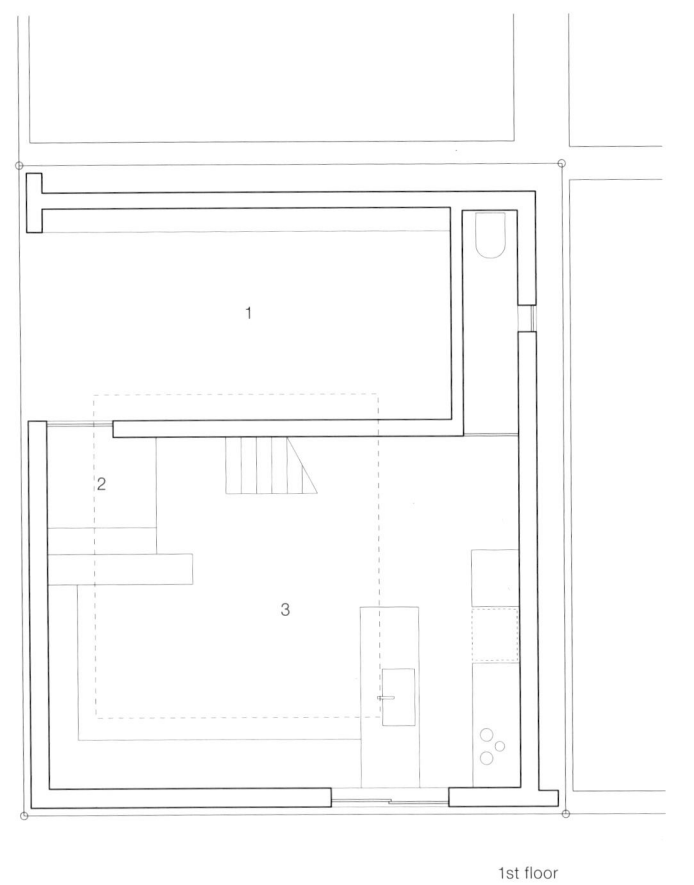

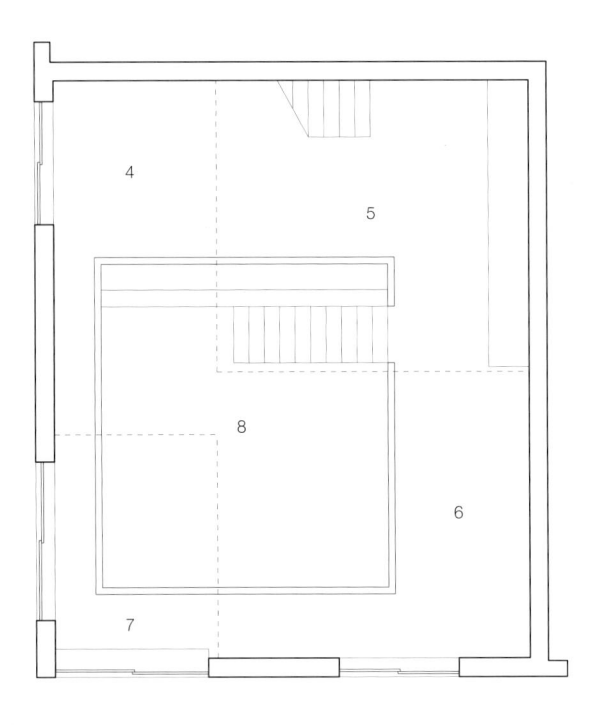

1st floor

2nd floor

N

1: garage 2: entrance 3: living room 4: children's room 1 5: play room 6: children's room 2 7: sunroom
8: void 9: study room 10: bedroom 11: closet 12: washroom 13: bathroom 14: terrace 15: skylight

Plan 1:100

3rd floor

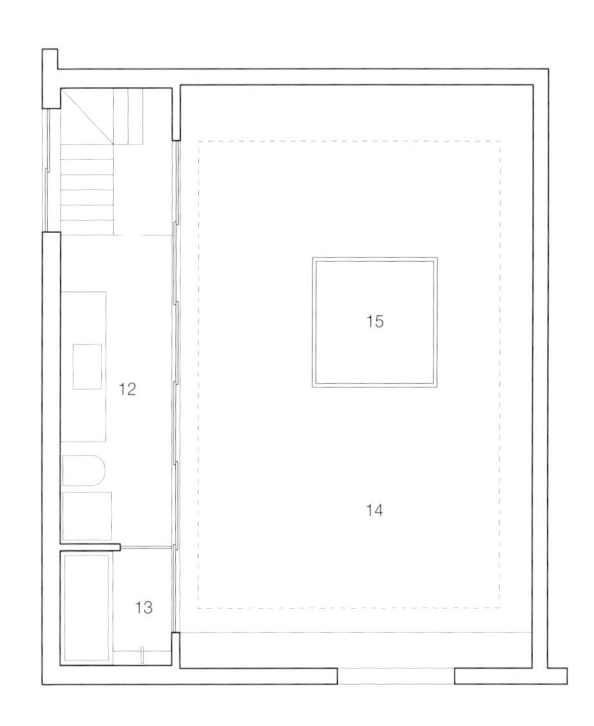

4th floor

1:車庫　2:玄関　3:リビング　4:子供室1　5:プレイルーム　6:子供室2　7:サンルーム
平面図　1:100　　8:吹抜け　9:書斎　10:寝室　11:クロゼット　12:洗面室　13:浴室　14:テラス　15:トップライト

2nd floor

3rd floor

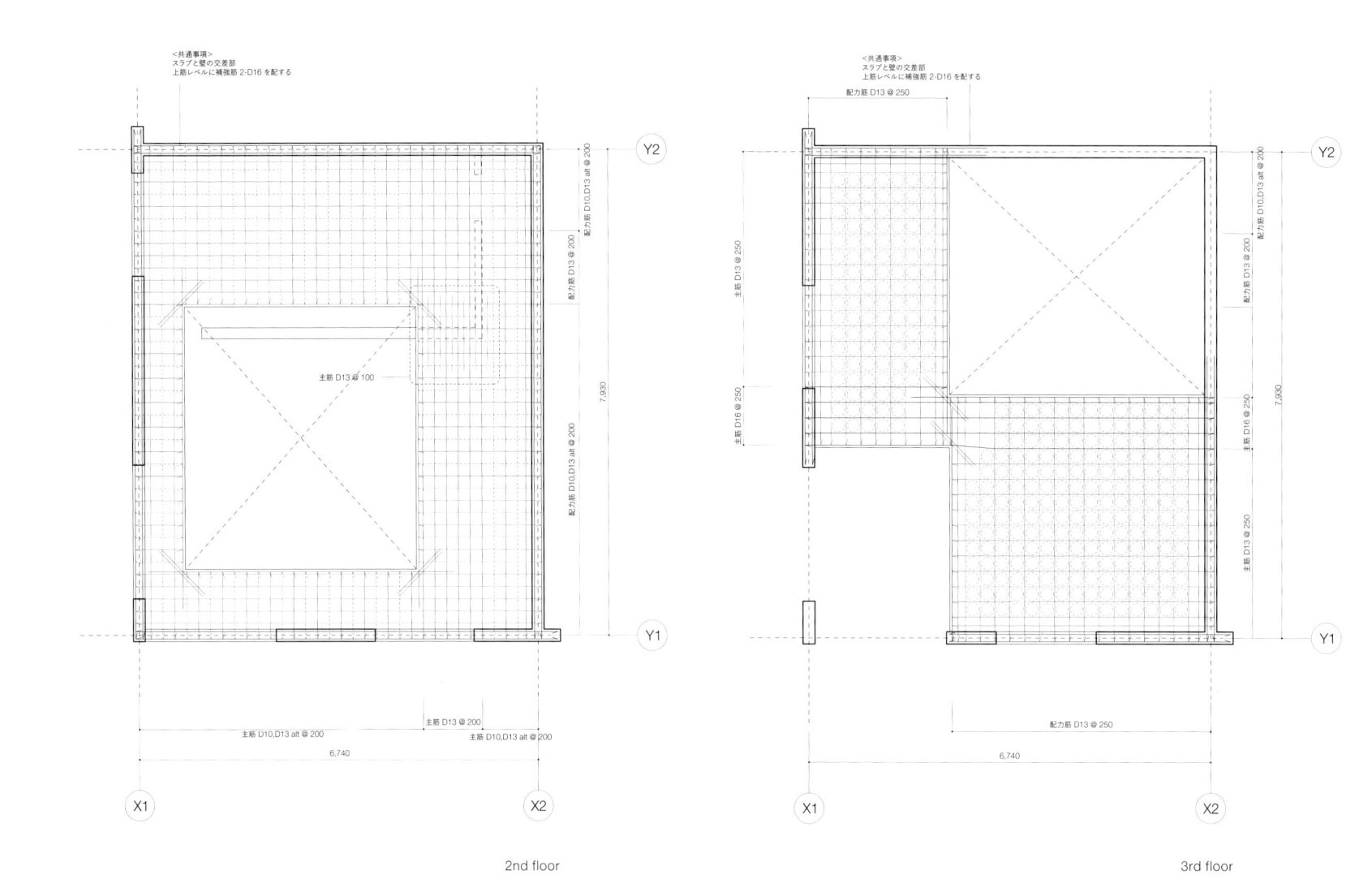

Bar arrangement plan 1:100

4th floor

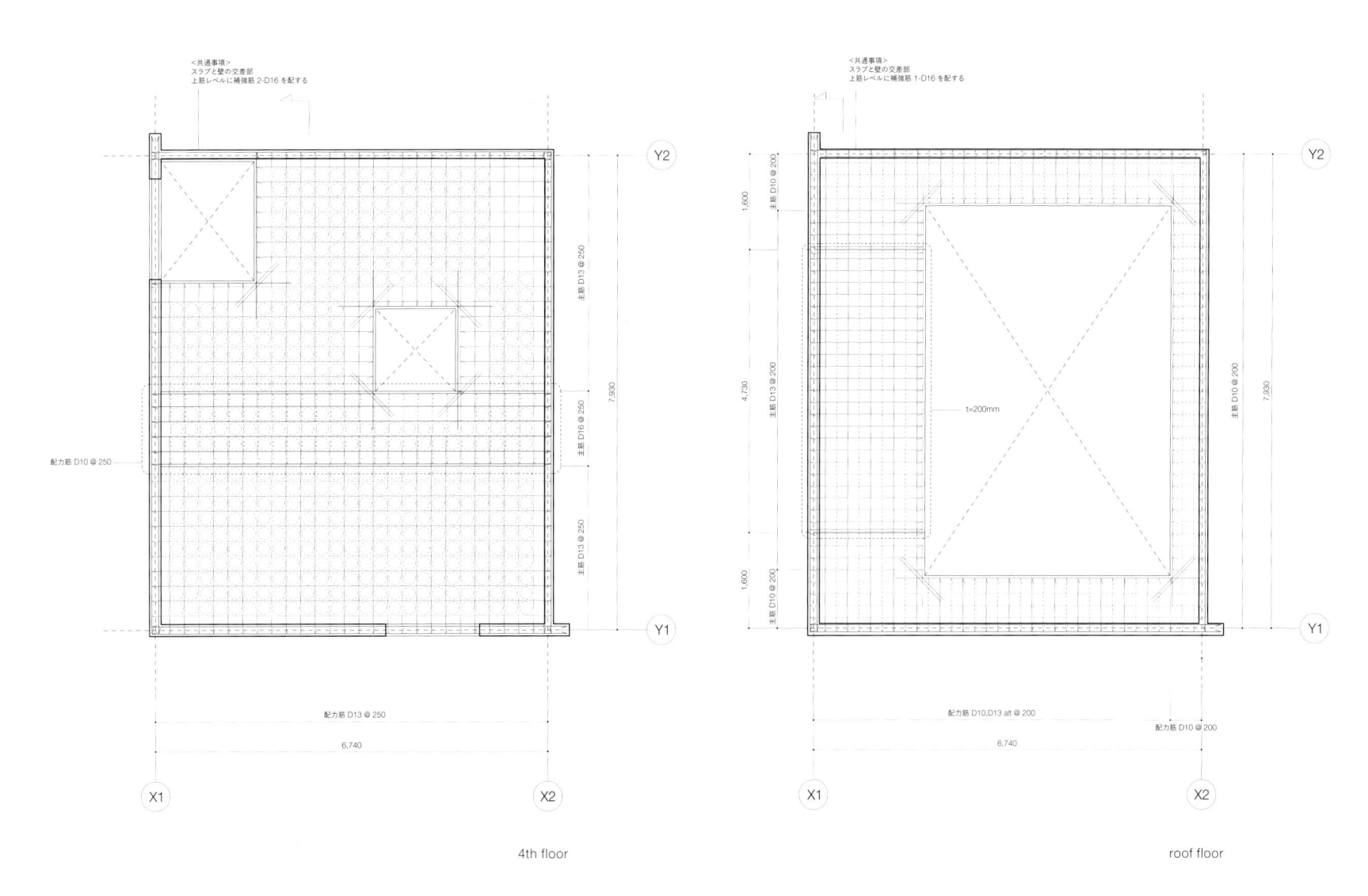

roof floor

特記なきスラブ厚はt=200mmとする

はD16(φ18)を示す

はD13(φ14)を示す

はD10(φ11)を示す

配筋図 1:100

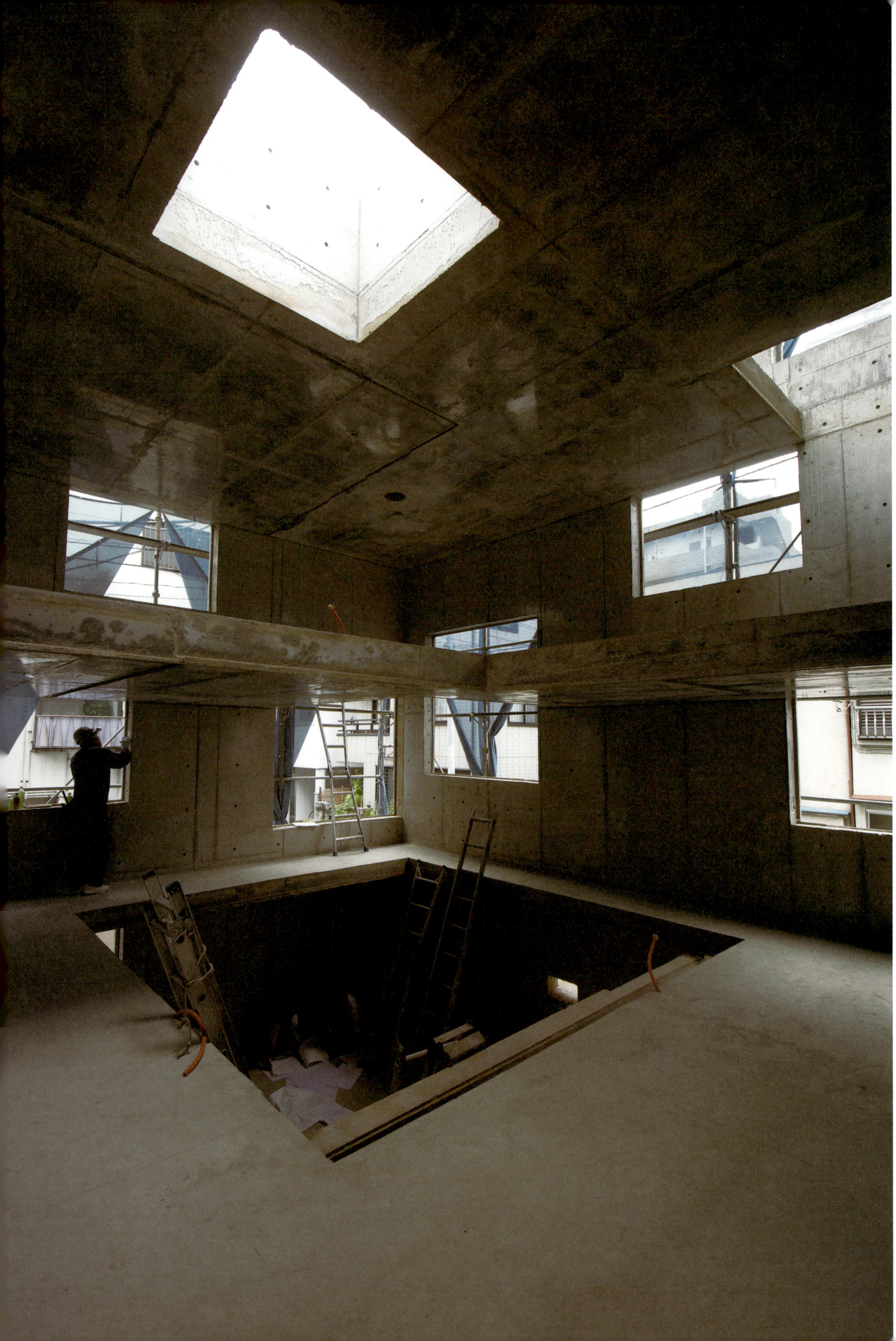

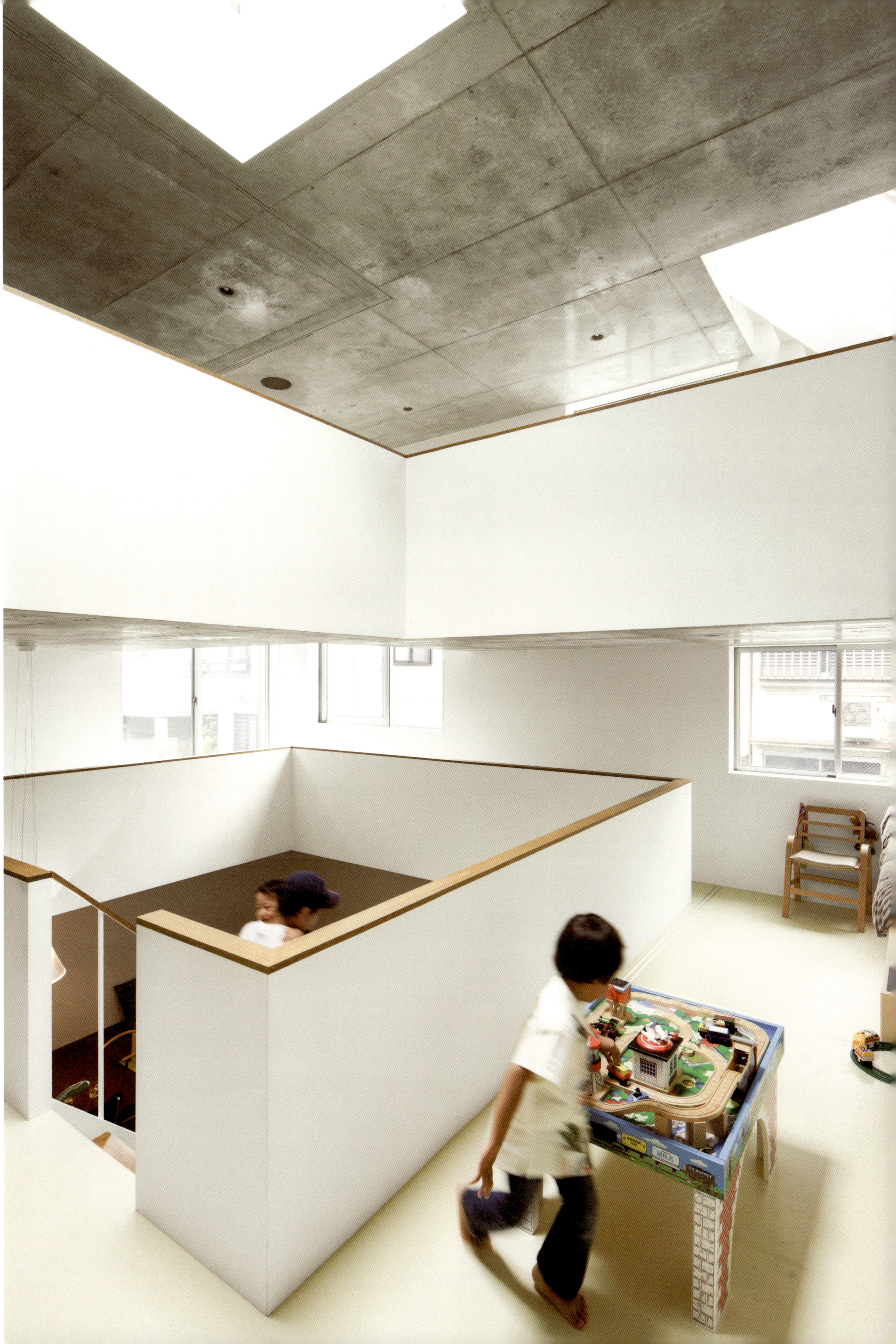
MILK

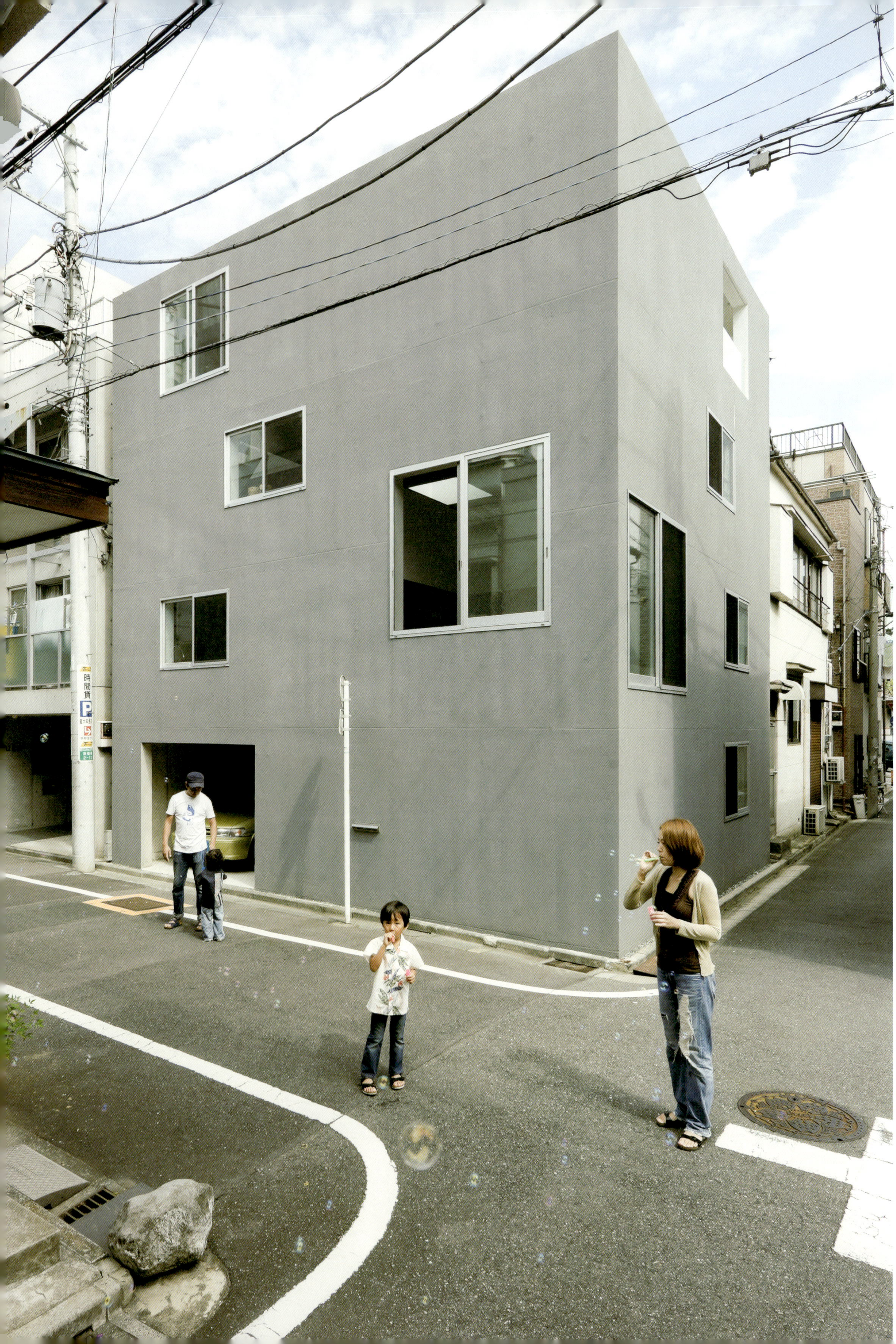

Townhouse in Asakusa

Location: Sumida, Tokyo
Principal use: Residential
Site area: 63.98m²
Building area: 53.45m²
Total floor area: 113.68m²
Number of stories: 4
Structure: Reinforced concrete

浅草の町家

所在地：東京都墨田区
主要用途：専用住宅
敷地面積：63.98m²
建築面積：53.45m²
延床面積：113.68m²
規模：地上4階
構造：鉄筋コンクリート造

House in Komazawa ｜ 駒沢の住宅

This house stands in a verdant residential district that contains a mixture of detached houses and low-rise condominiums. The east side of the lot abuts a grove of plum trees. While creating a two-story timber structure with a gabled roof that is common to the neighborhood, I tried to restructure the relationship between the first and second floor. First, I raised the first floor by one story to create a *doma*-like (earthen floor) space that connects to the ground. The rough space allows the residents to arrange their furniture and plants as they see fit on the stone-lined floor, and the open living room ensures a view out on the plum grove through the big window. In addition, the pitch of the roof is apparent in the second-floor attic space. With floors made of two-by-threes (38mm x 64mm) with gaps between them, half of the second floor is made up of a plywood-lined bedroom and wet area, and the remaining half houses a study with a louvered floor. The big window on the first floor and the top light on the second floor are linked via the louvered floor, allowing you to see the sky even when you're on the first floor and the neighborhood diagonally below you through the floor from the second level. In this project, I sensed a need for a contrast between the two floors (the light and expanse that is visible overhead from the first floor and the public atmosphere that you sense underfoot while on the second) that would create a mutual appeal and awareness in the environment.

戸建て住宅と低層の分譲マンションが入り混じる緑豊かな住宅地に建つ住宅。敷地の東側が梅林に面している。周囲と同じような切妻屋根の木造2階建てとしながら、1階と2階の関係を再構成している。まず1階は地面と地続きの土間のようなスペースにして階高を高くした。石張りの床のうえに置き家具や植物を自由に並べたラフなスペースは、大窓によって梅林への眺望を確保した開放的なリビングになっている。また2階は屋根勾配が室内に現れた小屋裏のような空間とした。床は2×3材（38×64mm）の小梁を隙間をあけて並べ、2階の半分は合板を張って寝室や水回りとし、もう半分はルーバー状の床の書斎としている。1階の大窓と2階のトップライトをこのルーバー状の床がつなぎ、1階にいても空が、2階からも床を介して斜め下方向に街が見える。1階にとっては頭上に明るさや広がりを、2階にとっては足元に公共的な雰囲気を、といったように、対照的な2つの階がお互いを環境として求め合い、意識し合うような状態になればと考えた。

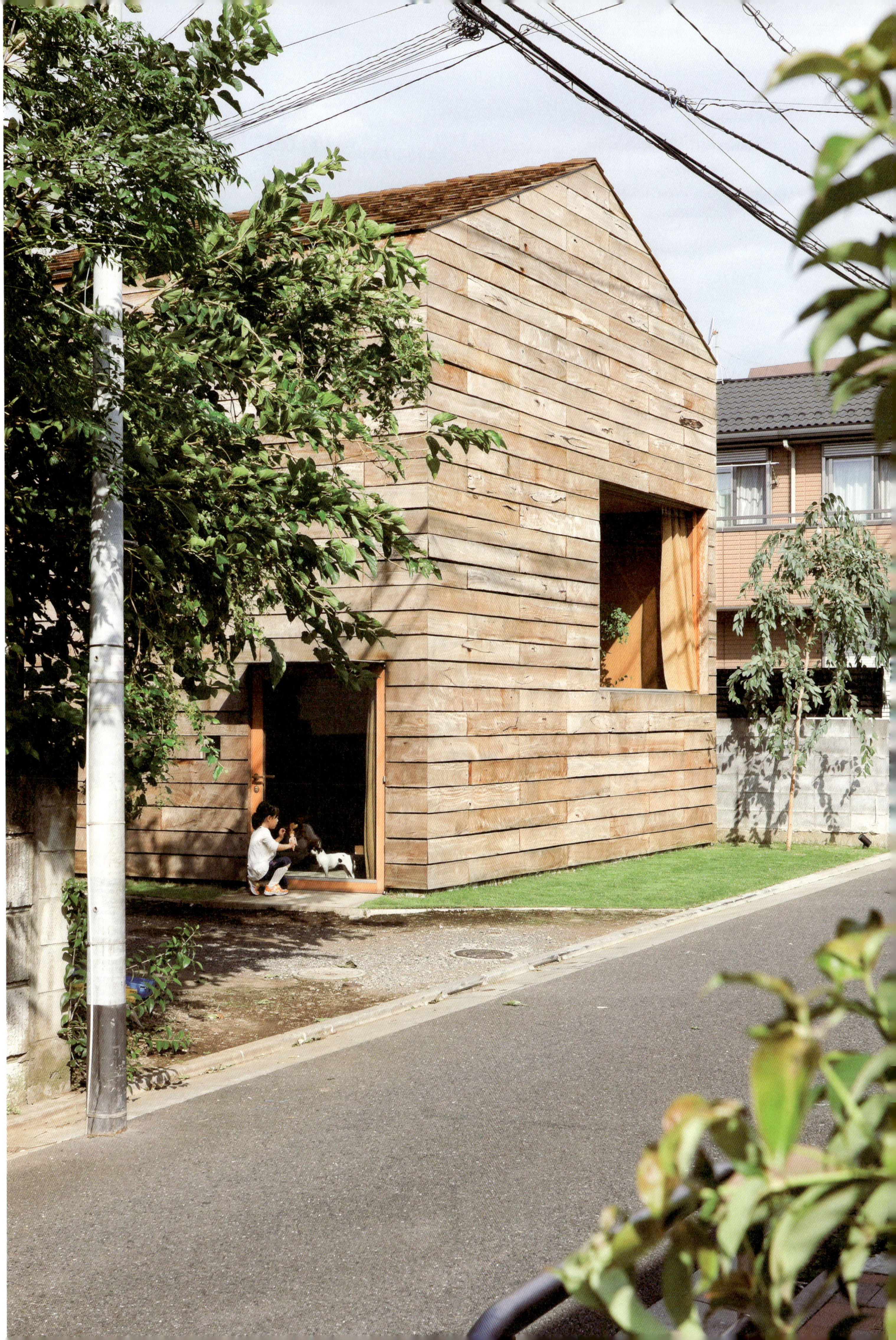

A—External walls: Eucalyptus t=36mm | Furring strips: 12×45mm @455mm | Galvanized steel sheeting t=0.25mm | Moisture permeable waterproof sheeting t=2mm | Plasterboard t=12.5mm | Structural plywood t=12mm | Column: 120×120mm | Insulation: Glasswool t=100mm (24kg/m^3) B—Roof: Red cedar t=24mm | Furring strips: 12×45mm @455mm | Asphalt roofing t=2mm | Structural plywood t=24mm | Beams: 210×120mm | Insulation: Glasswool t=100mm (24kg/m^3) C—Skylight: Aluminum single slider D—Walls: Fiber reinforced plastic waterproofing t=2mm, topcoat finish E—External floor: Korean lawn grass F—Ridge beams: Laminated veneer lumber 600×120mm, oil stain clear lacquer finish G—Ceiling: Lauan plywood t=9mm, oil stain finish H—Bifold door: Lauan flush t=30mm, oil stain clear laquer finish I—Suspending rod: Steel rod φ20mm @1575mm, polyurethane paint J—Timber sash K—Floor: Red cedar t=20mm, xyladecor finish | Fiber reinforced plastic waterproofing t=2mm, topcoat finish | Waterproof plywood t=12mm L—Floor: Double lauan plywood t=12mm, oil stain clear lacquer finish M—Batten (floor): SPF lumber 38×64mm @68mm, wax N—Beams: Steel flat bar 40×100mm @1575mm, polyurethane paint O—Stair tread: Steel plate t=22mm, polyurethane paint P—Wall: Lauan plywood t=3mm, oil stain finish Q—Floor: Quartzite t=10mm, wax | Structural plywood t=12mm | Floor joist: t=45×45mm @300mm | Leveling t=8mm | Concrete slab t=150mm | Insulation: Styrofoam t=50mm | Double polyethylene film sheeting t=0.2mm | Crushed stone t=60mm

Section 1:50   1: living room 2: balcony 3: bedroom 4: study room

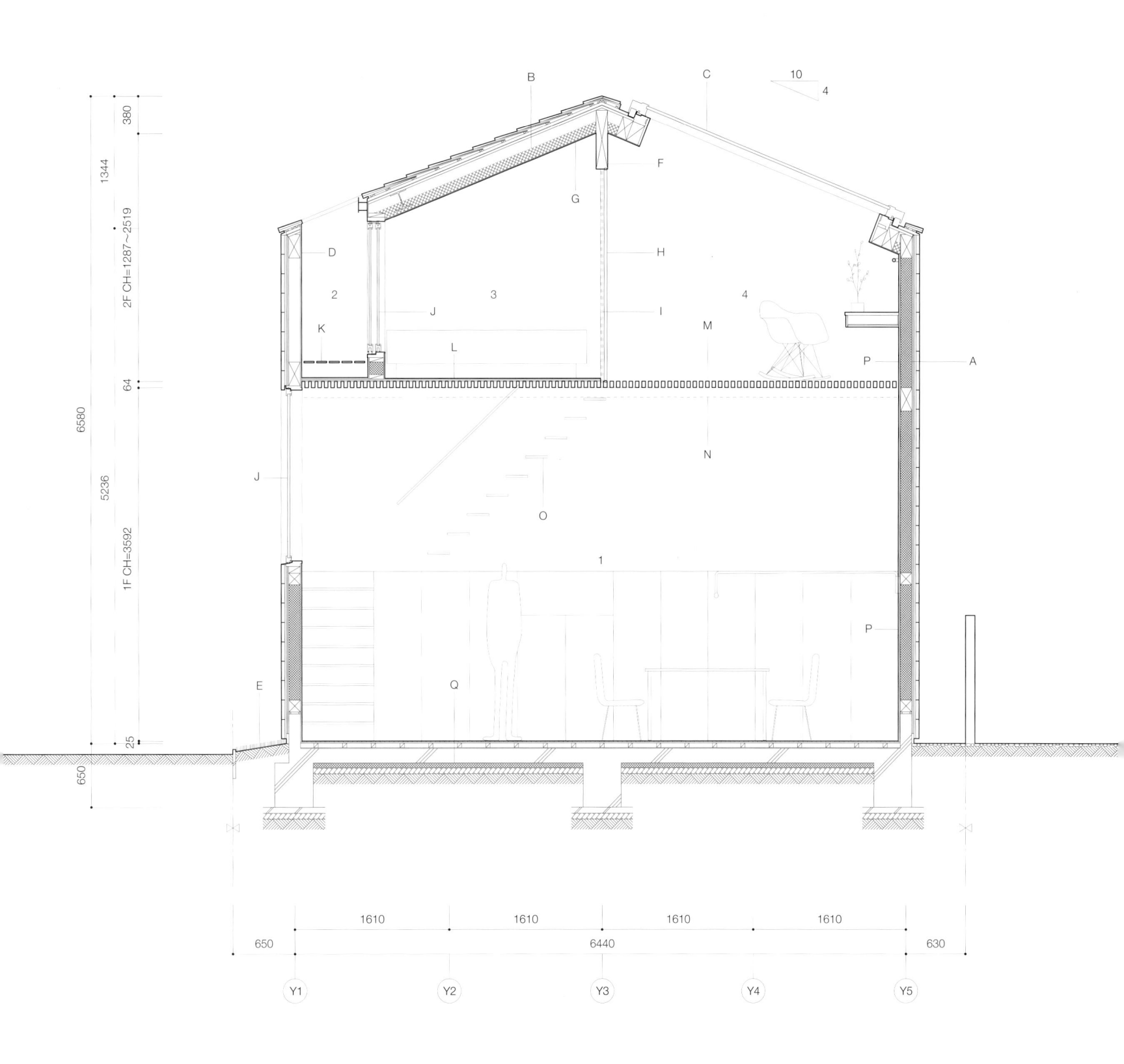

A—外壁：ユーカリ t=36mm｜胴縁：12×45mm @455mm｜亜鉛鉄板 t=0.25mm｜透湿防水シート｜プラスターボード t=12.5mm｜構造用合板 t=12mm｜柱：120×120mm｜断熱材：グラスウール t=100mm（24kg/m³）　B—屋根：レッドシダー t=24mm｜横胴縁：12×45mm @455mm｜アスファルトルーフィング t=2mm｜構造用合板 t=24mm｜梁：210×120mm｜断熱材：グラスウール t=100mm（24kg/m³）　C—トップライト：アルミ製片引き　D—壁：FRP防水 t=2mm トップコート仕上げ　E—外構床：高麗芝　F—棟梁：LVL 600×120mm OSCL　G—天井：ラワン合板 t=9mm OS　H—折れ戸：ラワンフラッシュ t=30mm OSCL　I—吊りロッド：St ロッドφ20mm @1575mm UP　J—木製サッシ　K—床：レッドシダー t=20mm XD｜FRP防水 t=2mm トップコート仕上げ｜耐水合板 t=12mm　L—床：ラワン合板 t=12mm 2枚貼り OSCL　M—小梁（床）：SPF材 38×64mm @68mm WAX　N—梁：St-FB 40×100mm @1575mm UP　O—階段踏み板：St PL t=22mm UP　P—壁：ラワン合板 t=3mm OS　Q—床：石英岩 t=10mm WAX｜構造用合板 t=12mm｜根太：45×45mm @300mm｜レベリング t=8mm｜コンクリートスラブ t=150mm｜断熱材：スタイロフォーム t=50mm｜ポリエチレンフィルム t=0.5mm 2重敷き｜砕石 t=60mm

矩計図 1:50　　1：居間　2：バルコニー　3：寝室　4：書斎

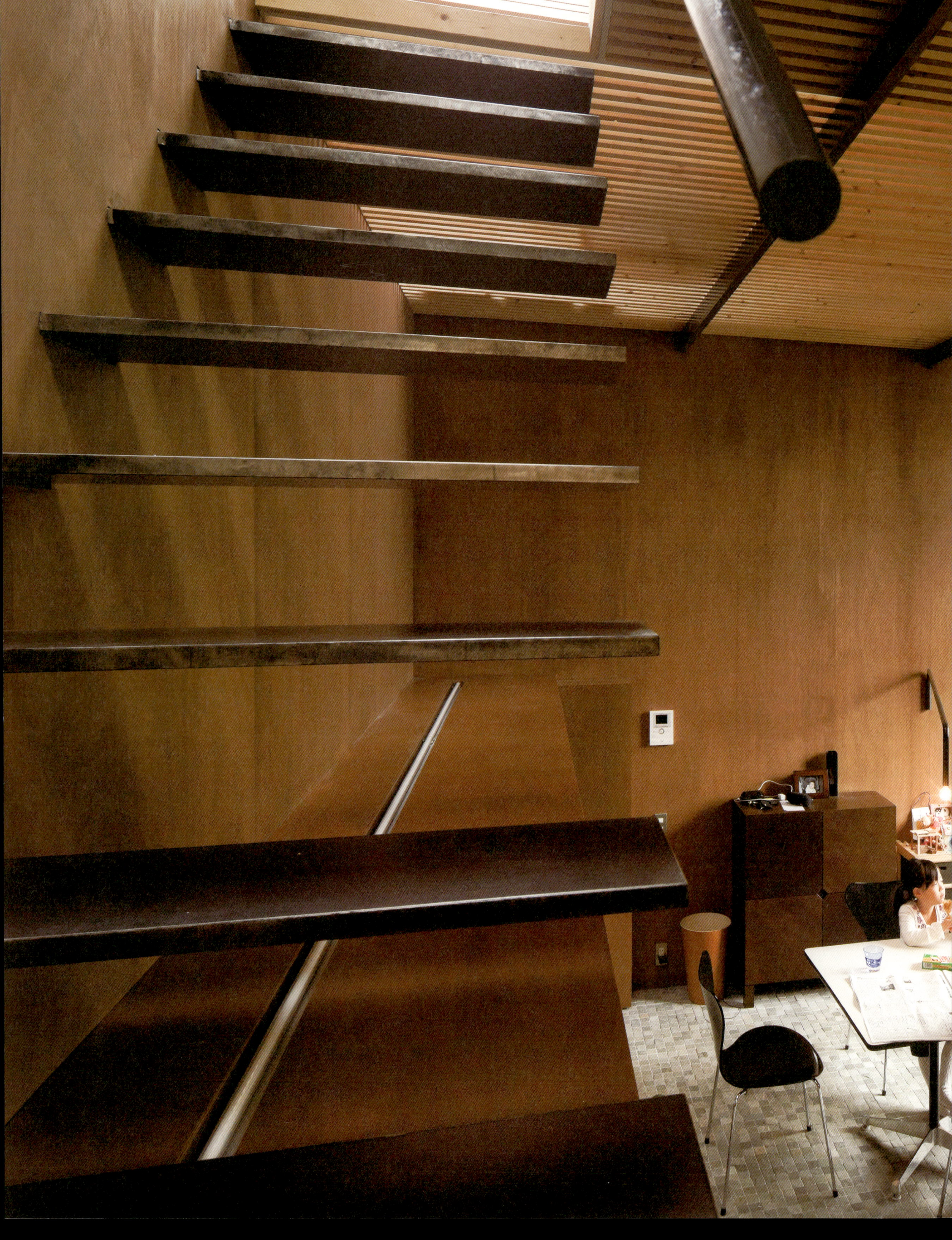

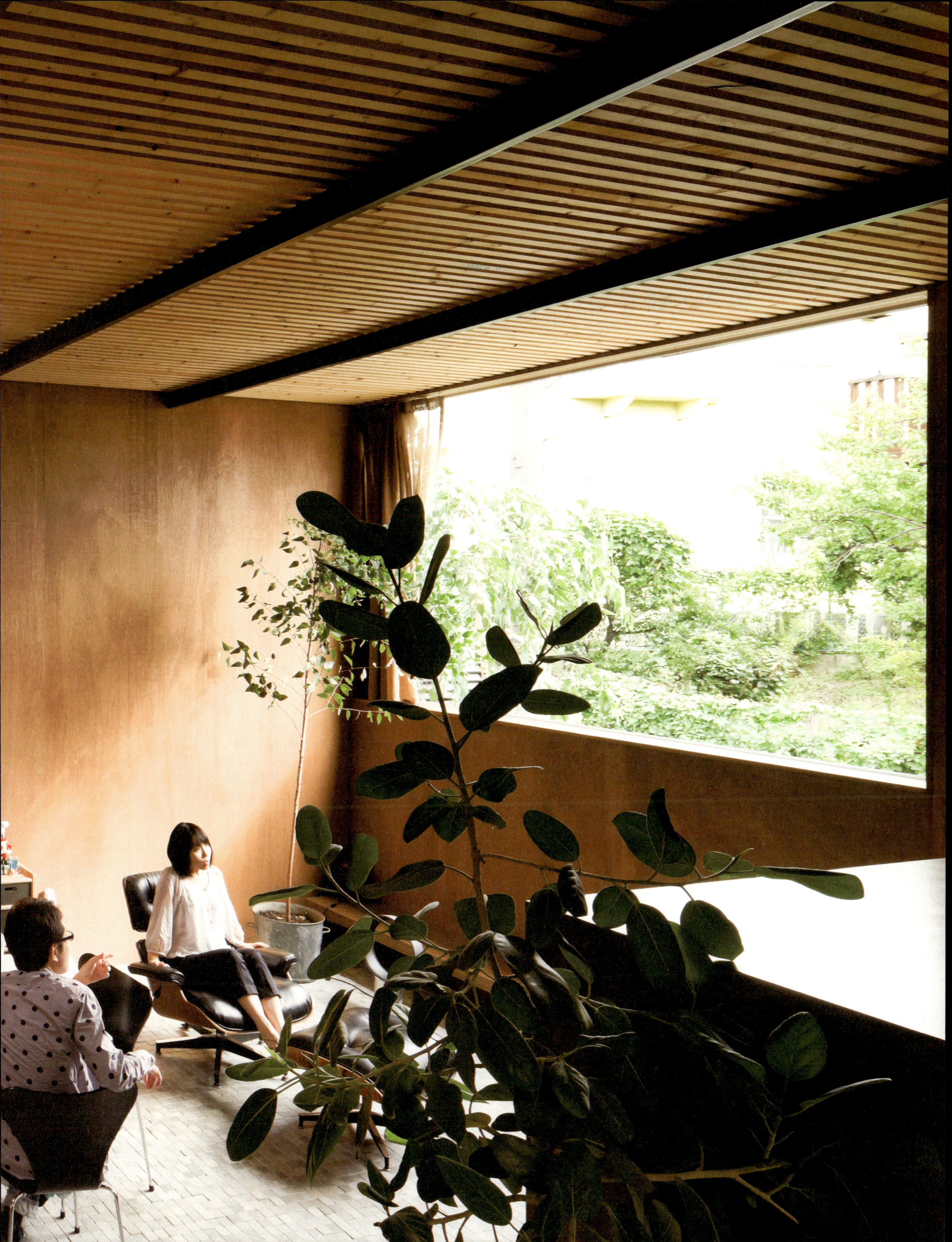

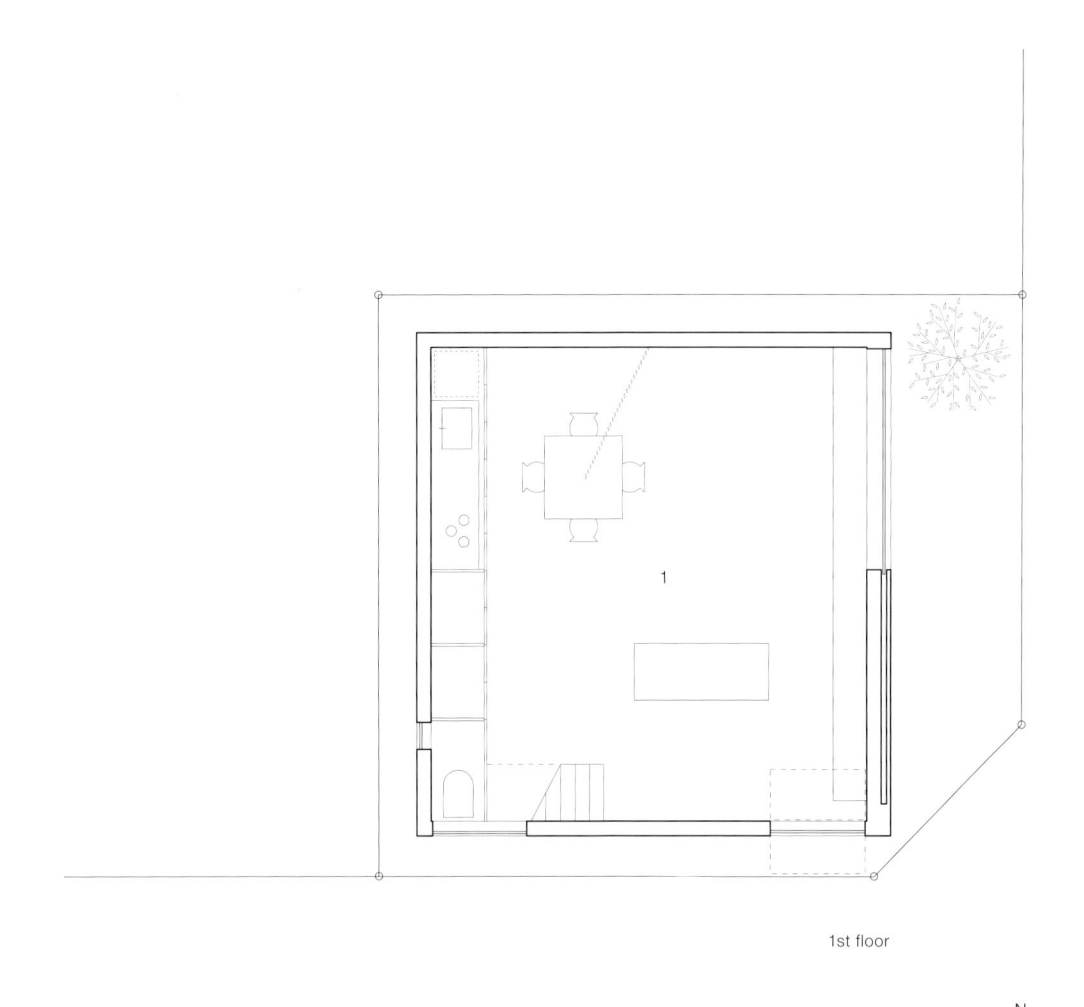

1st floor

N

128 Plan 1:100 1: living room 2: study room 3: bedroom 4: bathroom 5: balcony

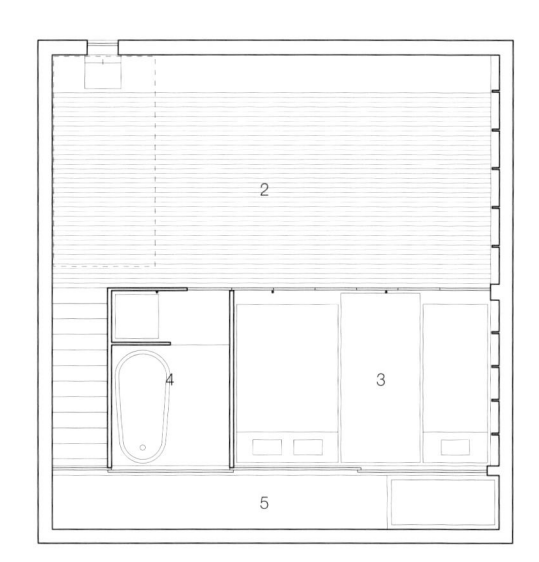

2nd floor

平面図　1:100　　1:リビング　2:書斎　3:寝室　4:浴室　5:バルコニー

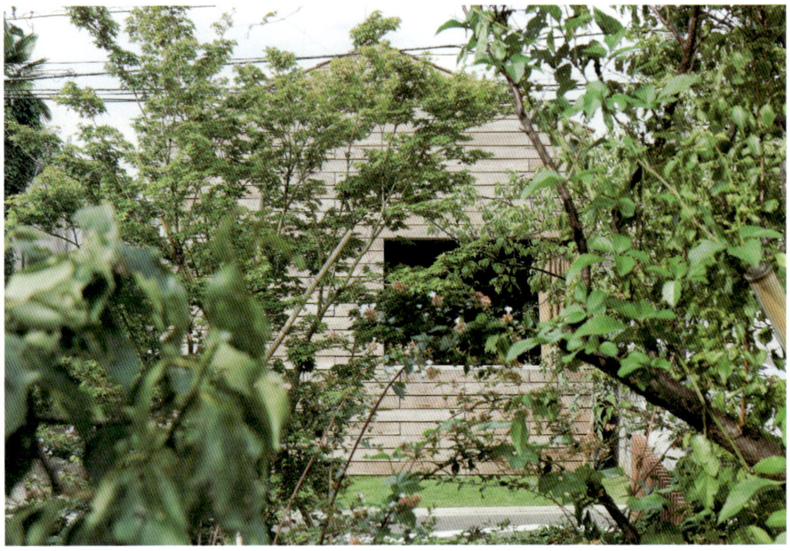
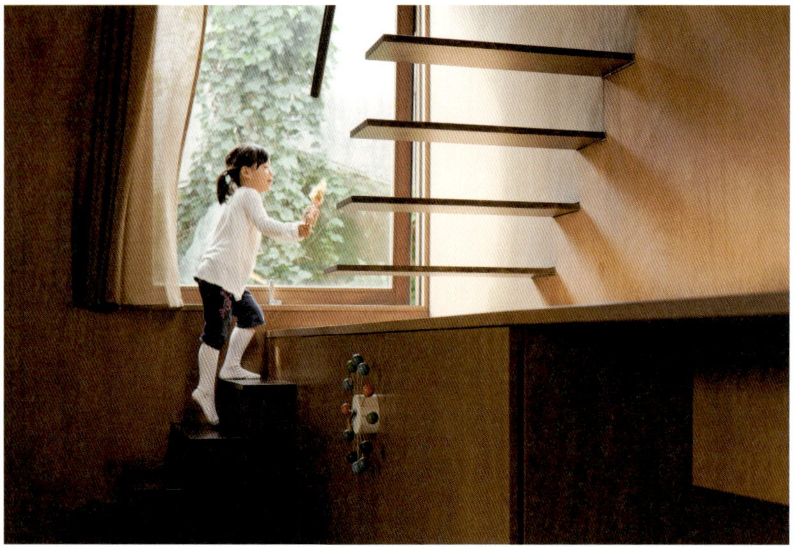
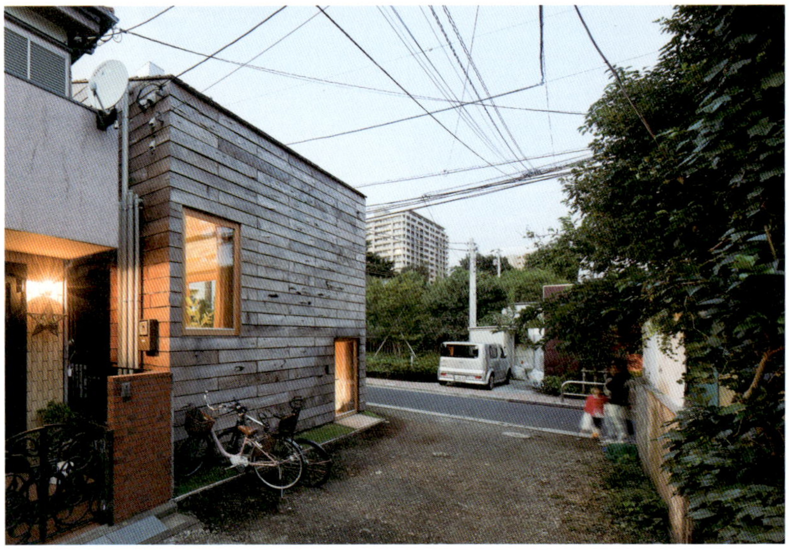
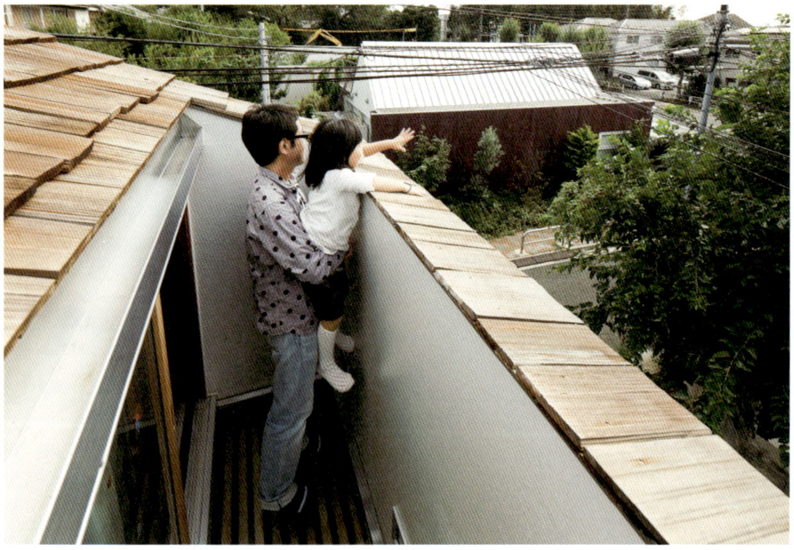

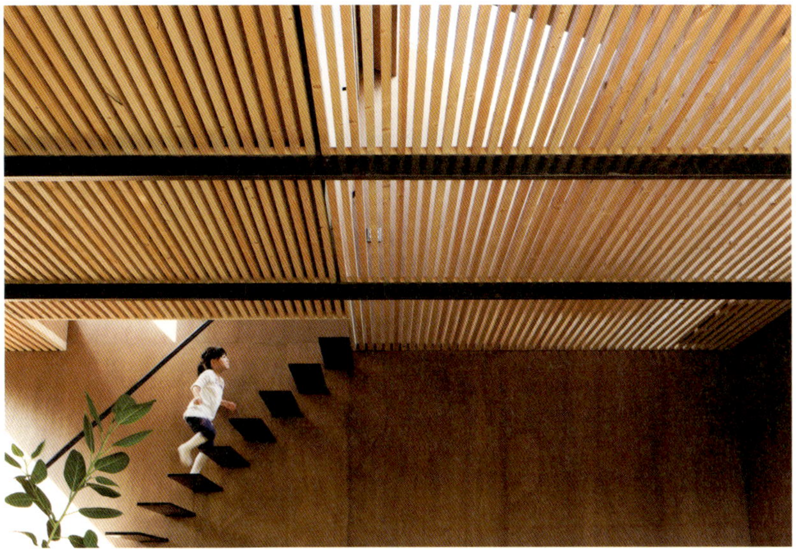

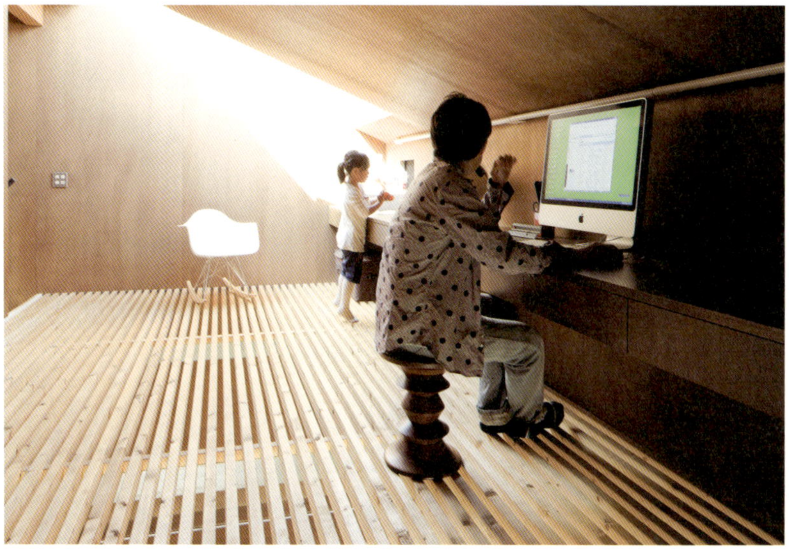

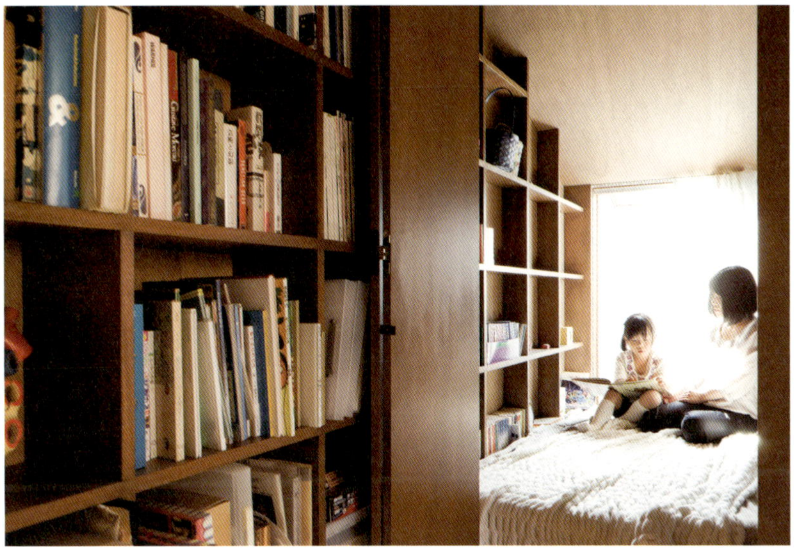

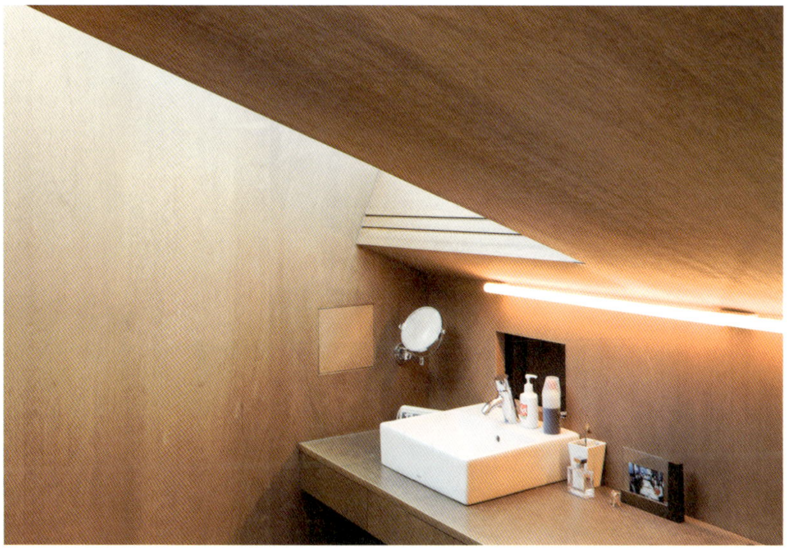

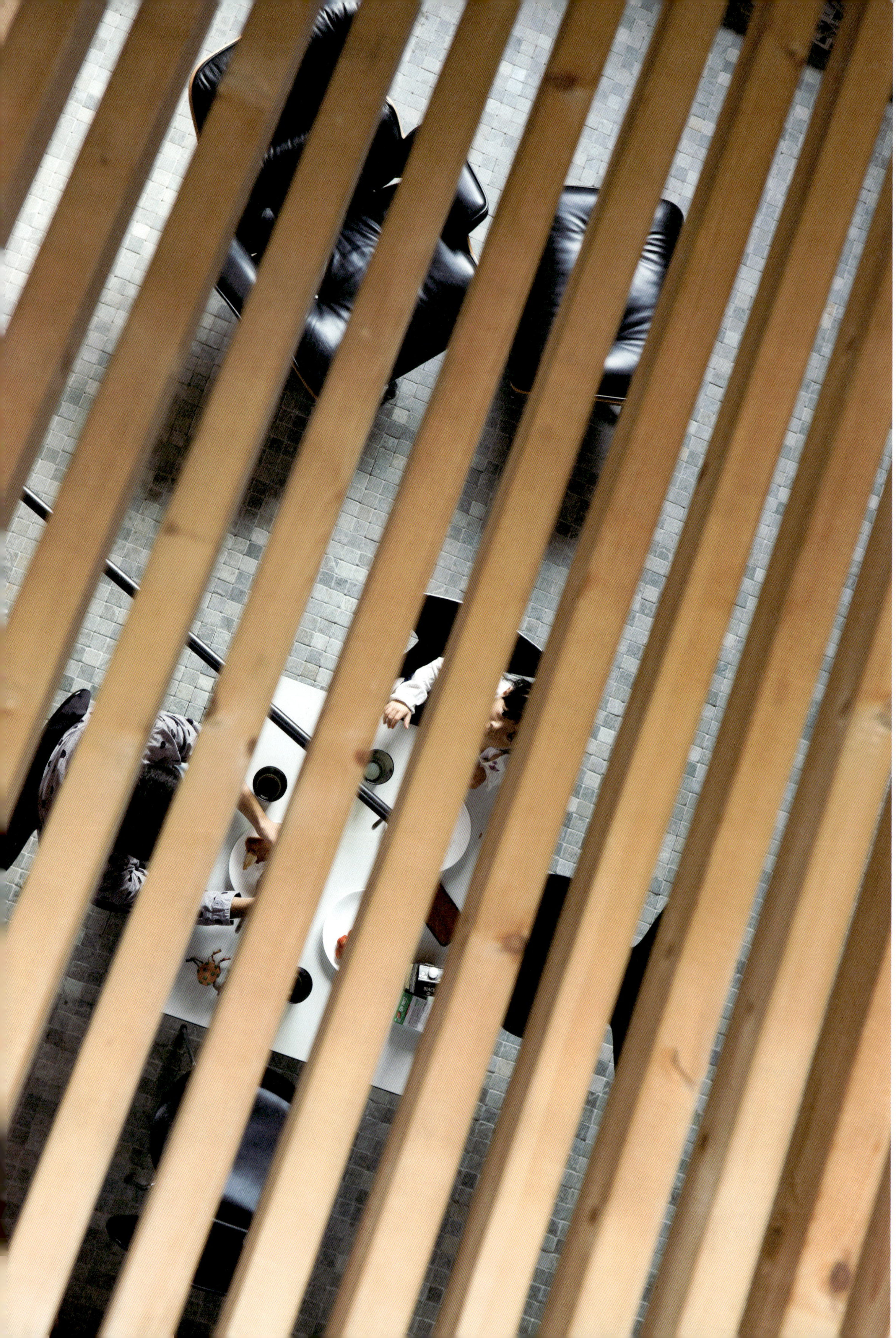

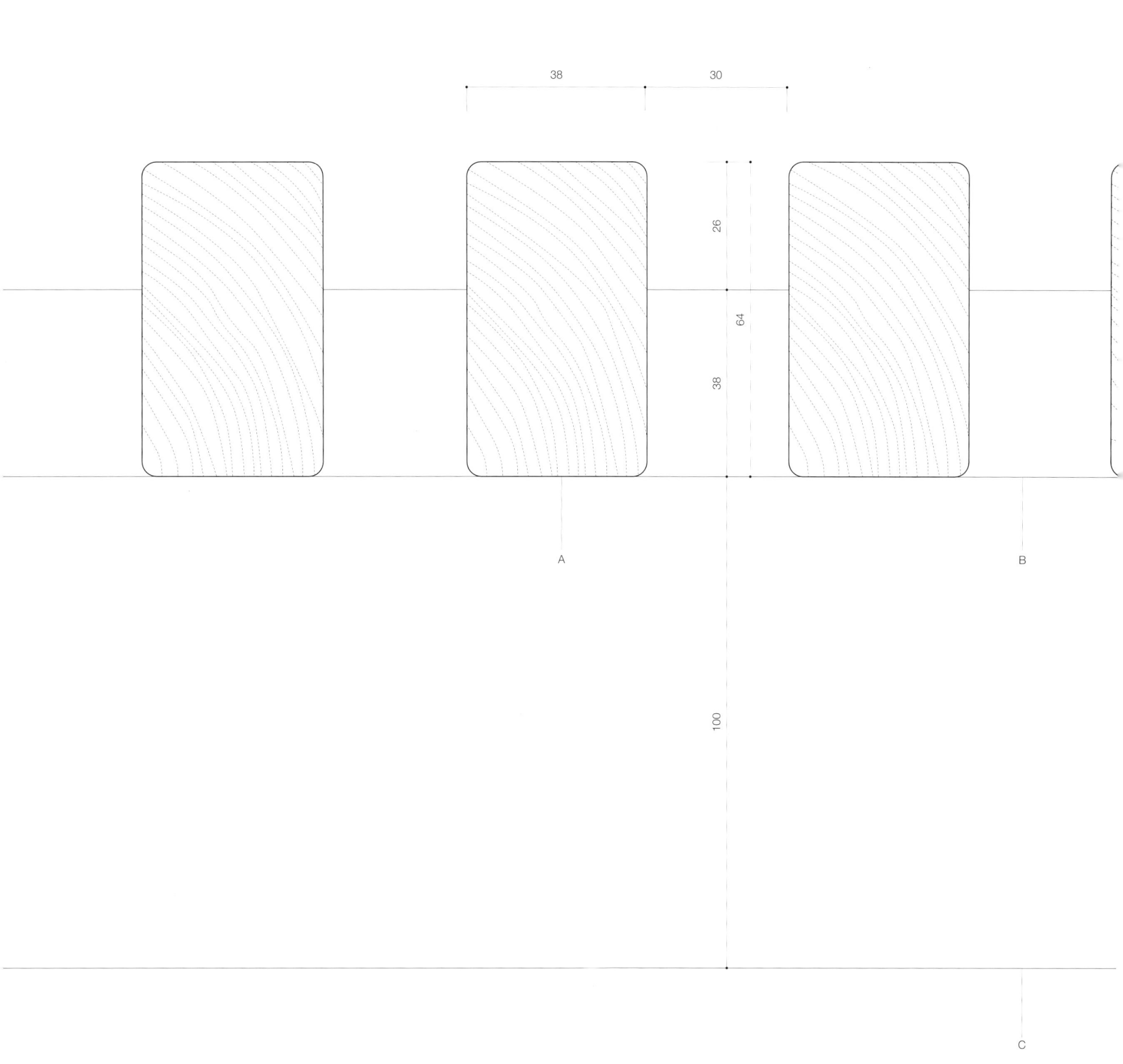

A—Batten (floor): 2" × 3" SPF lumber @68mm, wax finish   B—Spacer: 2"× 3" SPF lumber t=30mm   C—Beam: Black oxide steel flatbar 100 × 40mm, polyurethane paint

A—小梁（床）：SPF材 2" × 3"（38 × 64mm）@68mm WAX   B—スペーサー：SPF材 2" × 3"（38 × 64mm）t=30mm   C—梁：St FB-100 × 40mm 黒皮のうえUP

Detail of floor 1:1   床詳細図 1:1

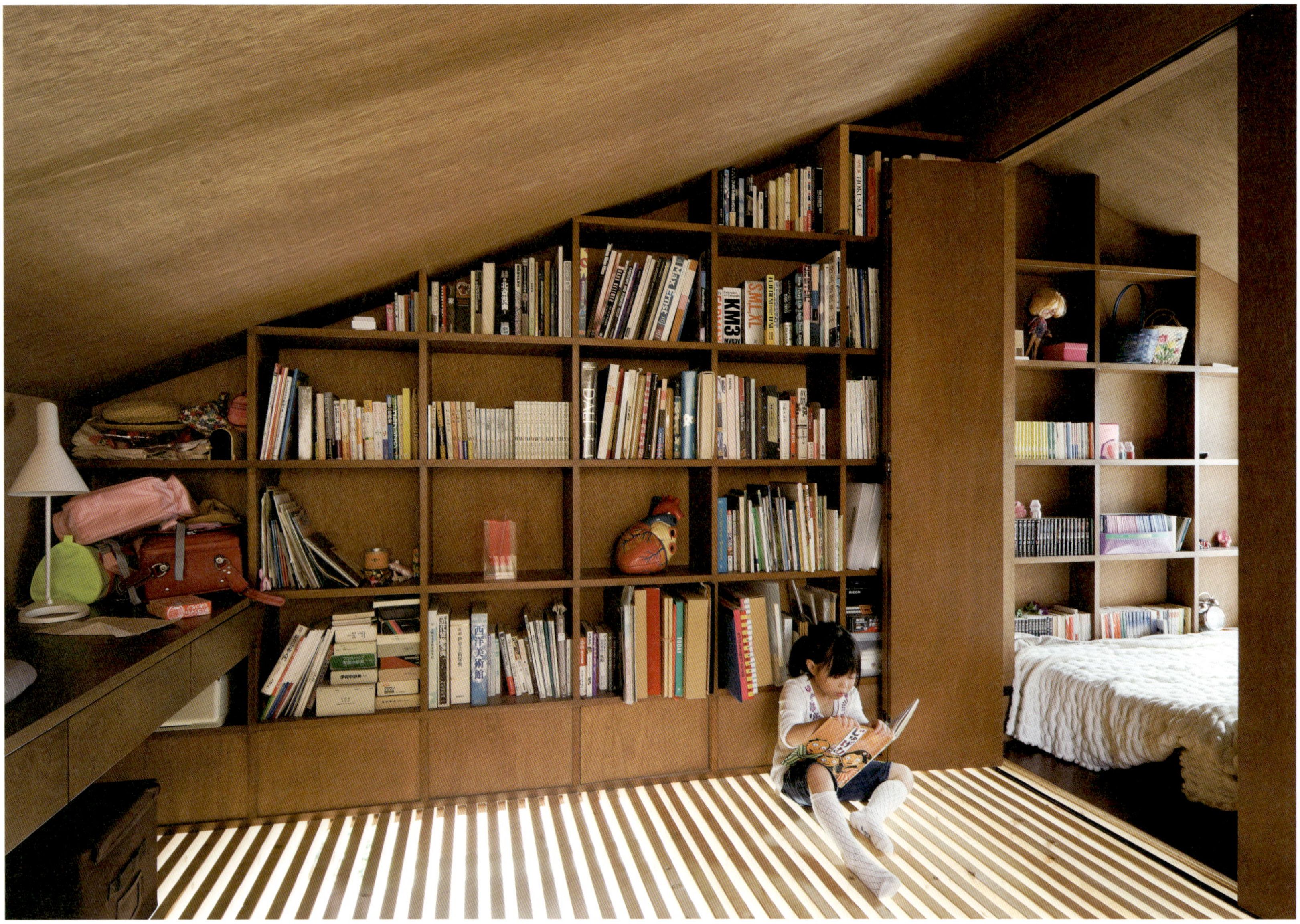

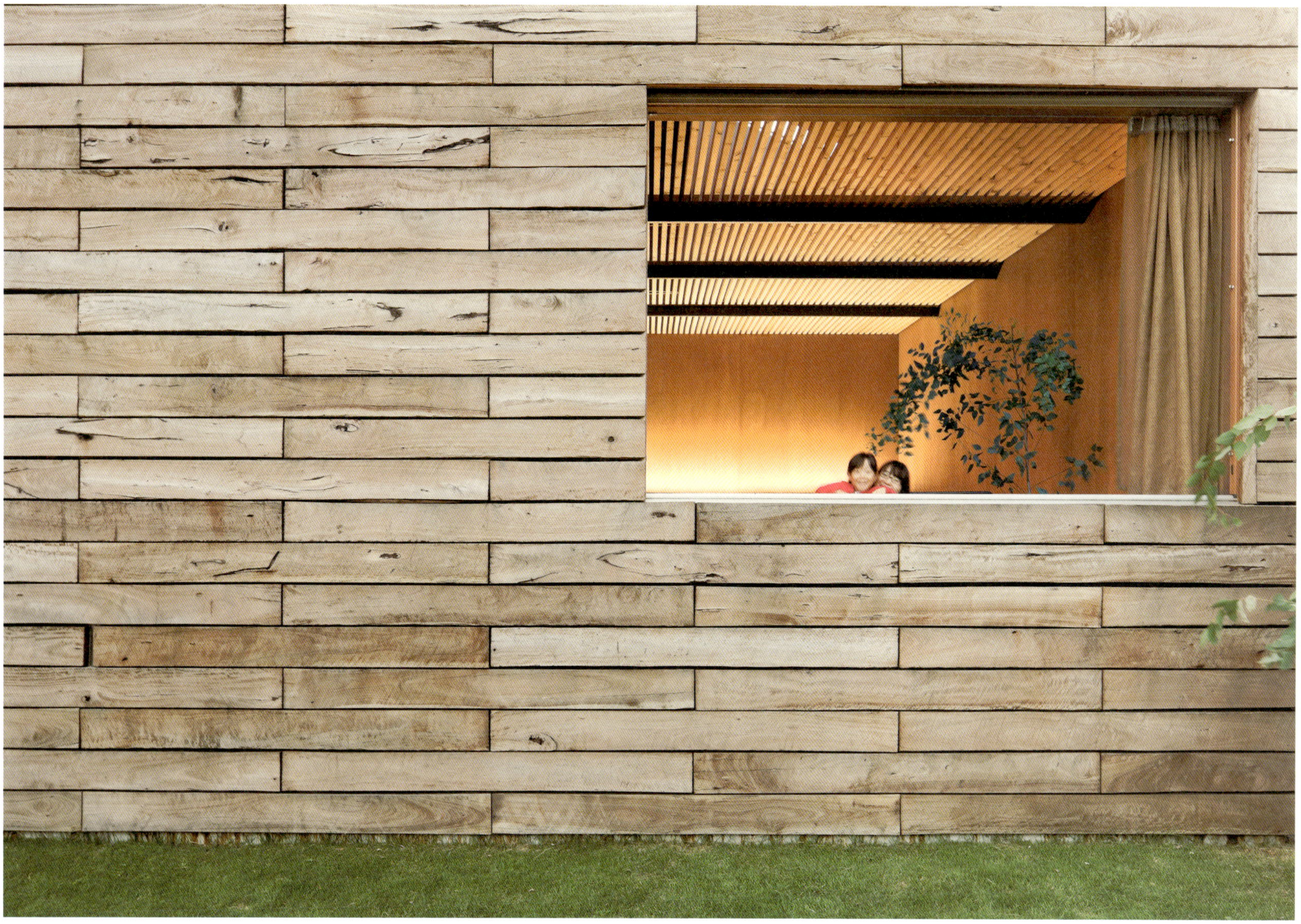

Site plan 1:1000　配置図 1:1000

House in Komazawa　　　　　　　　駒沢の住宅

Location: Setagaya, Tokyo　　　　　所在地：東京都世田谷区
Principal use: Residential　　　　　　主要用途：専用住宅
Site area: 66.12m²　　　　　　　　　敷地面積：66.12m²
Building area: 39.67m²　　　　　　　建築面積：39.67m²
Total floor area: 64.03m²　　　　　　延床面積：64.03m²
Number of stories: 2　　　　　　　　規模：地上2階
Structure: Timber frame　　　　　　　構造：木造

House in Kyodo ｜ 経堂の住宅

This small two-story house designed for a married couple stands in a quiet residential area with an abundance of greenery. As both of the residents are editors, they own a huge number of books. As as a result, I decided to make the entire first floor a book vault and insert the bathroom, sink area, entrance, study, bedroom, and closets in the gaps between the shelves. The couple lives in this library with a ceiling height of 1.8 meters. The shelves, about the same height as a person, create a closer relationship between the human body and the books. On the other hand, the second-floor living room and terrace is a spacious area gently topped with a thin, 60-millimeter roof made of steel sandwich panels. The silver roof softly reflects light and greenery from the neighboring garden on undersurfaces and the ground, and fills the interior of the house. The light and landscape are reflected on the ceiling like the surface of a pond, causing the roof to disappear, and imbuing the second floor the open quality of a rooftop. Both the interior and exterior walls are constructed out of fiber-reinforced cement panels, creating a standard size of three-by-six (910mm x 1,820mm) on the first floor and four-by-eight (1,220mm x 2,440mm) on the second. The couple spend each day going back and forth between the contrastive spaces of the nest-like area surrounded by their beloved books on the first floor, and the open, rooftop area on the second floor.

緑の多い閑静な住宅地に建つ夫婦2人のための2階建ての小さな住宅。2人とも書籍編集者のため所有している本がとても多い。そこで1階を全て書庫にして本棚の隙間に浴室／洗面／玄関／書斎／寝室／クローゼットを入れていった。天井高1.8mの書庫に住む。人間の身長と同じような高さの本棚が、身体と本の親密な関係をつくり出す。2階はリビングとテラスだけの広々とした空間になっており、鉄板のサンドイッチパネルでつくった厚さ60mmの薄い屋根がそっとかかる。シルバーの屋根はその下面に、地面にバウンドした光や近隣の庭の緑を柔らかく反射させ、室内に導き入れる。天井には水面のように光や風景が映り込み、屋根自体の存在感は消え、2階はまるで屋上のような開放感をもった空間になる。壁は内外ともに繊維強化セメント板とし、1階は3×6版（910×1820mm）、2階は4×8版（1220×2440mm）の規格寸法のものを並べている。好きな本に囲まれた巣穴のような1階と、屋上のように開放的な2階という対比的な空間を行き来しながら2人は生活する。

Site plan 1:1000　配置図 1:1000

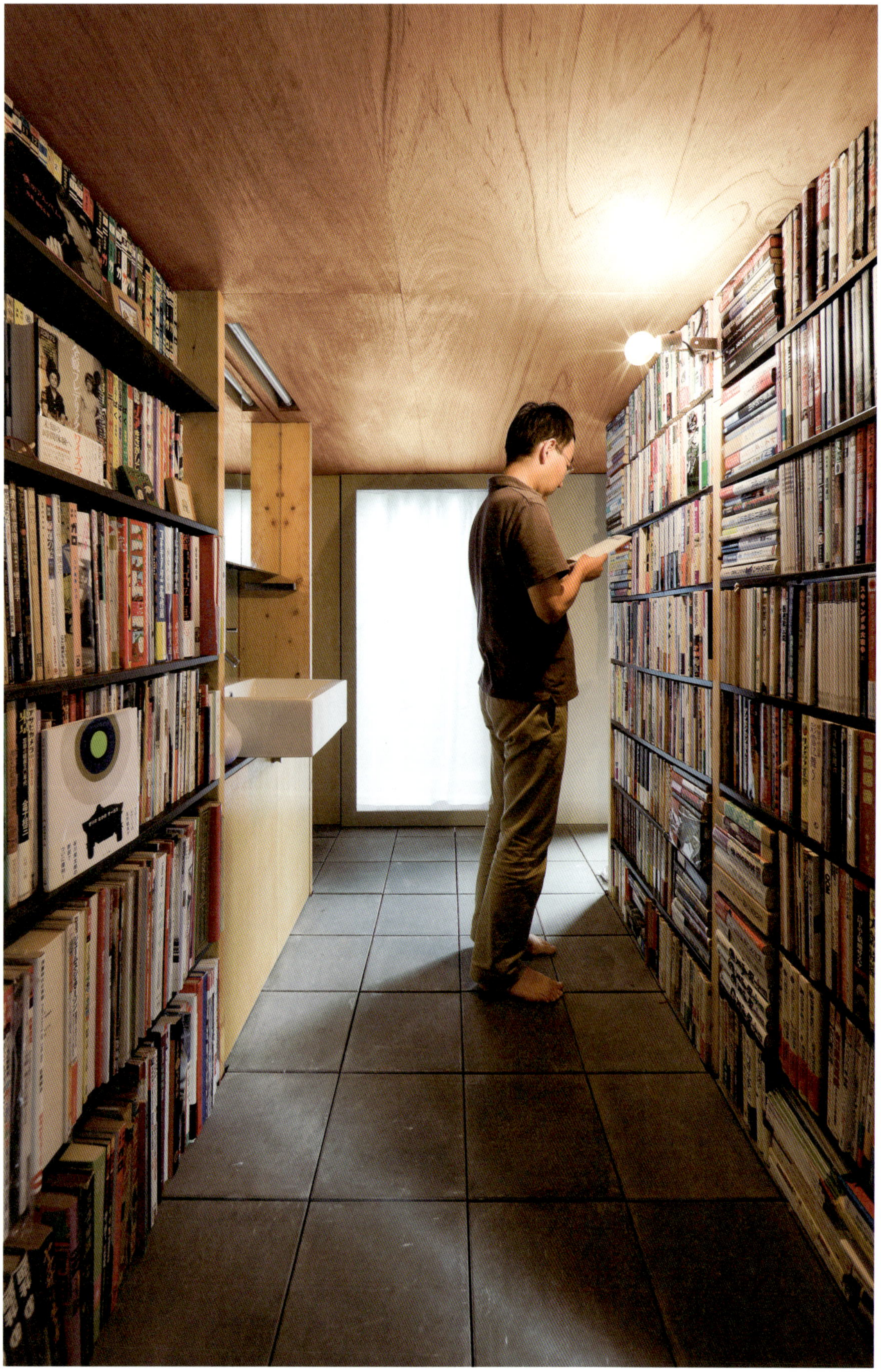

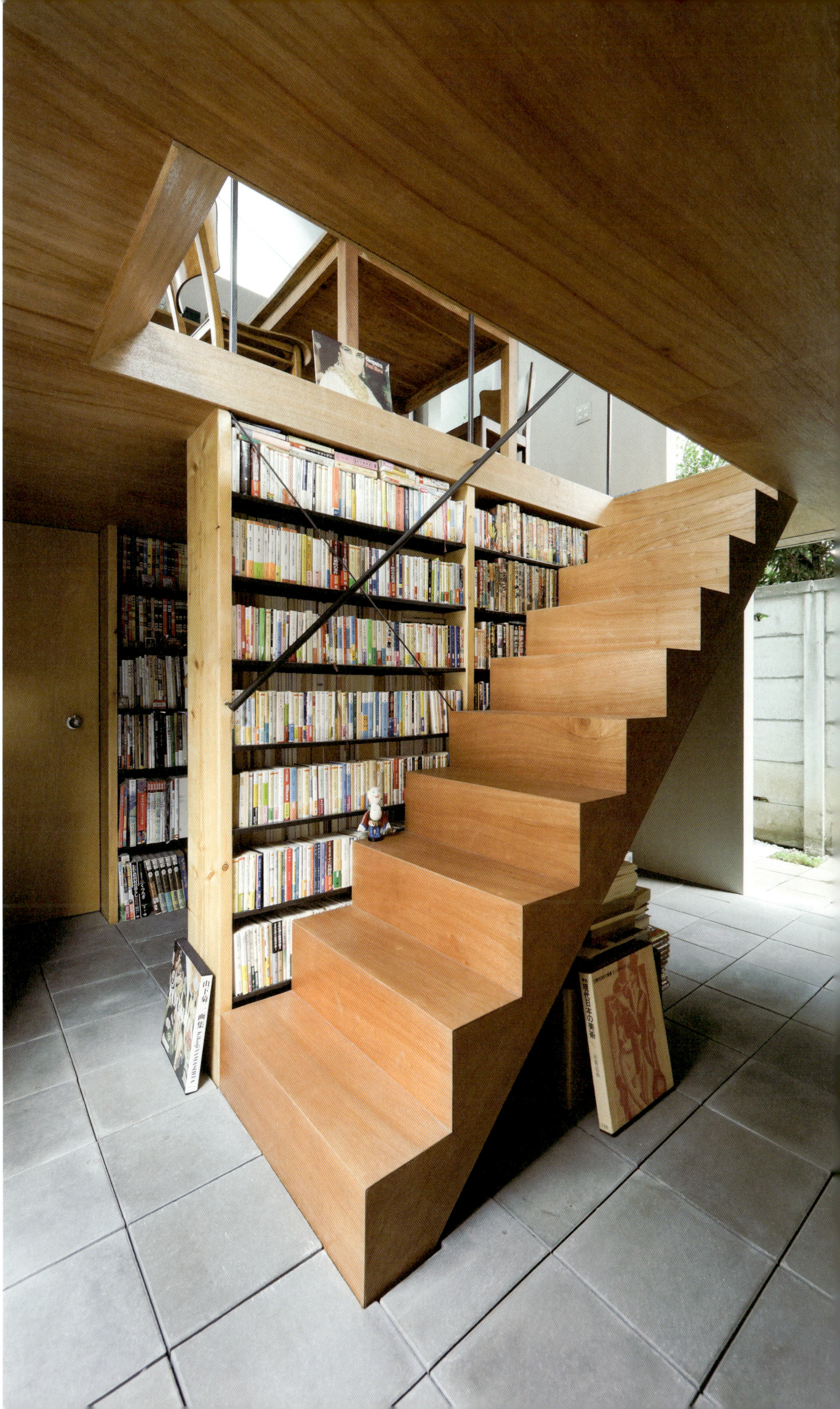

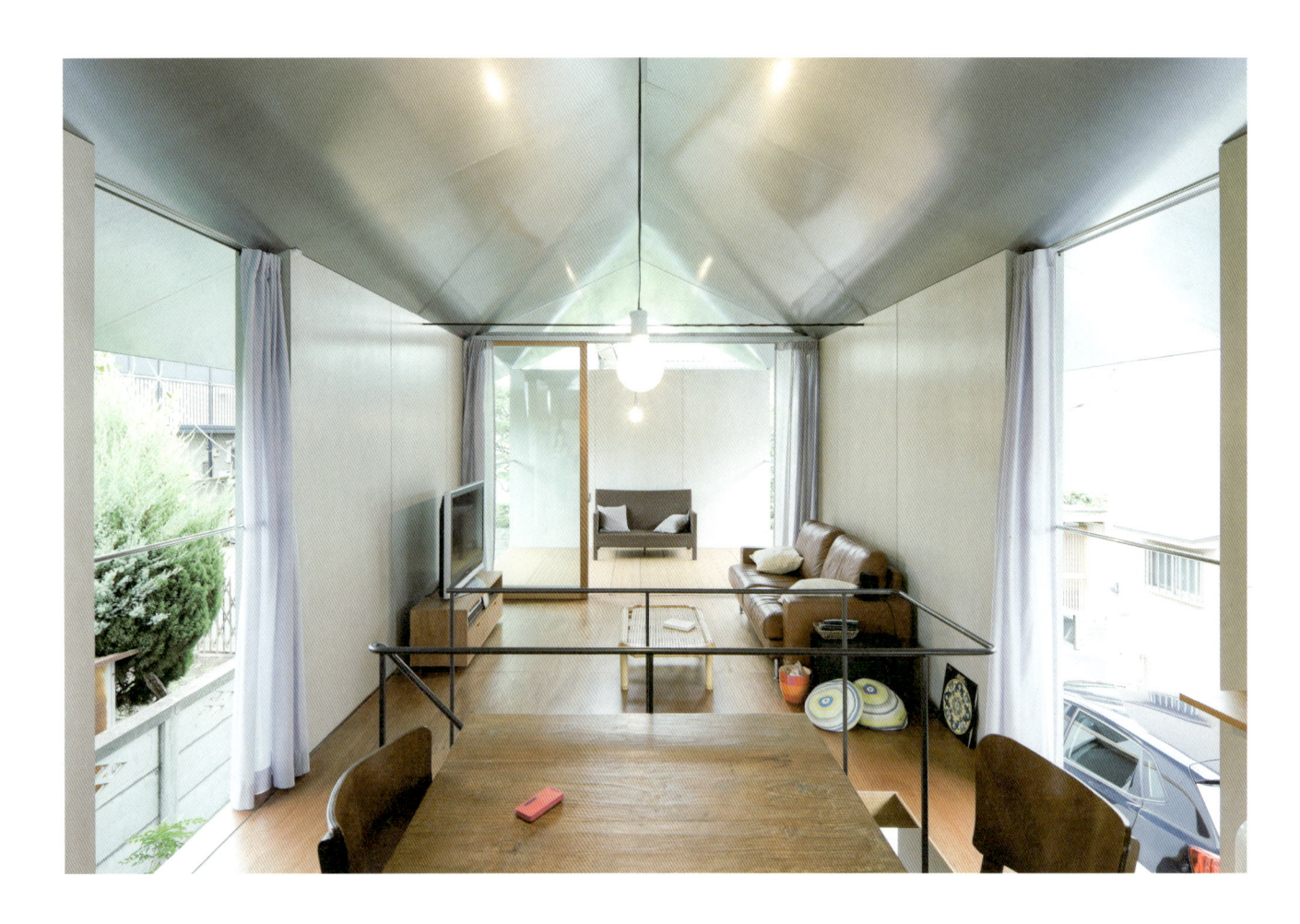

142   Plan 1:100   1: bathroom 2: washroom 3: entrance 4: study room 5: bedroom 6: closet 7: approach 8: garden 9: kitchen 10: living room 11: terrace

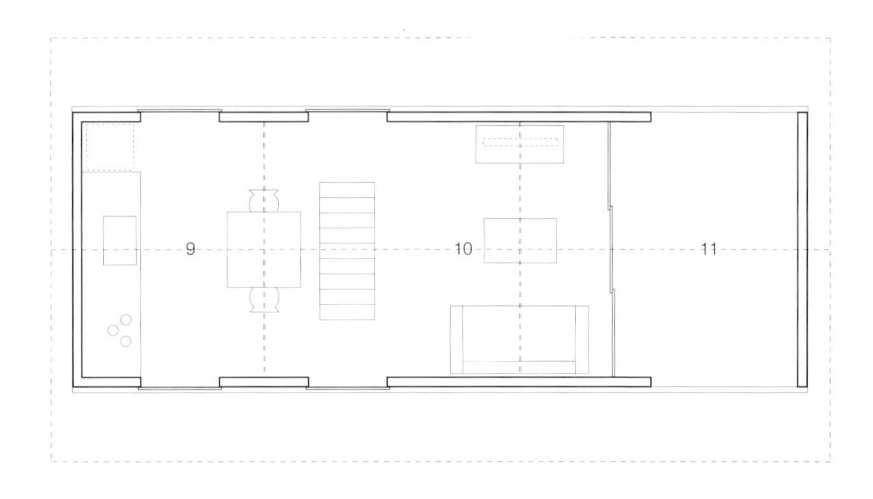

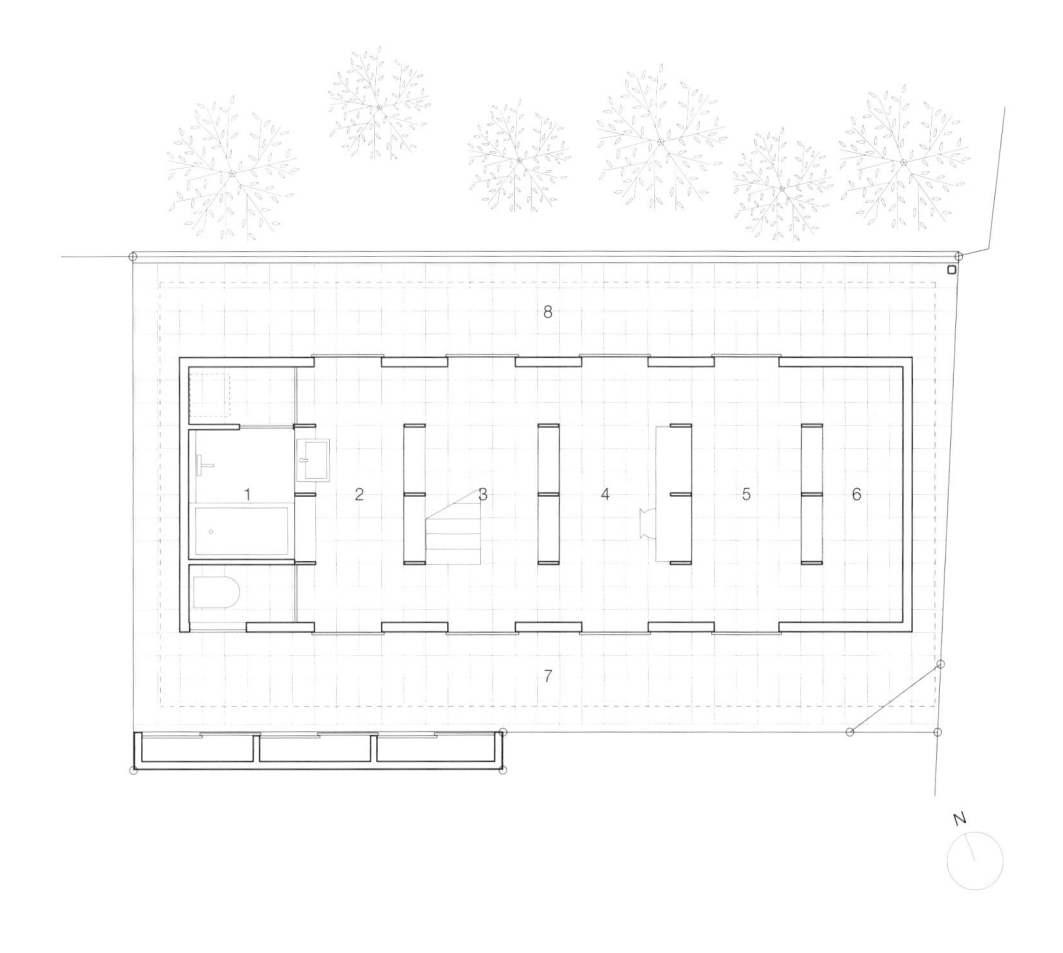

平面図　1:100　　　1:浴室　2:洗面室　3:玄関　4:書斎　5:寝室　6:クロゼット　7:アプローチ　8:庭　9:キッチン　10:リビング　11:テラス

A—Coping: Bent galvanized steel sheeting t=0.35mm B—Roof: Corrogated galvanized steel sheeting t=0.35mm | Furring strips: 18×45mm @455mm | Insulation: Aluminum thermal barrier t=8mm | Waterproofing membrane t=2mm C—Ceiling: Steel plate t=3.2mm (zinc coated steel sheet), polyurethane paint | Keystone steel deck plate h=25mm t=1.2mm | Steel plate t=2.3mm D—External floor: Concrete plate block 300×300mm t=30mm | Concrete underlaying t=50mm E—External walls: Fiber reinforced cement panel t=4mm (4×8), water repellent paint | Calcium silicate board t=8mm | Vent furring strips: 30×8mm | Moisture permeable waterproof sheeting | Structural plywood t=12mm | Column: 90×90 | Insulation: Polyurethane spray t=20mm F—Fascia: Lauan solid wood, xyladecor finish G—Ceiling: Steel plate t=1.2mm (zinc coated steel sheet), polyurethane paint | Plasterboard t=9.5mm | Ceiling joist: 30×30mm @300mm | Insulation: Polyurethane spray t=30mm H—Tie bar: Steel rod φ16mm, polyurethane paint I—Curtain rail J—Walls: Fiber reinforced cement panel t=4mm (4×8), water repellent paint | Plasterboard t=12.5mm K—Floor: Lauan plywood t=12mm (4×8), polyurethane paint | Plywood underlaying t=9mm | Floor heating panel t=9mm | Structural plywood t=24mm | Beams: 90×90mm | Polyurethane spray t=20mm L—Floor: Lauan solid wood t=18mm, xyladecor finish | Rubber spacer t=5mm | Fiber reinforced plastic waterproofing t=2mm, topcoat finish | Calcium silicate board t=5mm | Structural plywood t=24mm | Beams: 90×90mm | Insulation: Polyurethane spray t=20mm M—Ceiling: Lauan plywood t=5.5mm (3×6), polyurethane paint | Ceiling joist: 30×40mm @300mm N—Brace: Steel rod φ6mm, polyurethane paint O—Column (shelf): 2"×12" (38×286mm), polyurethane paint P—Floor: Concrete plate block 300×300mm t=30mm, water repellent paint | Plywood underlaying t=9mm | Floor joist: 30×60mm @300mm | Insulation: Polyurethane spray t=20mm | Concrete slab t=150mm | Polyethylene film sheeting t=0.2mm | Concrete underlaying t=50mm | Crushed stone t=80mm

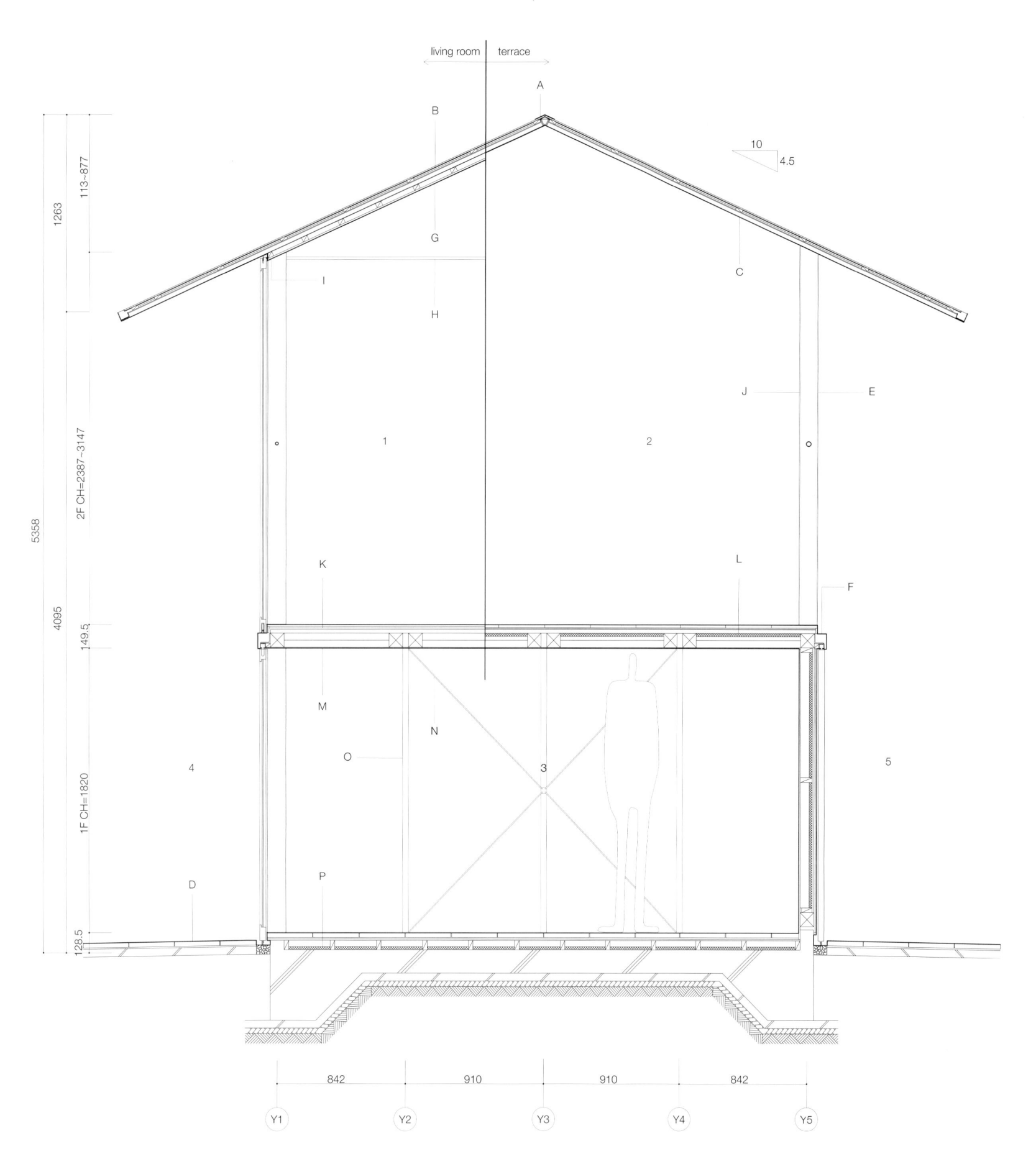

A—棟笠木：ガルバリウム鋼板 t=0.35mm マゲ　B—屋根：ガルバリウム鋼板 t=0.35mm 小波葺き｜横胴縁：18×45mm @455mm｜アルミ遮熱断熱材 t=8mm｜ガムロン t=2mm　C—天井・軒裏：St PL t=3.2mm（亜鉛引板）UP｜キーストンプレート h=25mm t=1.2mm｜St PL t=2.3mm　D—外構床：コンクリート平板 300×300mm t=30mm｜捨てコンクリート t=50mm　E—外壁：繊維強化セメント板 t=4mm（4×8版）撥水剤塗布｜珪酸カルシウム板 t=8mm｜通気胴縁：30×8mm｜透湿防水シート｜構造用合板 t=12mm｜柱：90×90mm｜断熱材：ウレタンフォーム吹付け t=20mm　F—鼻隠し：ラワン無垢材 XD　G—天井：St PL t=1.2mm（亜鉛引板）UP｜プラスターボード t=9.5mm｜野縁：30×30mm @300mm｜断熱材：ウレタンフォーム吹付け t=30mm　H—タイバー：St ロッド φ16mm UP　I—カーテンレール　J—壁：繊維強化セメント板 t=4mm（4×8版）撥水剤塗布｜プラスターボード t=12.5mm　K—床：ラワン合板 t=12mm（4×8版）UP｜捨て貼り合板 t=9mm｜床暖房パネル t=9mm｜構造用合板 t=24mm｜梁：90×90mm｜断熱材：ウレタンフォーム吹付け t=20mm　L—床：ラワン無垢材 t=18mm XD スペーサーゴム t=5mm｜FRP防水 t=2mm トップコート仕上げ｜珪酸カルシウム板 t=5mm｜構造用合板 t=24mm｜梁：90×90mm｜断熱材：ウレタンフォーム吹付け t=20mm　M—天井：ラワン合板 t=5.5mm（3×6版）UP｜野縁：30×40mm @300mm　N—ブレース：St ロッド φ6mm UP　O—柱（棚）：2"×12"(38×286mm) UP　P—床：コンクリート平板 300×300mm t=30mm 撥水材塗布｜捨て貼り合板 t=9mm｜根太：30×60mm @300mm｜断熱材：ウレタンフォーム吹付け t=20mm｜コンクリートスラブ t=150mm｜ポリエチレンフィルム t=0.2mm｜捨てコンクリート t=50mm｜砕石 t=80mm

矩計図　1:30　　1：リビング　2：テラス　3：玄関　4：アプローチ　5：庭

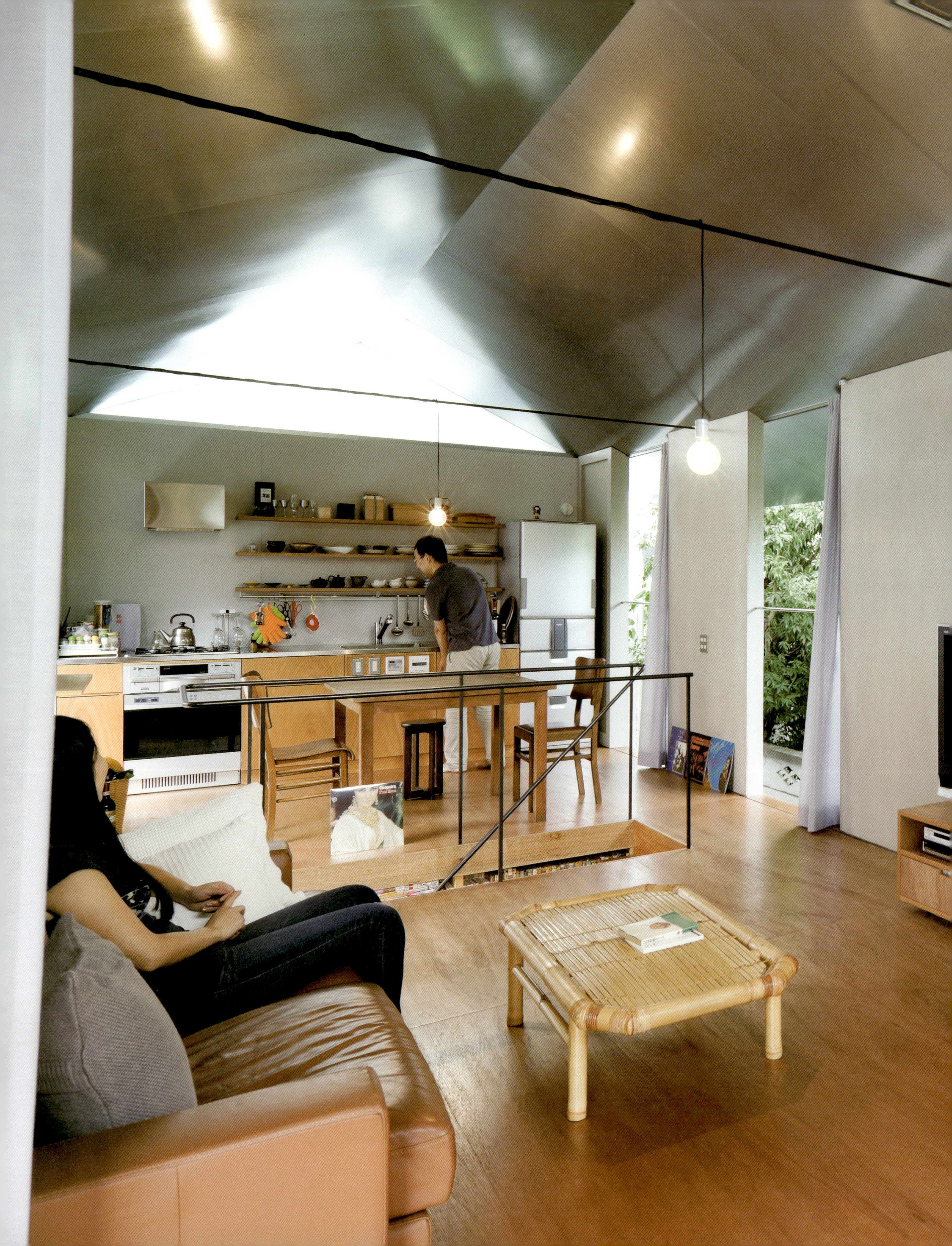

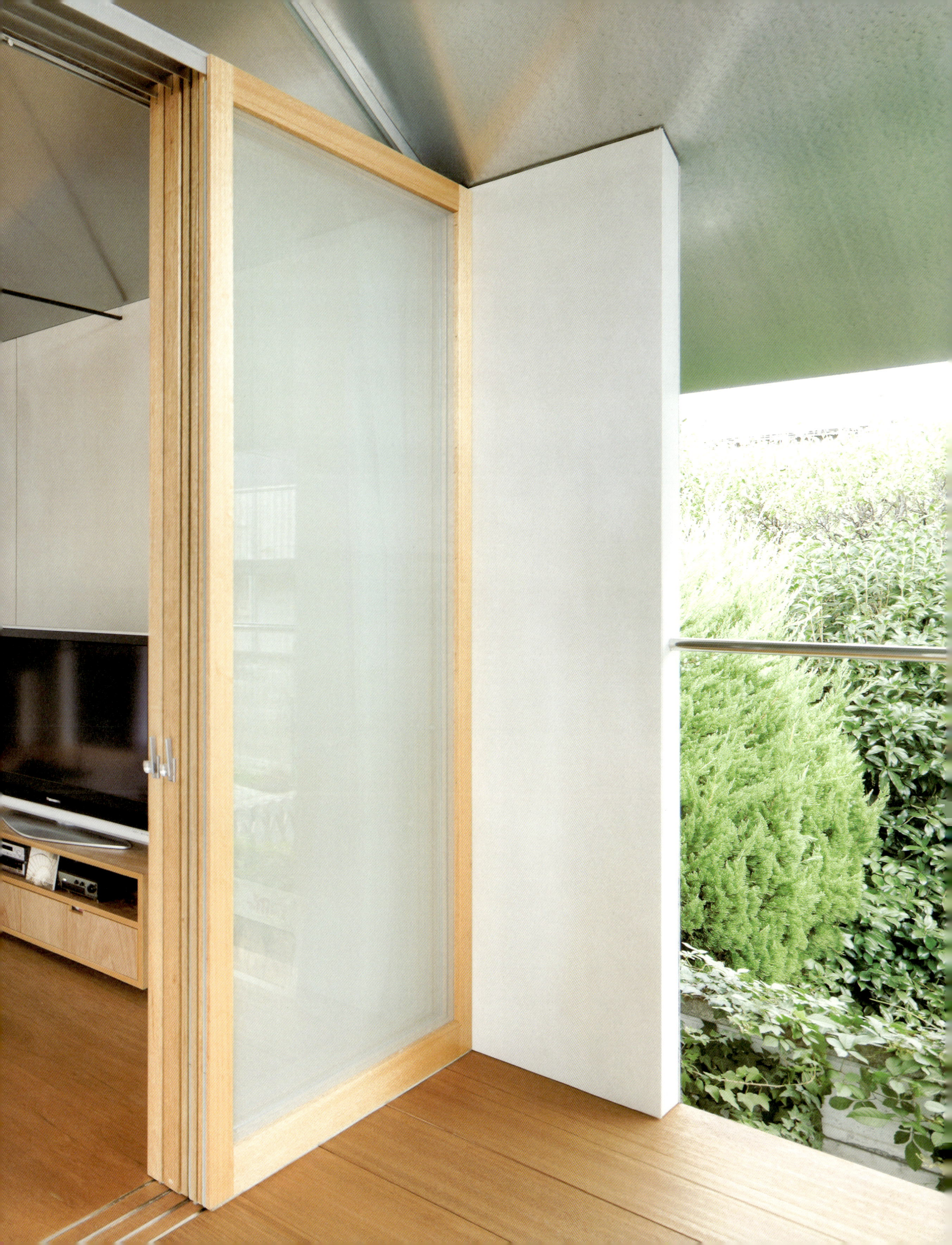

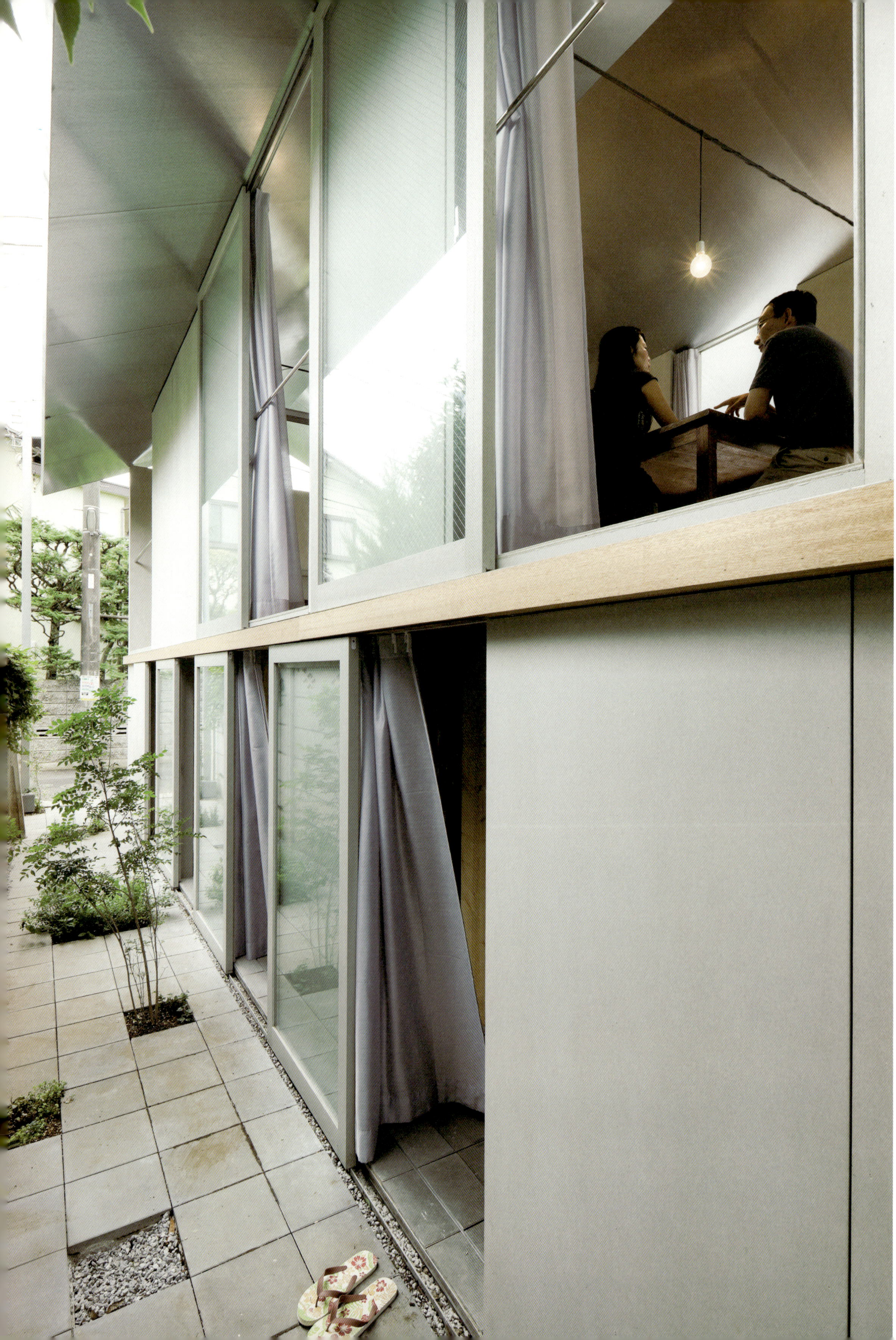

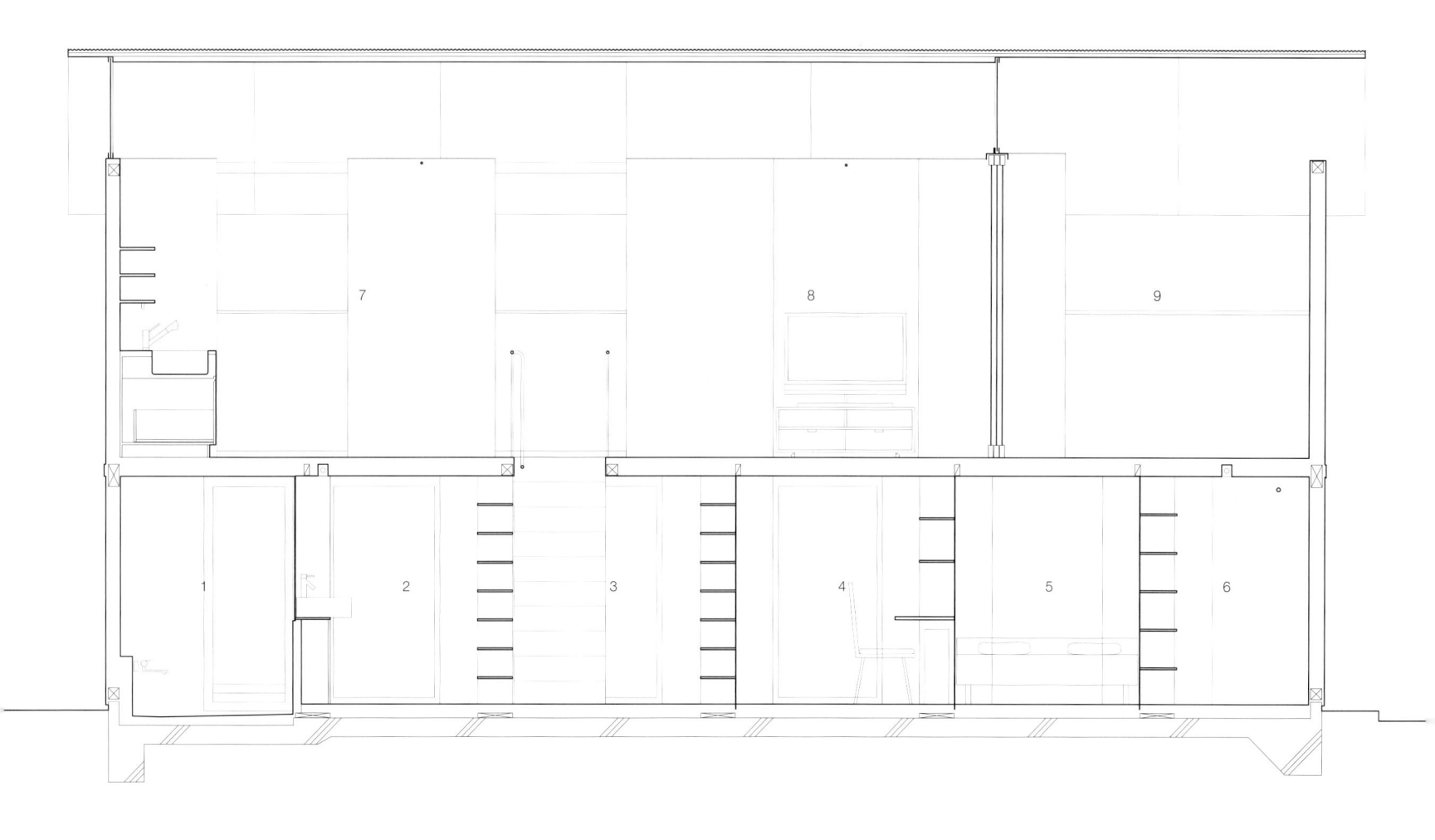

Section 1:50   1: bathroom 2: washroom 3: entrance 4: study room 5: bedroom 6: closet 7: kitchen 8: living room 9: terrace
断面図 1:50   1:浴室 2:洗面室 3:玄関 4:書斎 5:寝室 6:クロゼット 7:キッチン 8:リビング 9:テラス

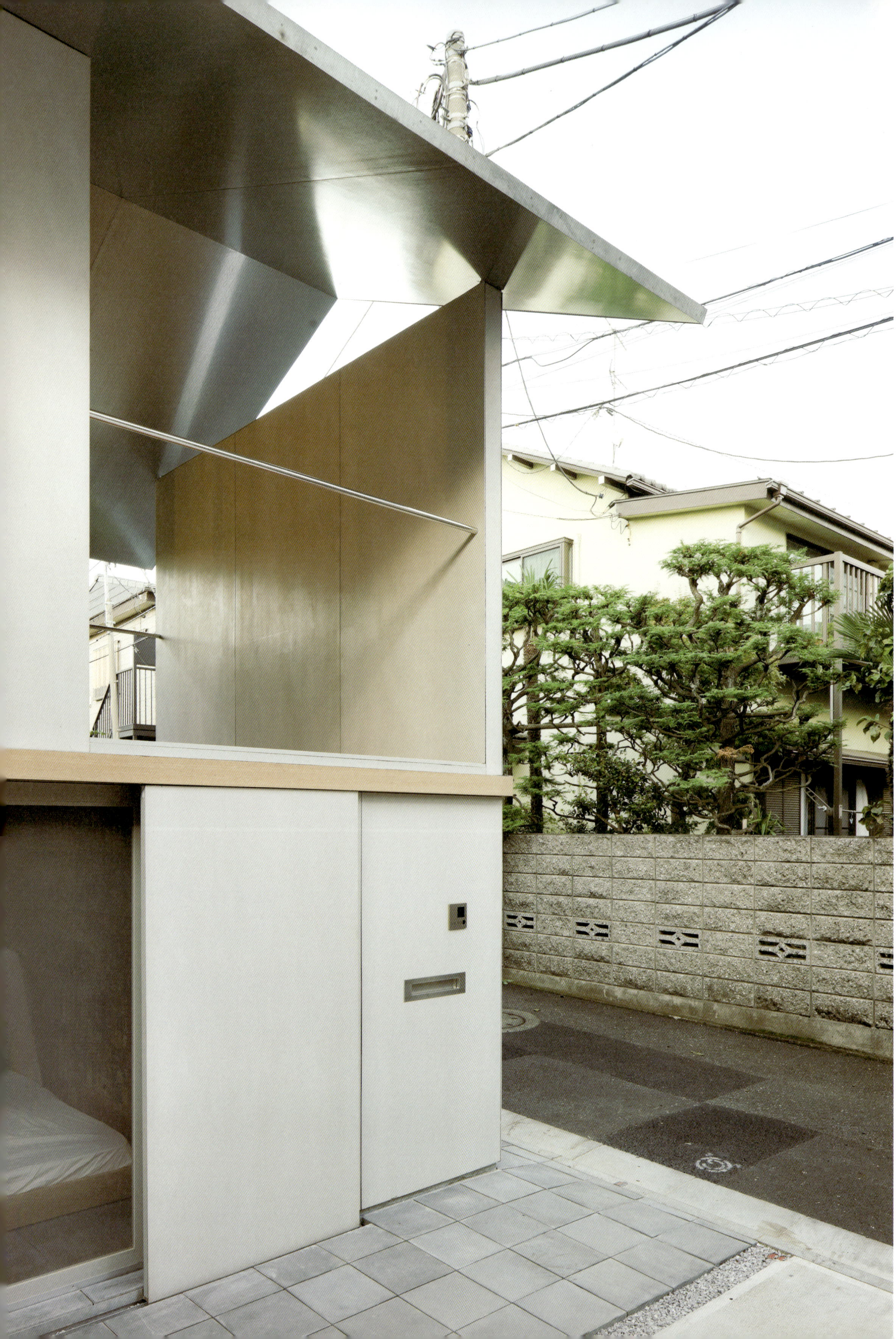

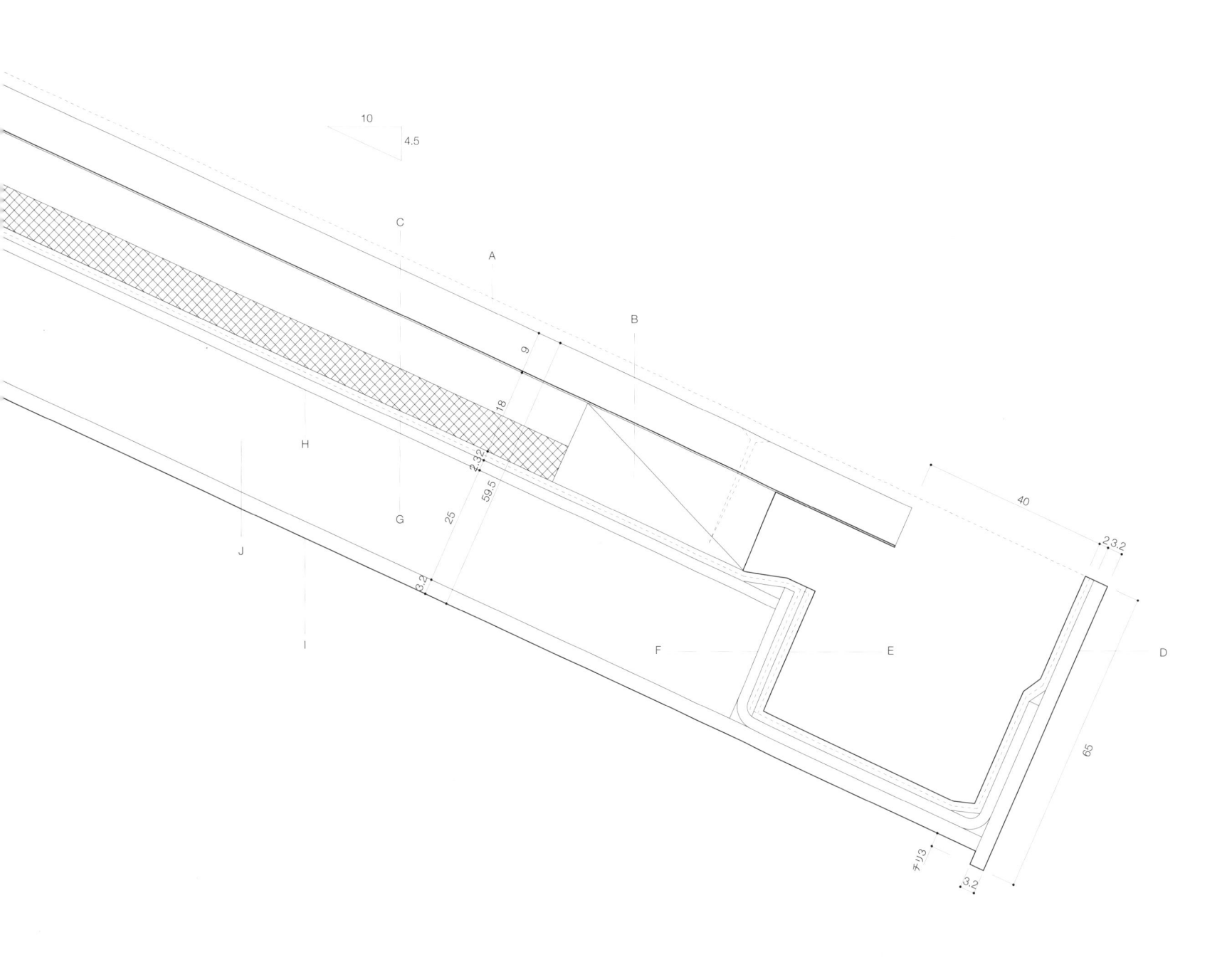

A—Corrugated galvanized steel sheeting t=0.35mm
B—Furring strips 18×45mm @455mm C—Insulation: Aluminum thermal barrier D—Fascia: Steel plate t=3.2mm, hot dip zinc E—Fiber reinforced plastic waterproofing t=2mm F—Steel U angle t=2.3mm (30×60mm) G—Waterproofing membrane t=2mm H—Steel plate t=2.3mm I—Insulation: Aluminum thermal barrier t=8mm I—Steel plate t=3.2mm (zinc-coated steel sheet), polyurethane paint J—Keystone steel deck plate h=25mm t=1.2mm

A—ガルバリウム鋼板 t=0.35mm 小波葺き B—横胴縁 18×45mm @455mm C—アルミ遮熱断熱材 D—鼻隠し:St PL t=3.2mm 亜鉛ドブヅケ E—FRP 防水 t=2mm F—St U-アングル t=2.3mm（30×60mm） G—ガムロン t=2mm H—St PL t=2.3mm I アルミ遮熱断熱材 t=8mm I—St PL-t=3.2mm（亜鉛引板）UP J—キーストンプレート h=25mm t=1.2mm

Detail of roof 1:1   屋根詳細図 1:1

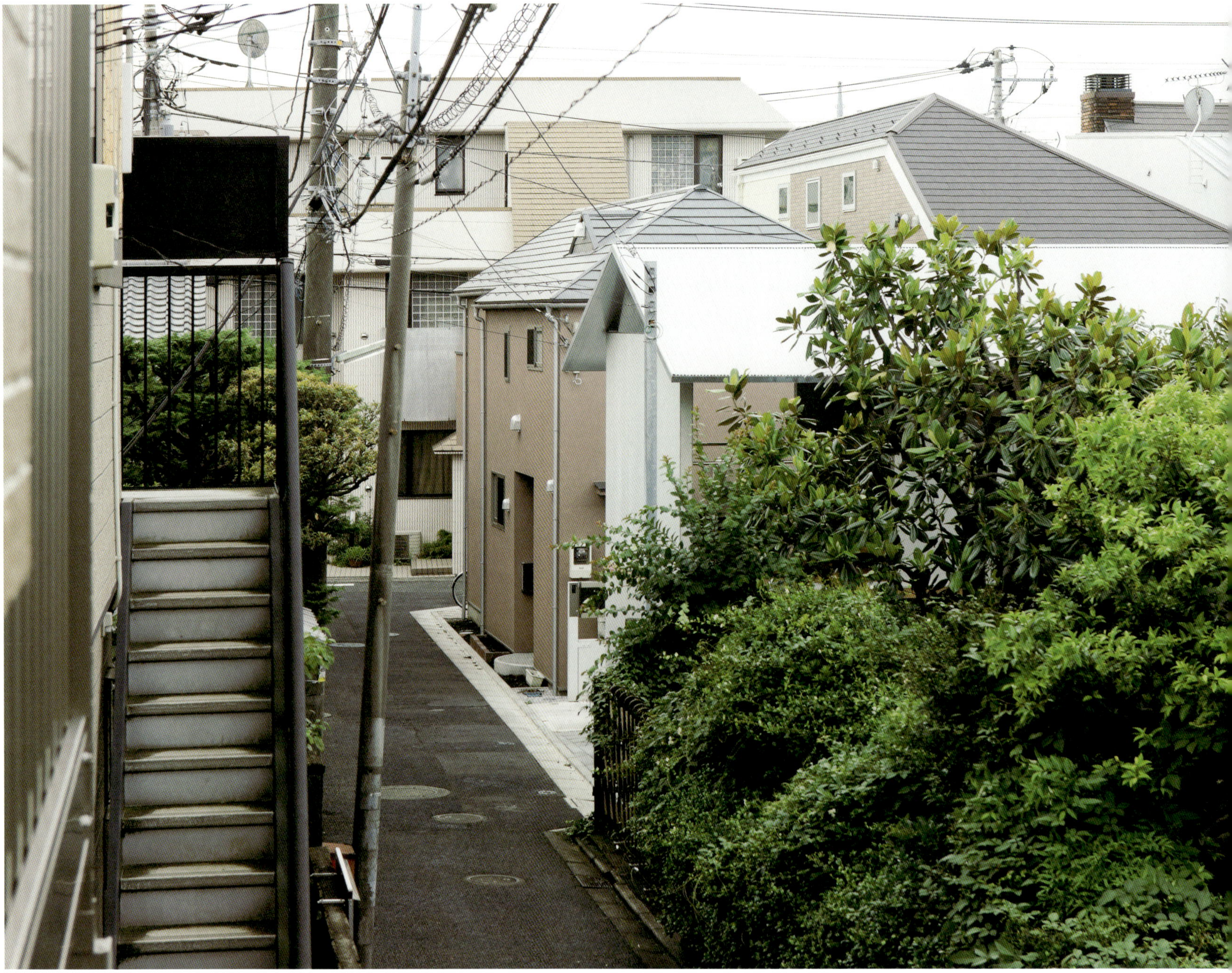

House in Kyodo

Location: Setagaya, Tokyo
Principal use: Residential
Site area: 72.89m²
Building area: 33.95m²
Total floor area: 67.90m²
Number of stories: 2
Structure: Timber frame

経堂の住宅

所在地：東京都世田谷区
主要用途：専用住宅
敷地面積：72.89m²
建築面積：33.95m²
延床面積：67.90m²
規模：地上2階
構造：木造

Nippon Design Center | 日本デザインセンター

This is the new headquarters for Japan's largest design firm. As the old building had deteriorated after over 40 years of use, the company decided to move to this multi-tenant, "skeleton" building stands at the Ginza 4-chome intersection. The firm occupies the upper six floors of the 13-story building on a long, narrow plane. I set out to create a comfortable office environment filled with natural light by making the most of a set of 54-meter, horizontally-connected windows. After calculating the potential amount of light on each floor, I altered the height and depth of the floor in each office space, and adjusted them to make even the lower levels of the building seem bright. Thus, the office areas take on a greater depth and height with each successive floor. In addition, by regulating the zoning, making the halls and other public areas as compact as possible, and placing the main office space on the fifth floor, I was able to leave the uppermost level completely empty. I designed this vacant space to be used freely right in the middle of Ginza. In addition to serving as a company library, a gallery to display posters and other works, and a hall for seminars, I conceived of a space that would continually allow the workers to think up new uses, and one that would function as a "living void" for the dispatch of new design.

国内最大のデザインプロダクションの新社屋。40年以上構えていた旧社屋の老朽化が進んだため、銀座4丁目交差点のすぐそばのスケルトンのテナントビルに移転する。細長い平面をもつ13階建てのビルの上部6フロアをつかう。各階ともに長さ54mの水平連窓を活かした自然光あふれる快適なオフィス環境を目指した。天空照度を測定したうえで、各フロアの執務空間の床の高さと奥行きを変化させ、下階でも明るい空間になるように調整した。上階ほど深く、高い執務空間になっていく。またゾーニングを整理し、さらに廊下などの共用部をできる限りコンパクトにして執務空間は5フロアにまとめ、最上階はワンフロアまるごと余白として残した。銀座のど真ん中に、自由に使えるがらんどうの空間をつくる。ここは社内の書籍をまとめたライブラリー、ポスターなどの作品を展示するギャラリー、セミナーなどを開催できるホールなどとして使われるほか、完成後も継続的に社員が空間の使い方を想像し、新たなデザインを発信していくための「生きた余白」になればと考えている。

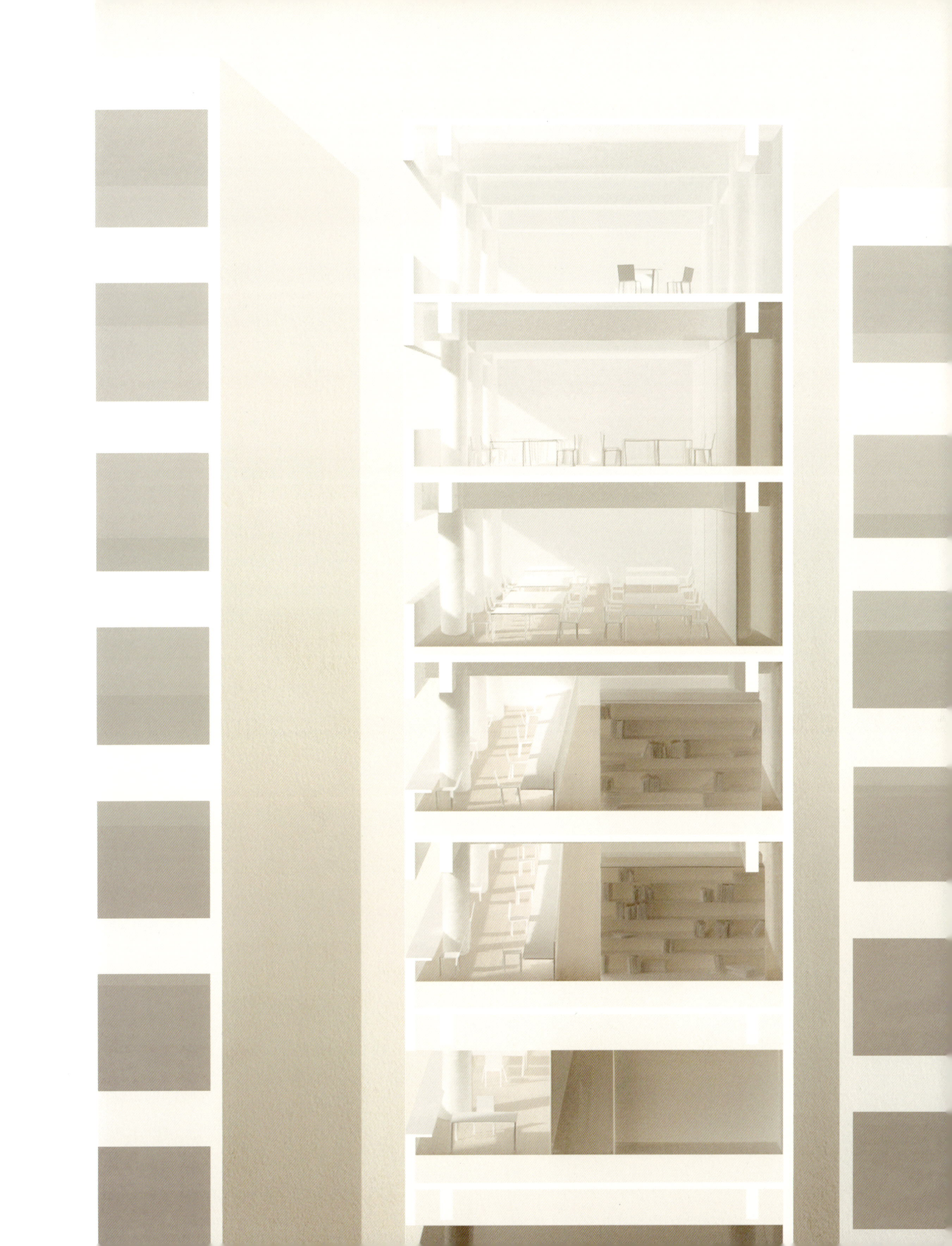

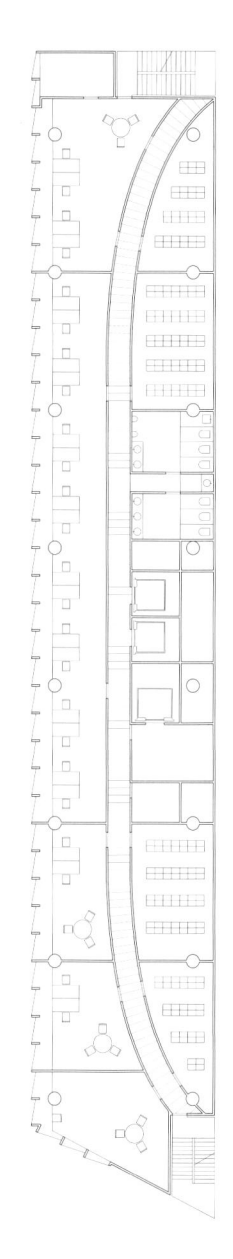

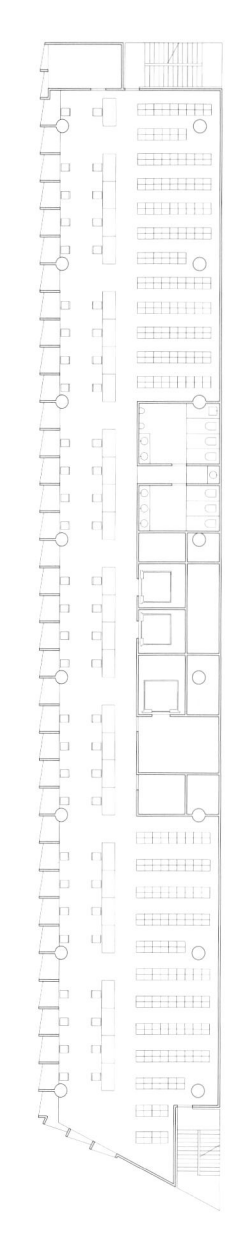

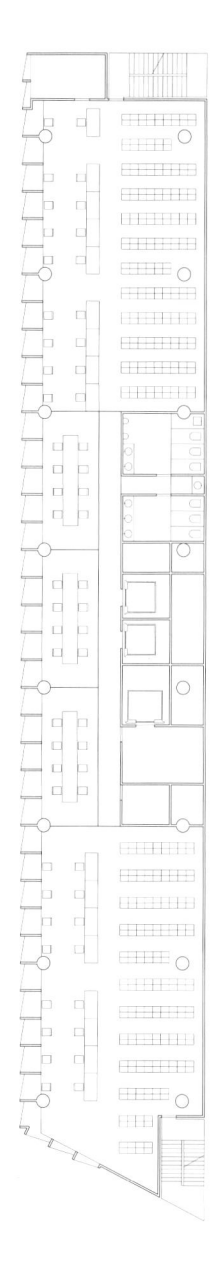

8th floor

9th floor

10th floor

Plan 1:400

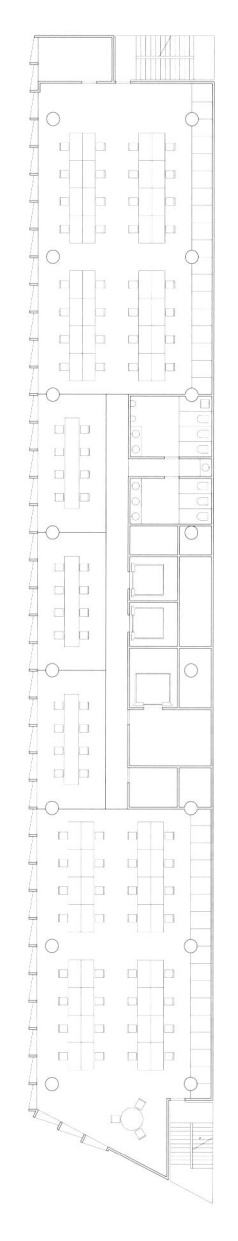

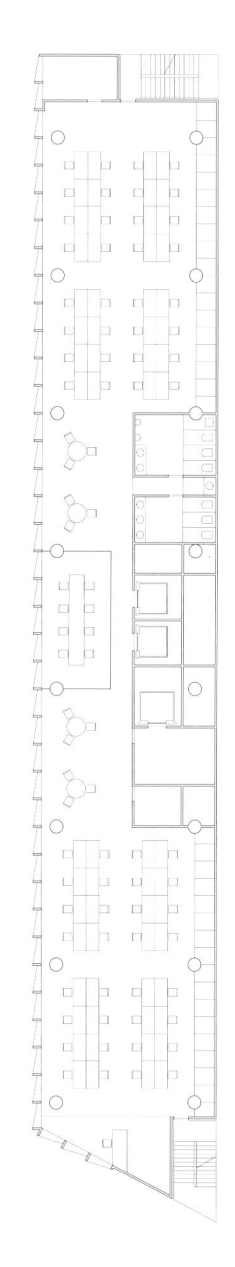

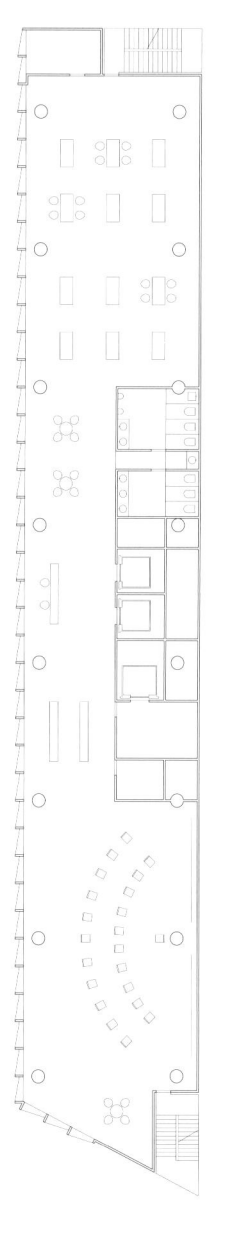

11th floor

12th floor

13th floor

平面図 1:400

Site plan 1:1000

配置図　1:1000

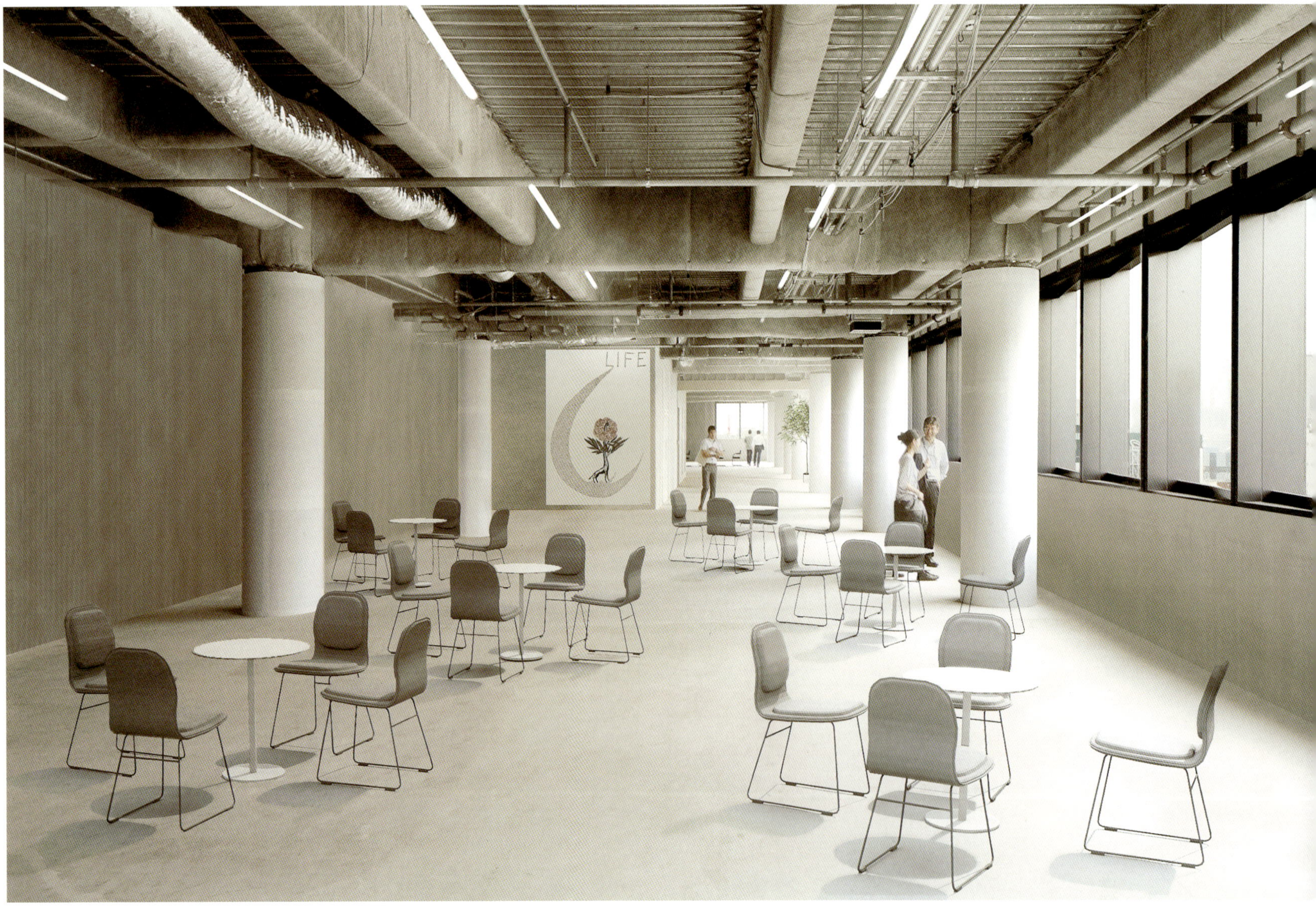
LIFE

Location: Chuo, Tokyo	所在地：東京都中央区
Principal use: Office	主要用途：オフィス
Site area: 694.21m^2	敷地面積：694.21m^2
Building area: 581.04m^2	建築面積：581.04m^2
Total floor area: 3,168.74m^2	延床面積：3,168.74m^2（8-13階）
Number of stories: 13 plus 3 basements	規模：地下3階　地上13階　のうち8-13階部分
Sturucture: Steel frame	構造：鉄骨造

Nippon Design Center

日本デザインセンター

Belfry in Ishinomaki | 石巻の鐘楼

This project involves the donation of a small building to a kindergarten in Ishinomaki, a city that was severely damaged in the Great East Japan Earthquake. Making use of a solo exhibition of my work that will be held at TOTO GALLERY・MA, I decided to start by building the structure in the gallery's courtyard. Then, after the exhibition ends, the building will be moved to Ishinomaki. Following about six months of discussions with the couple who are the principals of the kindergarten and the teachers there, I decided to create a building with three functions, saving as a kind of play equipment for children, a belfry that symbolizes the restoration of the city, and a verandah that would be open to the students' parents and other local residents. Considering the location of the building and its relationship with the neighborhood, the budget, and other factors both in the kindergarten and the gallery's courtyard, I devised a tower-shaped structure consisting of a planar triangle with a width of 4.9 square meters from which the sound of a bell will resound through the town. The five-story, child-scale tower will have a floor height of 1.75 meters. The first floor will be a verandah, where the children's guardians and neighborhood residents can relax; the second, equipped with a large balcony, will serve as the children's secret base; and the atrium that stretches from the third to the fifth floor will be a room from which the bell is rung. The floors will have a louvered form, the roof will be completely glass, and from the verandah you will be able to look up at the bell and the sky overhead. In addition, to ensure easier construction, dismantling, and reconstruction, I decided to make use of a layered, glued-laminated timber structure (900mm x 1,750mm, with a thickness of 60mm) that would fit inside an elevator.

東日本大震災で被害を受けた石巻市の幼稚園に小さな建物を寄贈するプロジェクト。TOTOギャラリー・間での個展を利用してまずギャラリーの中庭に建て、それを会期後に石巻に移築する。約半年間、園長夫妻や保母さんと話し合いを重ねて、子供たちのための遊具、街の復興のシンボルになる鐘楼、園児の父母や地域の人に開かれた縁側、の3つの機能をもつ建物をつくることになった。石巻の園庭とTOTOギャラリー・間の中庭という2つの敷地における配置や周辺との関係、予算などに配慮して、広さ3畳の三角形平面とし、また鐘の音が街に響くよう塔状の建物にした。階高1.75m、5階建ての子供のスケールの塔を建てる。1階は保護者や近隣住民が気軽に寛げる縁側、大きなバルコニーがついた2階は子供たちの秘密基地となる部屋、3〜5階の吹抜けは鐘を鳴らすための部屋とした。各床はルーバー状にして、屋根は全面ガラスにしており、縁側からも頭上の鐘や空を見上げることができる。またエレベーターで搬入することのできる900×1750mm、厚さ60mmの構造用集成材を積層する構造とし、設営や移築が容易になるように配慮している。

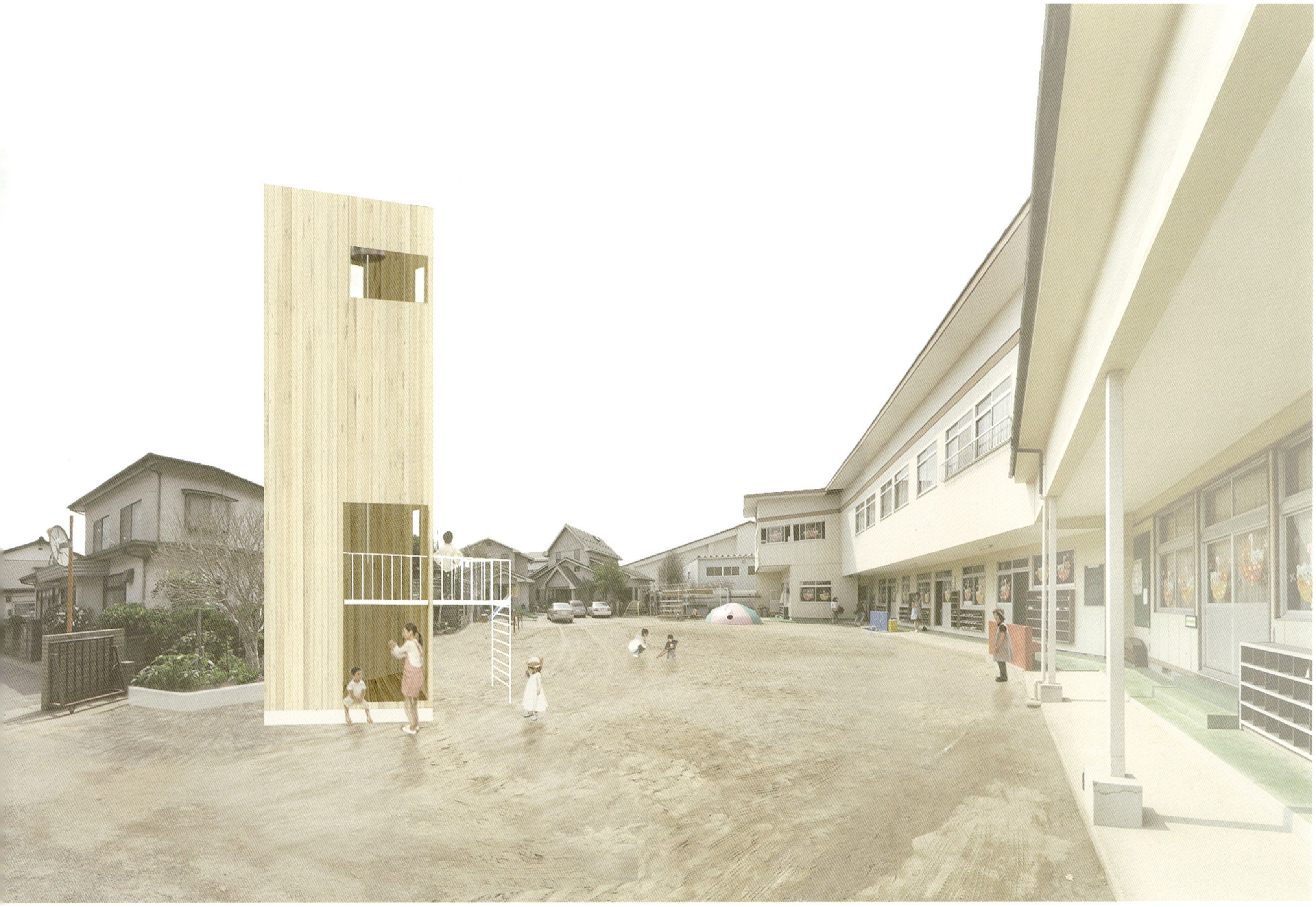

Site plan 1:150   1: belfry 2: flower bed 3: hall 4: kidergarten 5: chapel 6: parsonage 7: garden

配置図　N:150　　1:鐘楼　2:花壇　3:講堂　4:園舎　5:礼拝堂　6:牧師館　7:園庭

Elevation 1:50   立面図 1:50

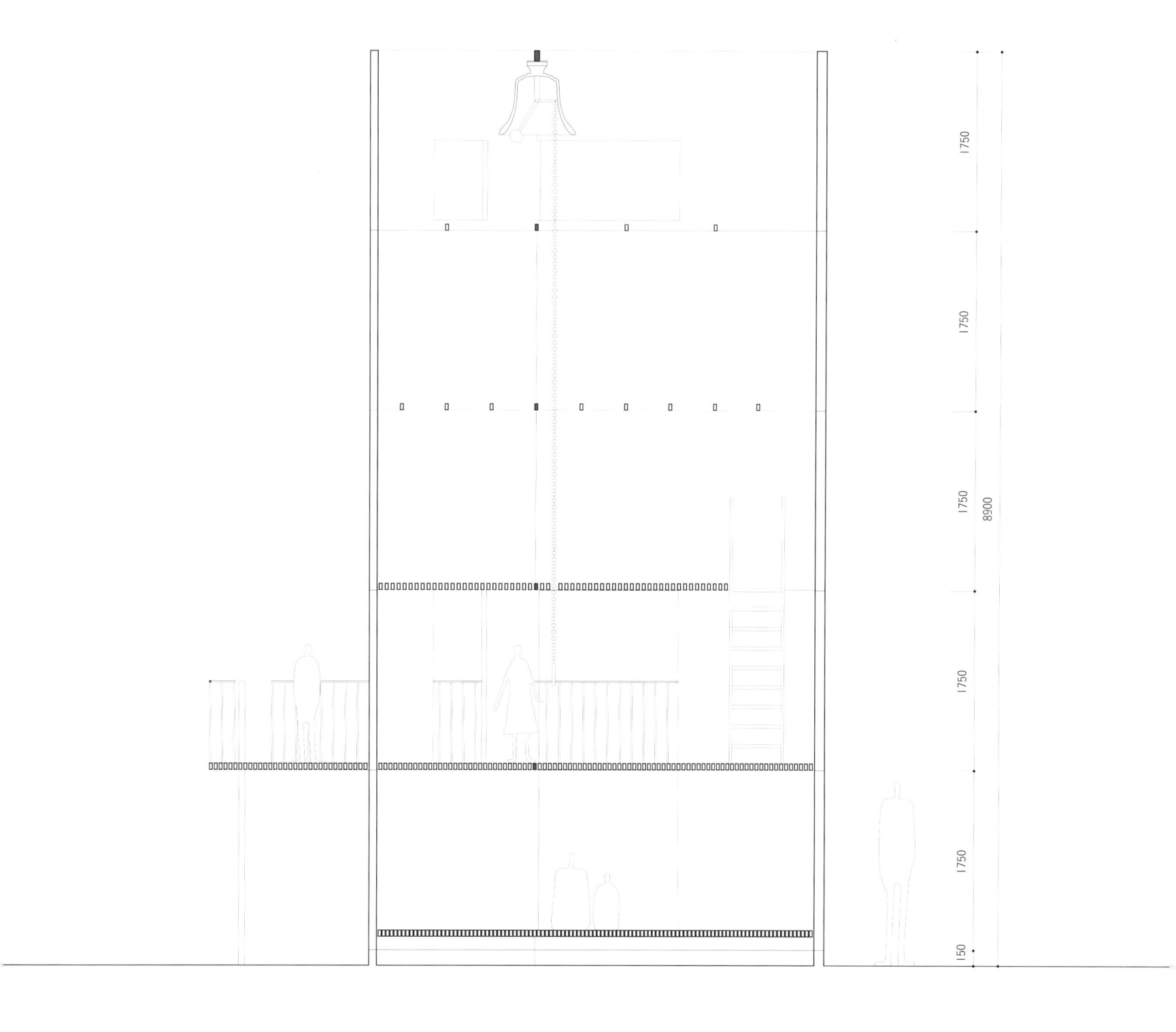

Section 1:50　断面図 1:50

Site plan 1:1000   配置図 1:1000

Belfry in Ishinomaki

Location: Ishinomaki, Miyagi
Principal use: Belfry
Site area: 356.69m²
Building area: 4.86m²
Total floor area: 14.58m²
Number of stories: 5
Sturucture: Timber frame

石巻の鐘楼

所在地：宮城県石巻市
主要用途：鐘楼
敷地面積：356.69m²
建築面積：4.86m²
延床面積：14.58m²
規模：地上5階
構造：木造

Credits | クレジット

Work Credits

10–25
House in a Forest
Design period: 2005.01–2005.08
Construction period: 2005.09–2006.01
Architect: Go Hasegawa
Structural engineer: Kanebako Structural Engineers
Construction firm: Kiuchi Contractor

26–41
House in Sakuradai
Design period: 2005.10–2006.04
Construction period: 2006.05–2006.10
Architect: Go Hasegawa
Structural engineer: Kanebako Structural Engineers
Construction firm: Uemura Contractor

42–57
House in Gotanda
Design period: 2005.09–2006.04
Construction period: 2006.05–2006.11
Architects: Go Hasegawa, Junpei Nosaku
Structural engineer: Kanebako Structural Engineers
Construction firm: Fukazawa Contractor

58–73
House in Komae
Design period: 2007.03–2008.07
Construction period: 2008.08–2009.02
Architects: Go Hasegawa, Junpei Nosaku
Structural engineer: Kanebako Structural Engineers
Producer: Shigeru Oshima
Construction firm: Misawa Homes Tokyo, Kudo Contractor

74–89
Apartment in Nerima
Design period: 2007.12–2009.03
Construction period: 2009.04–2010.03
Architects: Go Hasegawa, Junpei Nosaku
Structural engineer: Kanebako Structural Engineers
Facility design: System Design Laboratory
Producer: Shigeru Oshima
Construction firm: Misawa Homes Tokyo

90–105
Pilotis in a Forest
Design period: 2009.05–2010.03
Construction period: 2010.04–2010.09
Architects: Go Hasegawa, Shu Yamamoto
Structural engineer: Ohno Japan
Construction firm: Niitsu-gumi

106–121
Townhouse in Asakusa
Design period: 2009.04–2010.04
Construction period: 2010.05–2010.11
Architects: Go Hasegawa, Hayako Ohba
Structural engineer: Kanebako Structural Engineers
Facility design: Air Conditioning and Heating Laboratory
Construction firm: Fukazawa Contractor

122–137
House in Komazawa
Design period: 2010.04–2010.09
Construction period: 2010.10–2011.03
Architects: Go Hasegawa, Shu Yamamoto
Structural engineer: Ohno Japan
Construction firm: Taishin Contractor

138–153
House in Kyodo
Design period: 2010.06–2011.02
Construction period: 2011.03–2011.08
Architects: Go Hasegawa, Hayako Ohba
Structural engineer: Ohno Japan
Construction firm: Taishin Contractor

154–161
Nippon Design Center
Design period: 2011.08–2011.11
Architects: Go Hasegawa, Shu Yamamoto
Sign design: Nippon Design Center Hara Design Institute

162–169
Belfry in Ishinomaki
Design period: 2011.06–2011.12
Architects: Go Hasegawa, Marina Takahashi
Structural engineer: Ohno Japan
Construction firm: Kudo Contractor

Book Credits

Photos
Iwan Baan: 76–77, 84, 86, 88–91, 100–103, 108, 110–113, 119–121, 123–124, 126–127, 130–132, 134–135, 140–142, 144, 146–148, 150, 152–153
Go Hasegawa & Associates: 10–11, 16–18, 20–22, 118
Mie Morimoto: 2-3
Takumi Ota: 44–45, 52
Shinkenchiku-sha: 28–29, 34-38, 40-43, 46, 50–51, 54–55, 60–63, 68–70, 80–82, 92–95, 98

English Translation
William I. Elliott & Kazuo Kawamura: "A House" (poem by Shuntaro Tanikawa)
Christopher Stephens: Descriptions of works

Drawings
Go Hasegawa & Associates: Go Hasegawa, Marina Takahashi

作品クレジット

10–25
森のなかの住宅
設計期間：2005年1月〜2005年8月
施工期間：2005年9月〜2006年1月
設計担当：長谷川豪
構造設計：金箱構造設計事務所
施工：木内工務店

26–41
桜台の住宅
設計期間：2005年10月〜2006年4月
施工期間：2006年5月〜2006年10月
設計担当：長谷川豪
構造設計：金箱構造設計事務所
施工：上村工建

42–57
五反田の住宅
設計期間：2005年9月〜2006年4月
施工期間：2006年5月〜2006年11月
設計担当：長谷川豪、能作淳平
構造設計：金箱構造設計事務所
施工：深澤工務店

58–73
狛江の住宅
設計期間：2007年3月〜2008年7月
施工期間：2008年8月〜2009年2月
設計担当：長谷川豪、能作淳平
構造設計：金箱構造設計事務所
プロデュース：大島滋
施工：ミサワホーム東京、工藤工務店

74–89
練馬のアパートメント
設計期間：2007年12月〜2009年3月
施工期間：2009年4月〜2010年3月
設計担当：長谷川豪、能作淳平
構造設計：金箱構造設計事務所
設備設計：システムデザイン研究所
プロデュース：大島滋
施工：ミサワホーム東京

90–105
森のピロティ
設計期間：2009年5月〜2010年3月
施工期間：2010年4月〜2010年9月
設計担当：長谷川豪、山本周
構造設計：オーノJAPAN
施工：新津組

106–121
浅草の町家
設計期間：2009年4月〜2010年4月
施工期間：2010年5月〜2010年11月
設計担当：長谷川豪、大庭早子
構造設計：金箱構造設計事務所
設備設計：科学応用冷暖研究所
施工：深澤工務店

122–137
駒沢の住宅
設計期間：2010年4月〜2010年9月
施工期間：2010年10月〜2011年3月
設計担当：長谷川豪、山本周
構造設計：オーノJAPAN
施工：泰進建設

138–153
経堂の住宅
設計期間：2010年6月〜2011年2月
施工期間：2011年3月〜2011年8月
設計担当：長谷川豪、大庭早子
構造設計：オーノJAPAN
施工：泰進建設

154–161
日本デザインセンター
設計期間：2011年8月〜2011年11月
設計担当：長谷川豪、山本周
サイン計画：日本デザインセンター 原デザイン研究所

162–169
石巻の鐘楼
設計期間：2011年6月〜2011年12月
設計担当：長谷川豪、高橋真理奈
構造設計：オーノJAPAN
施工：工藤工務店

長谷川豪作品集クレジット

写真
太田拓実：44–45, 52
新建築社写真部：28–29, 34–38, 40–43, 46, 50–51, 54–55, 60–63, 68–70, 80–82, 92–95, 98
イワン・バーン：76–77, 84, 86, 88–91, 100–103, 108, 110–113, 119–121, 123–124, 126–127, 130–132, 134–135, 140–142, 144, 146–148, 150, 152–153
長谷川豪建築設計事務所：10–11, 16–18, 20–22, 118
森本美絵：2–3

英訳
ウィリアム・I・エリオット＆川村和夫：谷川俊太郎氏の詩
クリストファー・スティヴンズ：作品解説

図面
長谷川豪建築設計事務所：長谷川豪、高橋真理奈

Go Hasegawa

1977   Born in Saitama, Japan
2002   Completed a master's course at the Graduate School of Science and Engineering, Tokyo Institute of Technology
2002–04   Joined Taira Nishizawa Architects
2005   Established Go Hasegawa & Associates
2009–   Lecturer at Tokyo Institute of Technology, Tokyo University of Science, Hosei University

Awards

2005   The Kajima Prize for SD Review 2005 for *House in a Forest*
2007   Grand Prix, Tokyo Gas House Design Competition for *House in a Forest*
2007   Gold Prize in Residential Architecture Award, Tokyo Society of Architects & Building Engineers for *House in a Forest*
2007   Gold Prize in The 28th INAX Design Contest for *House in Sakuradai*
2008   The 24th Shinkenchiku Prize for *House in Sakuradai*

長谷川豪

1977　　　埼玉県生まれ
2002　　　東京工業大学大学院　修了
2002-04　 西沢大良建築設計事務所　勤務
2005　　　長谷川豪建築設計事務所　設立
2009-　　 東京工業大学　東京理科大学　法政大学　非常勤講師

受賞歴

2005　　　SDレビュー2005鹿島賞（森のなかの住宅）
2007　　　東京ガス住空間デザインコンペティション1等（森のなかの住宅）
2007　　　東京建築士会住宅建築賞金賞（森のなかの住宅）
2007　　　第28回INAXデザインコンテスト金賞（桜台の住宅）
2008　　　第24回新建築賞（桜台の住宅）

Go Hasegawa Works──長谷川豪作品集

2012年 2月24日　初版第1刷発行
2016年12月10日　初版第3刷発行

著者：長谷川 豪
発行者：加藤 徹
ブックデザイン：色部義昭
印刷・製本：株式会社サンニチ印刷

発行所：TOTO出版（TOTO株式会社）
〒107-0062 東京都港区南青山1-24-3 TOTO乃木坂ビル2F
［営業］TEL：03-3402-7138　FAX：03-3402-7187
［編集］TEL：03-3497-1010
URL：http://www.toto.co.jp/publishing/

落丁本・乱丁本はお取り替えいたします。
本書の全部又は一部に対するコピー・スキャン・デジタル化等の
無断複製行為は、著作権法上での例外を除き禁じます。
本書を代行業者等の第三者に依頼してスキャンやデジタル化することは、
たとえ個人や家庭内での利用であっても著作権上認められておりません。
定価はカバーに表示してあります。

© 2012　Go Hasegawa

Printed in Japan
ISBN978-4-88706-323-5